Advance Acclaim fo

"Erin Healy's *Motherless* is a complex and emotional web that dre...
and kept me spellbound. Mysterious, rich, and compelling. A masterfully
told story."

—KRISTEN HEITZMANN, BESTSELLING, AWARD-WINNING AUTHOR
OF *THE BREATH OF DAWN* (A RUSH OF WINGS SERIES)

"A story of the tales we tell ourselves—those we believe, and those we
must let go. Haunting, beautiful, and revelatory. With wrenching turns
you won't see coming, *Motherless* is Healy's best yet."

—TOSCA LEE, *NEW YORK TIMES* BESTSELLING AUTHOR

"*Motherless* is part supernatural mystery, part romance from beyond the
grave, and will keep you guessing until the very last minute. Erin Healy is
an artist who paints magnificent images with her words."

—THOMAS LOCKE, BESTSELLING AUTHOR OF *EMISSARY*

"*Motherless* by Erin Healy is a mesmerizing story about secrets and the
lies we tell ourselves. If you loved *Gone Girl*, you will gobble this one up.
Highly recommended!"

—COLLEEN COBLE, *USA TODAY* BESTSELLING
AUTHOR OF THE HOPE BEACH SERIES

"In this intricately-woven tale of life, death, and redemption, Erin Healy
lays bare the complicated bonds of family, the devastating effects of
secrets kept, and the saving power of grace and love. At times chilling,
at times heartrending, *Motherless* delves into the depths of identity, both
false and true, and the lasting effects of what we believe."

—LISA WINGATE, NATIONAL BESTSELLING AUTHOR
OF *THE PRAYER BOX* AND *THE STORY KEEPER*

"*Motherless* packs an incredible one-two punch as Healy delves into
the darkness of our humanity and the enormity of our need for grace,
redemption, and love. Her vivid imagery, compelling characters, and deft
hand at suspense keep you turning the pages to the very end."

—KATHERINE REAY, AUTHOR OF *DEAR MR.
KNIGHTLEY* AND *LIZZY & JANE*

Acclaim for Erin Healy

motherless

Other Books by Erin Healy

Stranger Things
Afloat
House of Mercy
The Baker's Wife
The Promises She Keeps
Never Let You Go

With Ted Dekker

Kiss
Burn

motherless

ERIN HEALY

THOMAS NELSON
Since 1798

NASHVILLE   MEXICO CITY   RIO DE JANEIRO

Published in Nashville, Tennessee, by Thomas Nelson. Thomas Nelson is a registered trademark of HarperCollins Christian Publishing, Inc.

Published in association with Creative Trust Literary Group, 5141 Virginia Way, Suite 320, Brentwood, TN, 37027.

Thomas Nelson titles may be purchased in bulk for educational, business, fund-raising, or sales promotional use. For information, please e-mail SpecialMarkets@ThomasNelson.com.

Publisher's Note: This novel is a work of fiction. Names, characters, places, and incidents are either products of the author's imagination or used fictitiously. All characters are fictional, and any similarity to people living or dead is purely coincidental.

Library of Congress Cataloging-in-Publication Data

Healy, Erin M.
  Motherless / Erin Healy.
     pages cm
  ISBN 978-1-4016-8959-9 (paperback)
  1. Mother and child--Fiction. I. Title.
  PS3608.E245M68 2014
  813'.6--dc23

                            2014018967

Printed in the United States of America

14 15 16 17 18 RRD 6 5 4 3 2 1

For anyone who has ever believed a lie.
May truth find you on waves of grace.

One day the ocean left us.
She unplugged the drain
And ran out
Took her lullaby waters and salt perfume
To a less demanding world.

Now we abandoned boats tilt in crusty sand
Punished
Guilty of needing the sea

But
Underneath one half-buried hull
Gritty grains still hold water.
They are wet enough to grow belief
That truly the ocean once was here
And that even now
She remains.

—DYLAN BECKER, "MOTHER" FROM
HOW TO SURVIVE PEOPLE

1997

Locals have been saying for years that this stretch of sand called Monastery Beach is anything but a sanctuary. It's the Venus flytrap of the California coast. The ocean cuts into the land here, and the sudden postcard view that pops up in front of the highway has caused many a driver to drift across the center line. Travelers make the spontaneous decision to stop for a stretch and a family photo: just look at that gorgeous blue backdrop, that sultry smile of coastline, that easy walk from the car to the packed sand.

For heaven's sake, it's called Monastery Beach. Who could know at a glance how deadly it is?

I hear the diving just offshore is amazing, though that adventure is for the experienced only, those who know what they're diving into. Those people have seen the uncommonly steep underwater drop-off here, hidden by the surface. They understand the powerful undertow, the wintertime dangers. They *expect* the sleeper waves to tower out of nowhere and smash them onto the sand, then grab them by the ankles and drag them into the instant depths. They know about the tragic drownings and the doubly tragic rescue attempts. They've seen the death toll climb year after year.

But the happily ignorant vacationers? They turn their backs

on the monster to smile for the camera. Once a single wave swallowed a family of four. In spite of posted signs that diagram the danger, too many don't heed the warnings.

I park on the shoulder of Highway 1, under the low branches of an old salt-whipped tree. People park here all the time—in summer vehicles line the road door-to-door and bumper to bumper—but it's nearly winter, and no one's here yet, if anyone will come at all this morning. The sun isn't shining even though it has recently risen. The winds are spitting sleet across my windshield, and clouds press down heavily. The beastly surf rattles its cage, daring me to come closer.

I take what's mine and leave what I want others to find. I close the door and leave the empty car unlocked. Why frustrate the search?

The old monastery sits right there on the other side of the highway. I stand on this skinny strip of asphalt, the only thing separating life from death. I could turn in either direction. Strange hope swells in me, then settles back into the sea. Yesterday I might have looked for refuge in that place where they believe God welcomes sinners. But not now.

Like the unwitting visitors who make the mistake of taking their eyes off the water, I put the monastery at my back and face my fate. Unlike them, I am fully informed.

See, the locals call this place Mortuary Beach, and I am here to save my children from my sins.

2014

Almost seventeen years had passed since Garrett Becker last saw his wife. More exactly, he had survived for sixteen years, six months, two weeks, and a day since grasping at her as she made her devastating exit. He had cried, sobbed actually, begged her for forgiveness. Bargained, negotiated, pleaded with her not to go.

Her ears were deaf to him then, and her eyes didn't see him now as she came down the sidewalk through heavy rain toward his SUV. They faced each other, their routes about to pass so closely, separated by just a few feet. And by eons. It would have been their twenty-second wedding anniversary.

The intensity of this summer storm was unusual for the region and the time of year. Overflowing gutters, the construction of a new skyscraper, and traffic clogging the downtown Los Angeles streets brought Garrett's vehicle to a standstill. He stared at his wife through the glass.

The sight of her, the possibility of her, set off Garrett's pulse. A landslide of anxiety came down behind his ribs.

Rain sheeted his windshield, and the rhythmic wipers couldn't keep up. Silvery water distorted the view of her face. Behind him someone honked, and he inched forward.

But she held his attention captive. Her outfit was identical to the one she wore the day she departed. Dark-blue jeans and a soft sweater, rich pink, the color of bougainvilleas. Moisture glittered her thick black hair. Crystal spray flew from the ends of her bouncing ponytail. Murky puddle water splashed around her quick feet, clad in her favorite pair of ballet flats, magenta like the sweater and studded with flashy rhinestones.

She glided over the sidewalk, this ghost from his past. Dusk conspired with the overcast sky to keep her expression in shadow. Her gait was graceful but urgent and she hugged herself, shoulders hunched, sheltered by the awnings of downtown shops that poured waterfalls of runoff between her and Garrett. As she hurried, she leaped through the gaps between awnings, because the downpour would drench her if she didn't keep moving.

The red taillights of the car in front of him brightened. He took too long to hit the brakes. When he did, his Suburban fishtailed in the street's gathering river.

At the near collision she lifted her face to Garrett's window for the space of a blink, then kept going.

In that breath her portrait was so clear. She looked so young, for all the years Garrett had aged since she'd gone. Her light step was untroubled. Stable. Free of the problems that twisted her mind and turned her heart wild after the births of their children.

He twisted around in his cab to watch her, but she was lost to him, hidden by the rain and the traffic and other pedestrians. Garrett wrenched his attention back to the busy street. He moved his left hand to open the door. His body was already leaning to spring out of the Chevy and chase her down.

But he stopped himself. There was no way in this world, in the known laws of the universe, that it could be her. There was no difference between giving in to wishful thinking and being delusional, and he wasn't the one who was delusional.

If he could see the tiny scar on her left cheek, he'd know for sure, but that side of her profile faced away.

He forced his attention to the construction zone just on the other side of oncoming traffic, where a skyscraper would soon rise from the earth like a sprouting tree. At the moment, a tall chain-link fence surrounded a thirty-foot-deep pit that occupied half a city block. The massive hole was to become the skyscraper's foundation and basement. The task of overseeing this mighty project was Garrett's work, the job he had finished for the day.

His wife appeared in his rearview mirror. She reached the street corner behind him and looked left, down the avenue where boutiques gave way to office buildings, then right, toward the excavated pit. A passerby on the crowded sidewalk bumped into her shoulder. A man in an outdated maroon beret. He brought to mind the film director Ingmar Bergman in the early years of his career. Built like him too. Tall, slim, angular. He carried an umbrella. Garrett's wife twisted toward the man, and they exchanged apologies.

Garrett's self-restraint snapped. The woman was no ghost. And he was *not* delusional.

The car in front of him finally inched ahead, and Garrett used the margin to yank his steering wheel into a U-turn. His wedding ring, the ring she'd once slipped onto his finger with a promise, bit into his skin as he pulled.

The oncoming driver of a small, energy-efficient hybrid lay on the horn and gesticulated, but yielded to the brute size of the Suburban. Garrett forced his way through. A chorus of offended drivers objected, but what could they do to stop him, really?

The engineering part of his mind also raised a ruckus. It knew he didn't have enough space to complete the illegal turn. His vehicle was too big, his steering radius too long. But Garrett was committed. As he came around, he drove up onto the opposite sidewalk and met the chain-link barrier that surrounded the pit. His headlights cut across the dripping gray mesh, and then his bumper pushed against it. The metal groaned before pushing back and taking some paint off of his passenger-side fender.

The old asphalt street was coated with excavated dirt that had escaped the dump trucks and turned to mud in the downpour. The back end of Garrett's vehicle slipped a little as he stepped on the gas. He leaned across the steering wheel, eyes straining through the liquid windshield. He guessed she would turn left, around that corner, in which case he'd lose sight of her. He'd have to abandon the car and follow her on foot.

But she surprised him. She asked the man in the beret a question. He pointed at the work site. She nodded a good-bye and stepped off the street corner, then cut through gridlocked cars toward the construction zone. She began to run toward the skyscraper pit, open like a sore, as if it could give her shelter. Within two splashing steps, raindrops doused her.

The traffic had nowhere to go, so Garrett kept his SUV on that sidewalk, where pedestrians were temporarily barred. He accelerated. The passenger-side mirror rattled that fence like a boy with a stick. Husband and wife moved toward the same point, their paths on collision as she aimed for the barrier. She approached without breaking stride, then reached up her hands and stuck her long, narrow foot into one of the links. She began to pull herself up.

He couldn't guess what she was doing, but he feared she might go over the top. Did nobody see? Would no one step in?

"No!" Garrett's shout was loud in the confined space. Then louder, "Wait!"

Driving was the fastest way to reach her. He unbuckled his seat belt, preparing to leap out. She had both feet in the chain links now, but she paused there. The whole fence vibrated as Garrett's mirror slid along its musical scale.

He opened his door and sideswiped a car in the lane he was trying to bypass. Metal squealed on metal, and muddy water splashed up into the footwell until Garrett corrected his error. He pulled the wheel to the right, and the Suburban leaned into the chain links. His door stayed open. The metallic groans on both sides deepened. He felt the right front tire leave the sidewalk and slip under the fence. Too late, he braked.

She turned her head to look at him, and no amount of rain could distort the connection their eyes made. Garrett believed she saw him clearly. Saw him, knew him, and somehow had expected to meet him exactly like this and at precisely this moment as he drove his SUV into the fence like a stone into a slingshot's rubber pocket.

She sprang off the fence, eyes still on him. The flexible soles of her slim ballet flats stayed wedged in the links, like the chain-link memorials stuffed with tributes to loved ones after unthinkable disasters. The groaning metal extended to its limits.

His tires quickly left the solid ground. They chipped away the tiny lip of earth underneath the fence, above the excavation, and gravity took care of the rest. The vehicle tipped to the right. His door slammed shut. Everything strained, just long enough for Garrett to hope the chain-link slingshot might shoot him back onto the street. He might at least get the chance to say good-bye to his children, to explain a few things. They had never understood their mother's abandonment. How much less sense would his own exit make?

He looked for her. She had withdrawn, backing away into the frozen traffic, where all eyes were on his catastrophe.

The Suburban tipped past the point of no return. He tried again to open his door and found the weight of the world holding it against him. The fence posts whined and then collapsed, and his head crashed into the cab's ceiling as everything plummeted. His feet pointed to the sky. His arms braced for hell.

One

That SUV falls for years.

Like a burst of lightning I'm back at the twisted fence, pouncing on it, gripping the strained wire links, watching. Disbelieving. Terrified. This moment is so different from what I expected when the sun rose this morning and I made my way here. I rattle the fence with all my strength and have less power than a gust of wind. The barrier doesn't budge.

The metal is solid and real beneath my fingers. I can feel the pain of it cutting into my joints. The world resists me. Each raindrop strikes me like hail that strips a tree of its leaves. Within seconds I've been pounded off the fence. I have to seek shelter. But first, I have to watch.

The Chevy dives headfirst into the excavation, where everything will soon be laid to rest in a casket of concrete. Hard-hatted workers still finishing their workday scatter. The vehicle finally hits the bottom. It bounces off the exposed net of crosshatched rebar and tumbles twice, the ground sledgehammering the cab.

The final, fatal, upside-down impact sends a shock wave that cuts me in half, and for a long minute, as the flattened SUV stills, the only thing I can do is try to breathe. Yes, the dead do breathe, just in a different dimension. Right now, it takes all my concentration.

A whispering voice at the back of my mind reminds me that I've been this way for some time. Dead, that is. The voice is fear, and it caresses my neck with cold secrets. Death is timeless and irreversible. It begins its work on the human heart long before it strikes its final physical blow. And by then, we're conditioned to hardly notice it.

For a sacred moment there's nothing but the sounds of my wheezing and the pattering of rain drumming on car tops, splatting in its own puddles, pinging the undercarriage of a destroyed car, a crushed life. The rain is shredding me to ribbons, causing pain without injury. I crawl between an outhouse and a piece of plywood tilted against it.

Gawkers are collecting on the sidewalk where they're not supposed to be. The especially stupid ones play with their own lives by leaning into the chasm opened up by the truck and the distended fence. The merely careless risk their electronics in the downpour for the sake of a picture or video. One phone slips out of its owner's hand and plummets into the site. How can these people value their own lives so cheaply? They can't see what's right in front of them, and they're going to call themselves witnesses. What do they know about what happened here today, really? They'll tell stories that might seem true but aren't even close, and no one will be able to point out the falsehood.

But even I feel confused about what just happened. The flimsy pink shoes jutting out of the twisted links look like a lie. Or at least a terrible misunderstanding. I crawl out from under the shelter and reach for them, thinking to pry them out, but I can't even wiggle the soft soles. My fingers are like floppy feathers trying to jack up a steel beam. I leave the shoes to rot and walk away with nothing, staggering under the pelting rain toward the shelter of a low awning on the other side of the street. The brick building embraces me.

The man in the beret who pointed out the work site is walking away under his umbrella. Did he know what would happen there?

The dead have a very broad view of the living, of actions performed out of sight, of thoughts believed to be private. Across the pit, someone standing at the front window of a store is praying. Fifteen cars behind the red light, a nurse has left her car door open and is looking for someone who knows the way down into the site. In the deli on the corner, a crane operator who stopped for dinner at shift's end has left half a sandwich on the plate and is rushing back to work. Behind me, where the street is jammed with people who want a good story to tell over drinks tonight, an off-duty highway patrolman in sopping wet street clothes is showing his badge to drivers and giving them instructions.

Eighty miles away, surviving family members are watching TV in a beach house, unaware that the curtain is rising on a terrible drama in which they will have to take center stage.

My children. Almost adults but not quite. Independent but not self-sufficient. Capable but in need of resources.

Who will take care of them now that both their parents are gone?

Who will tell them what happened here?

Raindrops fall from the awning onto my protruding feet, striking like stones. The pain is a living thing.

I've spent a lot of years thinking about what it would have been like to apologize to my kids courageously. Face-to-face, and with a happy ending. My fantasy looks like this: I'd unveil my secrets over cups of strong coffee, and they'd listen, and understand. We'd exchange weak smiles and awkward hugs all around. They'd get answers to their questions. I might eventually get mercy.

As I said, it's a fantasy.

The rain tapers off. It's safe to venture out. The skies are gray and night is near. Lights from cars and streetlamps and windows flicker on, resisting darkness. My weak hands smack a mailbox, a skinny tree growing out of the sidewalk, a newspaper stand, a parking meter. I make no sounds, leave no mark.

My children have believed a lie about me for years and years and years. After all this time I can still feel their hurt in my heart. The tether holding me to them is an old rope frayed by years of neglect. I have to find a way to make my confession before it snaps. What I did was unforgivable, but my own pardon is beside the point. My children deserve the truth, and more. They deserve what I could never give them: a mother's love. I want that much for them even at this late date. Because some part of us always needs mothering no matter how old we are.

My plodding walk quickly becomes a jog fueled by a new goal. I turn west and break into a run.

Two

By car the Rincon Point beach community is about an hour and a half northwest of LA, but I arrive on foot, unaware of how much time has passed or which route I took to get here.

The night sky is clear and sharp, and the scents of recent rain are almost as strong as the sea salt. The tiny, gated neighborhood is a quiet combination of year-round residents, snowbirds, and vacation renters. And surfers. Its crescent of rocky beach, rich with stones and real estate, juts into the Pacific just far enough to catch good, consistent waves.

By day dolphins leap through the surf. At night glittering oil derricks light up the ocean horizon.

The Becker house itself is a money pit, a modified (and modified, and modified some more) cottage first built in the fifties. It hasn't sucked up cash because it's a problem, but because it is a disappointment. The house has failed to be a home no matter how many improvements are made, no matter how luxurious the finishing touches. It is a showcase house. A facade.

This is only one of many reasons why I hate it. But it's my kids' home. And it's full of windows into their lives.

A wide clay-tiled porch leads to this door. Moonlight shines down on it through a redwood frame dense with bougainvillea vines that cast lacy shadows on everything. A small circle of light over the front door illuminates the three wide steps. Marina always remembers to turn the lights on.

She's responsible, capable. Twenty going on forty. My beautiful girl. Came out of the womb like that and will probably have her own funeral arrangements in order before she dies of a wise old age. And you know what? She will be that way whether I succeed or fail. She doesn't need me in the same way her brother does.

I know with a sudden, strange awareness that my sixteen-year-old son is upstairs reading poetry books that he has secreted away in the crannies of his room, because he needs some area of his life to be hidden from his sister's hovering, protective eye. It's not that she'd object to a few poems, it's that he wants the poetry to be his and his alone, even if thousands of people have had similar experiences reading them. Some things are just too sacred to be discussed with others.

There's also the fact that very few sixteen-year-old guys can make loving poetry look cool. Dylan prefers the people who know him to think of him as a brainy computer builder, gamer, and programmer. A quirky recluse who is too genius to leave his house.

I step onto the porch, which should be ocean-breeze cool, but the burnt-orange tiles are as hot as glowing coals. A soft hiss rises up beneath my feet, along with something like stage-trick fog. It seems like a warning, so I jump away and watch the smoky substance rise. It forms a barrier between me and the door before it finally dissipates. Of course. This house will be no different from the inanimate objects on the streets of LA—the fence, the newspaper box, the streetlamp. I can't turn a doorknob any more easily than I can pick up a pair of shoes. The door will deny me entrance. I'll have to find another way in.

The voices of Marina and her friend Jade come to me from the back patio, a partially enclosed area that overlooks the private beach.

"How come you never talk about her?" Jade is asking.

"*He* never talks about her. I've tried enough times."

My daughter's presence outside saves me. I circumvent the strangeness on the porch and go across the lawn to the brick footpath, which connects the front porch to the back patio. The path follows the front of the house and borders a small garden that Marina has planted and tended. Without the bougainvillea to shade them, the sweet peas, the snapdragons, the matilija poppies all glow in moonlight.

Tonight the light shines down on the memorial stone that sits among the flowers. A simple plaque mounted on granite:

In Memory of Misty
Wife, Mother, Friend
1971–1997

At the back of the house, a low wall topped with an acrylic windbreak surrounds the patio. A wraparound bench holds several potted plants, interesting pieces of driftwood, and dozens of seashells, whole and broken. A low gate with a simple latch grants access to the beach. In the far corner, Dylan's surfboard leans against the wall next to a couple of spares. Little pools of rainwater on the sandy wood slats reflect the wall-mounted floodlights. Overhead, the sunshades are retracted on their rolls and the stars shine down.

Marina and Jade sit on cushioned wicker chairs around an outdoor dining table. Marina has a dark beauty that is unapproachable when she wants it to be. Those heavily lined midnight eyes, the molasses hair that sits on her shoulders like a helmet, the velvet brows, and the Michelangelo mouth can all speak as one without uttering a word. She uses her fierce good looks to select which few people can have access to her heart.

In spite of her name, Jade is beach-bunny plain by comparison, blond and tan and dime-a-dozen pretty. She sits with her head down, half listening to Marina, half tending to something on her phone.

". . . says there isn't much to talk about," Marina is saying, her back to me. Her bare feet are propped up on the wraparound bench, and she's sipping natural soda straight from the can. "Mom committed suicide before Dylan even learned how to roll over."

Jade's eyes widen and abandon the phone. "She killed herself?"

Marina shrugs. "I guess she had a condition. A mental illness."

"So that's where Dylan gets his panic stuff from?" Jade asks.

"I don't know."

"Why not? Doesn't your dad know for sure?"

"As you already pointed out, we don't talk about it. What difference would it make?"

"But isn't that kind of thing genetic? If my head were screwed up, I'd want to know everything I could about why."

Marina's attention swivels toward the house, where the living room is bright but empty. She's looking for her brother, not knowing he's engrossed in a poem that's inspiring him with a new game concept. She lowers her voice.

"Dylan's not screwed up, okay? He's actually really high-functioning."

"I just meant it's a good idea to know your medical history."

"He worries about enough already. What good would it do if he started thinking he was his own worst enemy?"

"Doesn't he already?" Jade frowns at her phone. "Suicide is so sad. Aren't you even a tiny bit curious?"

Marina takes another drink and stares at the dark waters.

Jade sniffs. "Your dad still wears his wedding ring. He doesn't even *date*. You'd think he's still madly in love with her."

"Jade!" Marina laughs. She pulls her feet off the bench and leans in to the table toward her friend. "You have a sick crush on my dad!"

"No, I just think it's weird he doesn't talk about your mom. If I were crazy in love with a dead person I'd—"

"Well, you're not, or you'd know how much it hurts. Him and everyone else."

Marina's laugh is gone. Her warning is clear, but Jade's head must be full of air.

"C'mon, Marina. You told me you don't even have a *picture* of her."

My daughter's back stiffens and she pushes her soda aside. It's true, what Jade said about the pictures—and the letters, and the mementos, all of it—and the reason they are gone pains me too. It's nobody's business, though. Definitely not Jade's.

Still, Marina lets her off the hook. Sort of.

"When do you leave for Jakarta?" Marina asks.

"Three weeks from Monday." Jade grins. "If I decide to go."

"If? I thought it was all set."

"I don't know. You're not going. I still have to come up with that last payment. I met a guy."

"A guy." Marina scoffs. "You'd give up the trip of a lifetime for a guy?"

"I don't know if I'd call sleeping on dirt floors and helping to vaccinate snotty kids 'the trip of a lifetime.'"

"No, you probably wouldn't."

"He runs an auto shop up in Goleta. Says business has been really great and he can give me some work. Worst-case scenario, I'll scrape together enough for the last bill. But who knows? If he and I click, if the money's good, maybe I'll stay."

"Yeah, stay for all those broken-down cars. What's a few kids on the other side of the world?"

Jade reaches out across the table and gives Marina a playful shove. "You're the one who really cares about that sort of thing. It should be you on that plane."

"Too late. No money. Work. You know."

"No, I don't. Your dad's loaded. Unlike my delinquent parent, who dares to call herself my mother just because we live at the same address."

"You assume a lot. And your mom tries."

"Then Dylan must be your real excuse. Are you turning into an agoraphobe too? Seriously, Marina. He's sixteen, old enough to snap out of it so you can have a life. When's he going to get a job? Even a driver's license would be an improvement!"

Marina sighs. "He gets paid for some of his computer stuff. And if you had a brother with special needs maybe you'd understand."

The problem as I see it isn't that Jade doesn't have a brother, but that Marina doesn't have a mother. She's had to be both mother and sister since she was three. She has special needs even *she* doesn't know about.

The gate on the enclosed patio is shut. I stand there, as invisible to those girls as I am to everyone else, and place my hand on the Plexiglas. My fingertips flatten against the surface, but when I lift them away, my palm leaves no mark. No fleeting moisture, no oily smudge.

The sound of a car pulling into the driveway at the front of the house reaches my ears. Immediately I know who it is. Police officers, arriving with terrible news. I didn't get here soon enough.

"There's Dad." Marina pushes off the table and stands, blessedly ignorant for just one minute more, and collects her empty soda can. "I'm going to warm up some dinner for him."

"Doesn't he know how to operate a microwave?" Jade teases.

"Is that your way of offering to do it?" Marina grins and waggles her eyebrows before going inside. I make note of her smile and wonder how long it will be before I see it again.

I want to save her from this crushing blow, so I try to call her name. "Marina!" But my voice seizes up the way it does in nightmares, straining and soundless.

The black-soled steps of authorities drum a death march on the red-tiled porch. See, already I've messed this up. I should have gone to Sara first, then found a way to get her here. She could have been here when the kids got the news.

There was a time when Sara Rochester cared for my children just because I needed her to. She might have even loved them. I never asked. She never said. We didn't have time before the suicide.

Maybe there's time now.

Three

Sara is a success gliding among the successful. Though I still stand at the beach house, my forehead pressed against the patio windbreak, I close my eyes and can see her in a crowded room. She wears a simple black wrap dress with a swinging skirt that teases her knees, and her choice makes her the least flashy but most elegant person in this room full of black ties and burdensome accessories. Her black hair is cropped close at the back of her neck, much shorter and more sophisticated than when we last met.

On Sara's open palm is an antique silver tray filled with tiny squares of chocolate. Some are garnished with a candied orange peel twist, others with a curly sliver of a dried red chili. Tiny purple and yellow Johnny-jump-ups dipped in sugar sit on top of others. And she is passing them to guests, her eyes bright and her conversation easy. She is serving them and governing them at the same time. No one refuses her. Sara's treats cause even the skinniest, stuffiest, snobbiest guest to crack open a smile like a child's.

Where is this place? I look for clues, hoping her location is not so far for walking as Rincon Point from Los Angeles.

Sara's world is filled with earthy scents. Wine, cedar, rosemary, chocolate. A-frame ceilings with exposed wood beams steeple over the chattering party. There must be a hundred people inside the vast room. Most everyone holds quarter-full wine-glasses and tiny plates and each other's rapt attention. Beneath their feet: Welsh slate floors in five shades of iron. A floor-to-ceiling window showcases a staggering view that no one seems to be looking at: the persimmon sun is setting on acres and acres of rolling hills striped with rows of grapevines. Gold and purple, green and gold.

On the walls is a framed collection of much-larger-than-life-size wine labels, all from McCleary Vineyards. Each piece is a work of art. The bold, cheerful abstractions seem to represent the live music filling all the empty spaces. Something with a jaunty fiddle and a plucked harp and an Irish sort of rhythm.

McCleary Vineyards. An almost-local place on the other side of Santa Barbara's rolling foothills. A long walk.

Doesn't matter. When I open my eyes, I'm there. I can't begin to explain. In death there is no one to tell you how it works. But I'm standing by a potted fern that's been dragged from the window to prop open a side door. Fresh air moves over me, through me, carries me into the party. The muscles at the base of my neck tie themselves in knots. At least that's the sensation, a memory left over from when stress was physical.

Sara is stunning and talented and popular, but I never thought I'd see her like this, comfortably socializing. This is the woman who would rather be alone in a kitchen than at a dinner table with even two others. But here she is. Her beauty is like Marina's, though her approach to strangers is not. I wonder if she is still the same woman I knew seventeen years ago.

By all appearances she's done well with the money. Her family didn't exactly love her and, after the suicide, they took back that petty love and gave her cash instead. It looks like she invested it well. Or married it well. Maybe after all that she found someone decent.

An image forms in my mind. A house back in Santa Barbara, a well-appointed Spanish revival with her name on the mailbox. Her name alone, and no one inside to turn on the lights for her.

So maybe she never married. There's nothing on her fingers but a cocktail ring. What matters more is whether she's still generous. My children need a parent, and money to pay the bills, and a roof over their heads—that roof at Rincon Point in particular.

She offers up the candy it no doubt took her hours, days, to make with her own hands. She asks each person what he or she is drinking and recommends a chocolate based on the answer. They're holding dessert glasses. Cream sherry, says one. Marsala, ruby port. To those drinking dry whites she suggests they take a glass of water and the chocolate of their pick. This makes everyone laugh as they take sweaty glasses from the server who's following Sara around. I don't get the joke, but I also don't know the difference between a merlot and a cabernet.

A few of the partygoers recognize her and gush. Her chocolates can make orators out of monosyllabic teenagers. Imagine what they can do to educated adults. She still blushes with the praise, the way she did before her products became famous, and her modesty gives me courage.

I think of how to say how much I still admire her. How much I need her help. Can I speak to her the way death speaks to me, uttering a meaningful breath on the back of her neck?

She turns my direction and comes my way. She is so happy, so alive, I expect that when she reaches me she'll pause, offer me a chocolate and a napkin, and ask me how I've been passing the years.

I don't step aside in time. Her body passes through mine, reminding me just how solid the living are. Me, I'm little more than a gas. In a blink I become a scattered puff of smoke.

Sara utters a sharp, quiet gasp and pulls up short. The tray goes sideways on her palm while I hug myself back into one piece. Preventing yourself from coming apart is clumsy business, dead or alive.

The platter teeters, and the artfully arranged chocolates all slide to one side. The whole thing is headed for the floor.

The man who makes the save surprises both of us, crouching and swooping up under the falling tray in one quick, smooth motion. Sara snaps out of her brush with me and sees what's happening, lunges for the tray, and almost knocks it down again.

"Got it!" He elevates the chocolate to a safer height out of her reach and with his free hand helps Sara keep her feet.

"Ian." Her short laugh is one of relief. She brushes off the front of her skirt, ridding herself of our encounter just like that. "Thank you."

Ian presents the tray to her, a servant bowing before a queen. She smiles as she takes it. "Stop. I'm just a klutz."

"Aye. But you are the klutz who is the star of my show." His voice is cheerful, lightly accented. Like the Irish music in the background, adapted slightly to please American ears.

"Oh, I'm no star."

He gestures toward the contented guests. Every crease in his midlife face is a smile line. "They're here for your chocolate, not my wine. In fact, half of what you suggested I serve is stuff I don't even produce."

"Only for the chocolate round. Cocoa is finicky. But everything at dinner was yours."

"But they're all much happier now that you've been around, don't you think?"

"How much did you give them to drink at the main course?" she teases.

"More than I budgeted for," he says. "You are the strangest, most creative sommelier I have ever had the opportunity to work with."

This must be Ian McCleary, the vintner whose surname is all over the wine labels. He speaks to her so easily. Envy stabs me.

Sara shakes her head as she rearranges the chocolates on the tray, pulling them back to center and swiftly creating an artful design of orange peels and purple violets and curled chilies.

"Truth be told, I had to get outside help with the food pairings."

"You did? And who did you consult?"

"Your daughter."

Ian looks pleasantly surprised by that. "Denica? Wasn't it you who called her the most opinionated, hotheaded, unteachable—"

"I meant it as a compliment. After all, she gets it from you."

Ian's laugh is deep and rolling. "Then I guess I'll have to hire her."

"Well, she won't be caught dead working for *me*." Smiling, Sara turns toward an arched passage between this huge gathering place and a smaller room. Ian walks alongside her, and their shoulders bump together once before they find their stride. I follow, dragging my disappointment along.

"Are you referring to that blog she wrote accusing you of buying slave chocolate?" Ian asks. "You should forget about it."

"She's passionate about social justice. That's a good thing."

"Until it's not rooted in facts. These are the things that make a dad wonder if he's taught his kids well."

"You're a fine parent. But Denica and I are adults. We'll work it out."

"I'm sure you will," Ian says as they pass through into the next room. "It's good she helped you with the meal."

In here the lights are dim and the temperatures are cool. It's a much more intimate space. A wine bar backed by mirrors takes up a whole wall and reflects the TV screen on the opposite side of the room. A few scattered tables sit under gold light. The Celtic music sounds far away, muted by the baritone voices of men talking business.

Sara hasn't replied to Ian's last remark. The TV has grabbed her attention and sloshed distress all over her face.

"Sara?" Ian is saying. "Everything okay?"

On-screen a news station projects ribbons of financial information, headlines, and the closed-captioned words of the muted anchor. A telephoto lens zooms in on the undercarriage of an SUV, lying flattened on a bed of dirt and rebar. In the corner are head shots of two men. I recognize one of them.

My attention darts to the captioning.

. . . of Jim Davis following the accident in Los Angeles Friday night. City planners expect the fatality to delay the project, which could have further negative financial ramifications for a corporation already plagued with problems. A witness says site engineering manager, Garrett Becker, visited the excavated area Friday evening before the accident occurred . . .

"What day is it?" Sara murmurs, still staring at the screen.

I look at her. I have no idea what day it is. Or what month, or what year.

"It's Saturday," Ian says.

Saturday. A whole day has gone by since the accident. Is it

25

possible? Yes. I reached Marina last night after dark, but arrived here at the vineyard before the sun was setting.

So many hours of my existence are unaccounted for. So many days, years.

A man with a sauce stain on his tie approaches Sara's tray, eyes on the chocolate. He reaches for one. "May I?"

She holds the entire platter of chocolates out to him. He takes it as she spins away.

"I have to go. The children, there are children. I'm so sorry, but there's something I have to do."

The guest with the tray is happy to walk off with it, but Ian looks as stunned as I feel. She's speaking of my children. Her thoughts give her away. She sprints back out across the open room and flies through the open door. As she flees, she stumbles over the potted fern, jarring the makeshift doorstop. The heavy oak door falls shut. I am swift, I am spirit. I expect to slip through like a breath. But the door hits me with all the force of a baseball bat, and it knocks me back across the room.

I tumble, then roll to my knees, looking for another way out in time to follow Sara. I plant my hands on the floor and push myself up.

And I see something that looks like a miracle: there is blood dripping from my elbow. Gravity pulls one microscopic drop to the slate floor like a magnet.

Since when do the dead bleed?

Four

The slate floor where I am bent over on hands and knees turns red, but not from blood. The drop that has fallen from my body sizzles and evaporates like water on a skillet, then turns to misty fog. The fog becomes smoky and suffocating. The sun is tipping west, and the trellis of pink bougainvillea gives me no shade.

The beach house again. The front porch again. I don't like the porch.

The heat is unbearable, beating down on my back and rising up into my chest. I wonder what day it is now.

The front door opens, and Marina and Dylan step into the frame.

Twenty and sixteen are strange ages—no longer children, not yet adults. Or maybe the problem is that they are both.

Marina wears no makeup to hide the dark circles under her eyes, but she's pasted on a smile for Dylan. In shorts and a halter top, she bounds down the wide steps as if to show him how easily it's done.

"Let's go," she says. And she keeps going, right through the ankle-high layer of smoke as if it doesn't exist. For her, maybe it doesn't.

Dylan takes his time pulling the door closed, testing the knob, and making sure each keyhole is turned. He manages the steps just fine. It's the long walk to the end that kills him. An RV could park on this porch with a comfortable margin, it's so long and wide.

Light plays with Marina's hair as she passes under the bougainvillea. There are so many colors in black. My beautiful girl. She steps off the opposite end and goes around to the front of the garage, pulling her keys out of her favorite striped bag. The appearance of waiting for him will only make things worse. So she waits where he can't see her by going through the motions of opening up the car and rummaging for something in the trunk.

Sea air tousles Dylan's locks, black as his sister's. He wears it heavy around his face, brushed forward, because Marina says it's his best style. He's a good-looking young man, laid-back on the outside even when his insides are in knots.

Apart from the private beach in front of the house, Dylan doesn't get out much. It's amazing what can be done online. The therapists and tutors come here, and his closest friends, surfing buddies. He'll go to the doctor's office if he must, and he can manage short car rides from time to time—like going through In-N-Out for a burger and back. That's about all the energy he can put into leaving the house. The rest of the time he stays put, or he's on a surfboard in the ocean.

His sister keeps hoping he'll meet a girl he likes well enough to draw him out. But all of us know his condition isn't that simple. Phobias aren't logical. They don't fit into neat categories. They don't always have clear triggers. Take the surfing, for example. Dylan can't attend a concert in the park with a crowd of friendly picnickers, but he can float on a vast ocean that teems with very real threats. He can put himself in the pipeline of a wave on a flimsy fiberglass board and not fear drowning. I've never understood that sort of thing, but understanding it isn't the same as accepting it.

Today Dylan's progress across the porch is smooth until his leg cuts the smoke that I've generated, and his step stutters.

Marina hears the hesitation. By the time she emerges from the front of the house, his feet are rooted. Can he see the mist lapping his shoes?

I roll off the tile onto the brick pathway that borders Marina's flower beds. The smoke is transformed into sunlight as it clears away.

"What is it?" Marina asks.

Dylan takes a deep breath and holds it for a few seconds. Then he exhales. "Nothing," he says. He proceeds to the edge of the porch. And today, that's as far as he can go.

The fringe of hair that frames his face is collecting sweat at the tips. It's the only outward evidence that Dylan stands on the edge of a cliff and is worrying about being pushed off. Someone who doesn't know him might think it's just the heat. Or the grief of bad news.

"You do this every time we go out for a bite," his sister says gently.

"We're not going out for a bite."

"True. But you're going with me, in my car, and that's exactly the same. Come get in the car, then we can decide if you want to go any farther."

From where he stands he can see that she's already pulled it out of the garage. It's idling, waiting for him. Marina has a convertible but only drives with the top down when Dylan isn't with her. The vinyl is securely in place. It seems clear to me that he wants to get there, even if his legs won't obey. His breathing becomes more shallow, and not from the exhaust floating our direction.

"I can't."

It's been years since Marina stopped trying to talk her brother out of the way he feels, but she still aims to be helpful. She comes up onto the patio and leans against the trellis.

"We don't have to hurry. You set the pace. If things start to go south, I'll bring you straight back. You know I will."

Dylan nods. Marina has rescued him many times.

My heart sinks for my son. That coarse thread of mental illness runs through our family tapestry, and Dylan got caught in its weave. People like Jade think he's manipulative, that his refusal to leave the house except when it suits him is irrational. And it is, unless you're Dylan.

For starters, agoraphobia isn't exactly about the fear of being in a certain place, or of leaving a certain place. Agoraphobia is about being afraid of fear itself in a way Franklin Roosevelt probably never comprehended. It's the all-consuming dread of having a full-fledged panic attack in any location where there's no escape route, no shelter, no protection. For someone with this preoccupation, the very logical, rational thing to do is to stay in the sanctuary where he knows he can survive, without the risk of public embarrassment, should fear catch him off guard. Our family understands this, Marina most of all.

Sometimes I worry that Dylan's ability to float on the ocean is a subconscious death wish. What can a panicked man do on the ocean but drown?

"I know this is hard," she says. "I won't leave your side. You'll always have an out."

"Yeah," he says. "I know."

Still, he doesn't move. His fingertips are trembling, so he wipes them across his sweating brow.

"I thought you wanted to come," she tries.

"I do. I just can't."

Her gaze is sympathetic. "Is it that you don't want to see Dad like . . . like that?" Marina asks. "I don't want to either. But it's just us now, Dylan. We have to do this, and if we go together—"

"I can't leave Mom," he blurts, "not with things the way they are." His words bring me to my feet. Marina's face mirrors my own reaction: surprise, worry, disbelief. My eyes dart to the ocean.

"Mom's not here, Dylan." Marina speaks so patiently. "Mom's never been here."

"She's *always* been here. Ever since I can remember. You just don't feel it the way I do."

A painful silence passes between them.

Marina breaks it gently. "What brings that up now? You haven't mentioned Mom since you were in fourth or fifth grade."

"You don't like to talk about her. About what happened."

"But what does that have to do with . . . ?" She puts one hand over her mouth and then decides to give the argument to Dylan. "If we leave Mom here, just for a little while, she'll be here when we get back, right? Just like all the other times you've gone?"

"It's not the same now." He takes a step back from the edge of the porch. "I'm really sorry. Could we go tomorrow?"

"What will be different tomorrow?" There's frustration at the edge of her question.

He crosses his arms defensively. "Can Jade go with you?"

Marina's tense shoulders drop an inch at this suggestion. She closes the gap between her and her brother and encircles him with a hug that he doesn't return. "She's not the one I want with me for this." She studies her brother; he stares at his shoes. She looks over her shoulder as if she's heard a sound on the street, but really she's trying to hide her disappointment. Dylan already sees, but what can he do about it?

"I'll be back as soon as I can." Then Marina spins away.

Dylan shuffles back to the cushioned bench under the trellis and sits. He leans his head back against the wall and closes his eyes. I stay in the yard, staring at him until the tips of his sweaty bangs dry into stiff points and his fingers stop trembling and his tight breathing levels out again.

In my mind's eye I can see Marina entering the southbound lanes of the freeway. She's left the top of her car up.

Then I can see Sara, working alone in a kitchen. It seems to be a private residential kitchen, except that it's twice the size of any I've ever stepped foot in, and it contains equipment I don't recognize. There's no evidence she was thinking of my children when she fled Ian's party.

The blood on my elbow continues to ooze slowly. It's thick and black and seems to have forgotten how to clot. I blot it off with my fingers but don't know what to do with the smears. I try to wipe my hand clean on the grass, but it passes right through the green blades. They don't resist me like the hard, lifeless stuff of earth, but neither can I touch them. The grass is a living thing, like Sara. My fingertips can't touch its softness. I try to transfer the smudges to the trellis like paint. Though my contact with the wood is sure enough, nothing will transfer. What am I going to do with this blood?

Dylan gets up to go inside the house. This is my chance to get in. I time my move to slip in through the door before he might see smoke rise from this cursed porch. I can't be sure how much he sees but doesn't say.

He withdraws the house key from his jeans pocket, unlocks

the door, and pushes it wide. He steps inside and reaches back to close it without turning his head. I dart then, across the tiles and up the steps and into the house, and a breath passes through me as he pushes the door closed and displaces the air. I make it through.

Into someone else's home.

Five

An ornate black bench sits against a white wall in an alcove.
Above the bench, Spanish tiles hand painted with a yellow-and-blue motif frame an arched window that overlooks a garden.

Dylan isn't here, and I'm upset by that. Upset by the way I can't control my own comings and goings. I want to be with my son.

At my back is a heavy oak door. The door pull is vertical, an old, twisted bronze handle, straight and sturdy like the bar of a jail cell, and as effective at imprisoning me.

From somewhere deeper in the house, Sara Rochester's strained voice reaches me.

I'm in Sara's house?

On the black bench is a small stack of white mail. My fingers can read the texture of the linen paper, but when I try to pick it up, push it around, flip it over to check the address, the mail won't budge. The corner gouges my skin.

I close my eyes and think of Dylan and wait for the magic to snatch me away. He's sitting at the computer in his littered room, writing code for a game about orphaned kids whose parents left them a legacy of superpowers.

When my eyes open, the scene is the same. The black lacquered bench. The blue-and-yellow tiles. The closed door.

This must be what it's like when fear smacks Dylan in the face and he knows he can't escape it.

Sara's house is done up in the Spanish Revival style, with soft arches framing the windows, alcoves, and entryways. The plaster throughout is crisp and white. A few windows are open to the summer day, but they're barred with screens and decorative wrought-iron scrollwork. Plush area rugs soften the tile floors. Heavy, unpainted wood beams line the ceiling and frame the fireplace, and hammered-metal lampshades top the lamps. More tiles, colorful and hand painted, cover the risers of steps between the living spaces.

It's a pricey home. Small but perfect, professionally decorated. A symbol of success.

When I pass through the living room, a Siamese cat leaps off a sunny windowsill and mews, then runs out of the room toward Sara's voice.

"I'm just trying to find out about his children," she's saying. "The police were no help at all—they won't tell me anything."

A male voice coming over a speaker phone replies, "What's your connection with him again?"

"I'm a friend, but we've been out of touch. I'm trying to reach his family. All I need is a phone number. Everything's unlisted these days."

I track Sara's frustration to the large kitchen. In contrast to the pristine home, it's a mess that smells of scalded chocolate and burnt sugar. Her slim figure is covered in a stained white apron that sets off her rich-toned skin and striking features: stylishly short coarse hair, full lips, dark eyes naturally lined with dense lashes.

Sara's kitchen is a foodie's heaven. She has an industrial-sized stove, a hooded wood-burning oven, and miles and miles of stained-concrete countertops. One of these forms an island that nearly spans the width of the kitchen and supports an expansive wrought-iron pot rack loaded with dangling copper pots. Bar stools on the opposite side of the island suggest it might also serve as a dining table, or at least an invitation to socialize with the cook. But today there isn't an inch of clear space for a guest's cup, or fork, or elbows. The place is covered with used pots, stained candy forms, dirty thermometers, broken slabs of chocolate, and all manner of cooking utensils. Her phone sits on one corner, safe from her sticky hands if not from the rest of the mess.

Trails of fine white sugar and cocoa dust make an odd map on the floor as she paces through it. The cat has left paw prints that lead to the pantry. Odd equipment lines the back wall: a large stainless steel vat, an old chocolate enrobing machine, marble slabs standing on end. Next to the pantry is an alcove that holds a workspace, and a door that might lead to the garage. The workspace captures my attention. It's stacked with a chaos of papers and books. A computer screen peeks out through a mass of sticky notes. I wonder if the computer might offer a way to communicate with her.

The man Sara is speaking to says, "I'm the wrong person to ask for a number. I can't get an interview with the Beckers either."

"I'm not looking for an interview, or a scoop, or money, or anything like that. Honestly, I just want to know if they're okay. Maybe there's something I can do . . . to help."

"Give it time, then. I'm sure you can imagine their need for privacy right now."

Sara uses her forearm to push a loose lock of hair off her forehead. "Garrett Becker has two children. No mother. No one to look after them." She licks her lips. "Unless he remarried. Did he remarry?"

"After his wife's suicide?"

His question makes me bristle.

"That's right," she says quickly, but her golden skin pales.

"No. Unless he did it in secret, in which case no one's claiming to be married to him." The man chuckles. "Some of his coworkers are wondering if Becker's accident was suicidal in nature. Following his wife's path."

"He has *kids*."

"Not always a reason for people to stay. How old are they?" he asks.

Her answer is measured with caution. "You don't know?"

"I thought they were adults. What's your phone number again?"

Sara blinks and her lips part to answer, then she shuts her mouth and frowns. She has called him and doesn't want him to return the favor.

He continues, "Maybe you and I could help each other out. Would you be willing to answer a few questions, tell me what you know about Becker the family man? His past? Anything that might explain his state of mind when that accident happened? Apparently he kept his home life and his career pretty compartmentalized."

She puts her hands on her hips, transferring new smudges to her apron. "You seem to know more than I do."

"I doubt it."

"Where does he live?" she asks forcefully.

"Not LA. That's all I know."

Turning away from the phone, she mumbles, "I think you know and won't say."

"What's that?"

More clearly she says, "I read the piece you wrote for the *Times* yesterday. You interviewed a man who witnessed the accident. Maybe I could talk with him, if you're done?"

"Sure. Let me call him for you. I'll pave the way. What's the best number for him to reach you?"

Sara contemplates this for the space of a breath, then presses a dirty forefinger into the screen of her phone, ending the call. "No, thank you," she mutters to the empty kitchen.

A journalist's power to influence the beliefs of the masses frightens me. I don't like that this one played the suicide card.

The low-battery warning on Sara's phone beeps. She doesn't hear it. She stands in the sugar dust for a moment with her hands loose at her sides, then turns to the stove and looks into a pot filled with chocolate turned chalky and brittle. A spatula stands stiffly in the center of the pot. She pries it loose and begins to scrape the waste into a trash can.

The computer in Sara's alcove dares me to put it to use. How?

"Rough day in the test kitchen?" Ian McCleary's light brogue startles us both. She drops the pot. It thunks into the bin and she looks up at him, on the razor-thin brink between laughing and snapping.

At the sight of her conflicted expression, he hesitates. "Hope it's okay that I let myself in." The vintner has come in through the side entrance. Behind him I see a laundry room, and beyond that a door that stands open to the garage. I could leave through that door and walk back to Dylan, but not until I find a way to bring Sara with me.

"Of course it is. Come on in."

Ian pulls the door shut.

"I'm sorry for bolting last week," she says. "I was . . . it was nothing that couldn't wait."

"No apology needed," he says.

"I didn't even call to explain." Sara fishes the pot out of the trash and keeps scraping it. "I haven't been that unprofessional since I was a teenager."

"I just stopped by your shop to check on you, and they said you're on the doss."

This makes her grin. "They did? Well, I haven't played hooky since I was a teenager either. I told them I was sick. Guess I'm not very convincing." She carries the crusty pot to the sink. "What's the final word on your party? A huge success, from what I saw."

"We had fun, but those tales will keep. Are you going to tell me how you're faring? In all the time I've known you you've never left a job early, or stayed away from your shop."

Her back is to him. She fills the pot with hot, soapy water, then slowly washes her hands. Ian is patient. Sara's phone beeps again. Ian walks the length of the island to pick it up, then carries it to the arched alcove. I give him a wide berth. Her charger is there, still plugged in to the outlet. Ian hooks up her phone, then turns around to study her.

"It's not important," she finally says. "It'll pass."

"Don't make me meddle," he says.

She nods at the sink, smiling again. "Can I get you some coffee?"

"Aye, if you mean to tell me something interesting while we drink it."

"You know I never have anything interesting to say that isn't about chocolate. Would you like to know how to ruin a simple ganache? I've done it three different ways in the last hour."

He leans against the counter and crosses his arms and ankles. Sara dries her hands on a towel, opens a cupboard, and withdraws a coffee grinder and a bag of beans.

He looks around the kitchen and says, "I've known you almost two years now, Sara, and I still don't have an inkling what it takes to earn your trust."

She turns around and looks across the room at him with raised eyebrows that seem to say both *What do you mean?* and *Please don't.* The beans rattle as she pours them into the grinder.

"I trust you."

"Then have dinner with me."

She sighs. "We've eaten dinner together."

"Professionally. With colleagues. I mean just you and me."

"I don't date, Ian."

"Who's calling it a date?"

Sara grinds the beans.

He picks up again when she's done. "You live alone. You never speak of your family, or visit them—whoever they are, wherever they are—and they never come here. Everyone respects you, but you hold us off, the people who would like to be your good friends. You hold me off, Sara."

"You *are* my friend."

"I think we're just two people using each other to the advantage of our careers."

"Oh don't be melodramatic." Sara gives her apron strings a yank and then lifts the neck strap over her head. "Now you sound like Denica."

"You did say she gets her finer qualities from me."

"When is your son coming to visit?" Sara asks.

His smile broadens. "Couple of weeks."

"We should have dinner together. All three of you fine-quality McClearys and me."

The Siamese cat has come out of the pantry and is rubbing her arched back against Ian's leg, leaving a film of white hair on the tan cotton. Ian gives her a gentle shove with his foot, and the cat meanders off, insulted. Her erect tail vanishes underneath the desk, where there is more clutter: stacked boxes, a trash can, an overflowing paper shredder.

As if seeking consolation for Ian's indifference, the cat bats at a piece of plastic sticking out of the trash can and drags it loose with her claws. The plastic strip pulls the can over on its side, and the stack of boxes next to it comes crashing down on the cat, who rockets into the air and smacks her head on the bottom of the desk. A waterfall of papers tumbles from the surface onto the floor.

Ian steps aside. Maybe he's had experience with the claws of a frightened cat. This one is growing more anxious by the second: with a snake's length of plastic stuck to her paw and her head chirping with bluebirds, she can't get traction on the fallen papers. She scrambles on shifting ground. Fear comes off her in a cloud of fine hair. Forgetting myself, I try to grab her by the scruff of the neck.

My touch is the worst thing the poor cat might have wished for. When my hand passes through her body, the irritable growling transforms into a shriek. Her tail turns into a bottle brush, her ruff becomes a lion's mane. The cat drops her belly to the ground and withdraws beneath the desk, ears flat against her head and teeth bared.

"With this kind of free entertainment, I can see why you don't need to go out," Ian says as Sara, coming to her kitty's rescue, goes down on hands and knees to coax her pet out of its hiding place.

She tugs on the plastic strip and frees it from the cat's paw, then pushes the loose papers out of the way.

"I didn't name you Pandora for nothing, did I?" she coos. She keeps talking in a soothing voice: "You big, fat troublemaker, now look how much work you've given me to do. Come here, now. Come to mama so I can leash you up outside like a dog."

Ian is laughing at this. The cat has deflated to her actual size but still cowers at the back of the desk, half hidden by the scattered boxes. The beast's mew is pitiful and, I'm sure, designed to solicit Sara's pity. Not seeming too sorry for the cat's self-ordained predicament, she pulls the boxes out. One of them catches my eye: on the side is a photo of a stainless steel chocolate fondue pot holding rich melted chocolate. A strawberry stabbed by a silver fork is headed for a dunking. What other unpleasant memories will my foolishness unearth?

"You could just leave her there," Ian suggests.

"And next she'll be shedding in the vats," Sara announces. She finally gets her hand around the beast and, with only a soft bump on the back of her own head, emerges from beneath the desk with the wide-eyed cat tucked under one arm. She sits back on the floor, eyes on the fondue box.

The object brought to light cuts her heart open.

"When I was younger, I had an affair with a married man," she blurts. She nudges the box back under the desk with her foot and looks away. "He had two kids, one of them just a newborn. Gorgeous kids. The sweetest. When his wife found out, she killed herself. Walked into the ocean in winter and drowned."

The tale has a morbidly calming effect on the cat. Her stiff body relaxes in Sara's arms, and she settles down on her hip. Ian takes a seat on the desk chair and leans in, waiting for Sara.

"I killed their mother," she whispers.

Her claim opens up a dark scar in my heart that I have long ignored. I can't look into it. Ian nods slowly, but I don't think he is agreeing with her. "My wife died before Denica and Gabe reached their tenth birthdays," he says.

Sara is staring at the wall, or maybe at a memory. "I know."

"You don't know how. We were still in Ireland, had a night out at the theater, and then the pub with friends. I'd just worked a triple shift—trying to pull in some extra money. By the time we headed for home I was bushed. Fell asleep and hit a lorry. *That's* what it is to kill a child's mother, Sara."

Sara turns her attention to him. "How do you *live*?"

"Not the way you do," he says.

She looks away.

"Your children are lucky to have you," she says. "Whatever you did, you made it up. They love you."

"You can't make up for a lost life. A child's love for a parent may be unconditional, but it doesn't change the guilt."

The cat purrs as Sara strokes its head. "I'm no parent. They'll have no love for me. But now their father . . . They have no one, Ian. And I don't know what to do."

"You think you should help?"

"Yes, but after all these years? What do I have to give them that they could possibly need?"

Everything, I want to say. *Hope. Support. Survival tips.*

Ian rises and reaches for the cat, who doesn't resist being taken from Sara's arms. "What other family will step in?" he asks her. "Grandparents, aunts and uncles?"

"I am the family," Sara confesses. "Their mother was my cousin."

Ian is silent as he reaches for the laundry room door and opens it, depositing the cat next to the dryer. I slip out then, unable to stand the guilt that isn't Sara's to bear, though she's been carrying it around like a sack of rocks all these years. I'm the guilty one. To hope Sara Rochester will atone for my sins is all wrong.

Ian shuts me in with the cat, and the corner of the door clips my heel as he pulls it closed. It takes so little to knock me over anymore. I stumble face-first into the laundry basket, out of Sara's life, unable to see where I am going next.

Six

The laundry basket is in a closet that smells of shoe leather and dry cleaning. I've fallen into the empty plastic container nestled behind a sliding panel. The other half of the closet is open, and Dylan is kneeling in the gap, snatching what he needs out of the enclosed space without actually having to enter it. He's investigating a pile of boxes that blocks his access to a file cabinet. There are a half dozen containers on the closet floor and another six or seven forming a tower beside him. The stack forms a rickety staircase to an open window.

The window overlooks the beach house's side yard, where meaty aloe vera succulents grow atop a cinder block retaining wall. The sash has been raised, letting in salty scents and the dull roar of the surf.

Miles away, Sara is arranging a custom order of chocolates in its box. Not at home. In a store. She keeps making mistakes and has to put several of the pieces back.

Dylan's hair is falling into his eyes. The sunlight at his back casts shadows across the hems of hanging clothes. Marina sits nearby, beyond the closet in the bright room. She hunches over the desk, opening a stack of ignored mail and plowing through unpleasant paperwork. Bills. Debts. An inheritance no parent means to leave behind. We all think we have more time.

"Did Dad ever tell you there are three mortgages on this house?" she asks. A drawer rumbles closed on a track that needs to be oiled. "Of course he didn't," she mutters. "He didn't tell me." She sounds angry, but the truth is she's scared. Dylan's engrossed in the eclectic contents of the boxes. I lean forward for a closer look, unable to figure out what's so fascinating. Receipts, old business cards, shoe polish, golf tees. He fishes out a penny flattened into an oval shape by one of those souvenir machines. For fifty cents at the Child's Estate Zoo, you can have the penny stamped with a train engine, a sea otter, or a howler monkey. Marina liked the monkeys.

"Is three a lot?" Dylan asks. He caresses the penny, then tucks it into the front pocket of his jeans and sets the box atop the tipsy stack beside him. It tilts into the wall.

"I think so," she says. "When I have a family, I'm going to tell them everything while I can. Where all the important docs are, the accounts, the power of attorney, the will"—her voice is thick and drops in volume—"who to ask for help."

She sits in profile to her brother and me, leaning forward in a modern ergonomic chair, elbows propped on an antique oak desk. The room also holds a drafting table and a mess of blueprint rolls. Actually, everything here is a mess: engineering and city planning books on the floor, unopened mail stacked in front of the computer, a discarded printer and the empty box for the one that replaced it, a shopping bag with printer cartridges visible through the thin plastic.

Marina takes a deep breath. There are tears on her cheeks. She wipes them away and keeps her voice level.

"Any luck with Dad's stuff?"

"Not yet. I still say he wasn't the type to write down his passwords."

"Like you."

"I keep telling you, all you have to do is come up with a system. Say your favorite foods in alphabetical order, changing on the first of every month: 1tamale, 2in-n-outs. You can get fancy: 3C@r@C@r@or@nges, with *at* thingies for the *A*s."

"So what system would Dad use?"

"Poets," Dylan says quickly.

"Poets. Because that's the last thing anyone would associate with Dad."

"No, because he loves poetry."

It takes loved ones the longest to start using the past tense.

Marina swivels the chair to face him. "Since when does Dad love *poetry*?"

Dylan shrugs and says no more. My eyes go to a gap in the office bookshelf, which is missing books like a smiling man who lost his front teeth in a bar fight. I wonder when Dylan took those tattered old paperbacks as his own, each one inscribed the same: *To Garrett, who loves me through the fogs of my Misty life.*

"But he'd alphabetize," Dylan says confidently. "Angelou, Baudelaire, Collins—"

"It's June. Letter *F*."

He pauses to think. "Frost," he finally says.

Marina types the name into her keyboard. "No."

"Or Francis. Fletcher. Try numbers for letters. One for *I* and zero for *O*, you know?"

Hopeful clicking fills the room for a time. The box Dylan has picked up is filled with sandy, broken seashells nestled in facial tissue. Hairy blue-black mussels, open like butterflies. Tiny dried-up starfish. Faded augers with broken tips. Dozens of cockles and buttercups, chipped by the surf. Dylan's eyes linger on the worthless, common collection. The shells are tiny bowls brimming with memories of briefly happy times—this is their only value.

Marina sighs. "There's got to be a way to get them in a situation like this. Bypass all the security questions, reset them, something."

"Can't you call the bank and explain?"

"It isn't just a bank." Her worried tone goes up a notch to stressful levels. "He's got an attorney's business card here on the desk. Jamie Blythe? Does that name mean anything to you?"

"Nuh-uh."

"See if you can find a will," she instructs, reaching for the stack of mail. "That would tell us a lot."

Marina tears open an envelope and withdraws the contents. Dylan is holding a box full of CDs too old for his taste and too new to be cool. He gives these a cursory glance and sets them aside.

"What!" his sister cries.

"What?" Dylan asks, turning toward her. She thrusts a folded piece of paper in his face.

"Credit card bill," she says, pointing her finger at the five-figure balance.

"Whoa. Good thing it's not our bill," Dylan says.

Marina snatches it back. "But we're responsible for it now."

"I don't see our names on it."

"Becker. Right here. That's our name."

"I didn't mean that."

"I know what you meant. We didn't buy any of this stuff, whatever it is." As she scans the charges, she murmurs, "But in other ways . . ."

Dylan pulls open the top drawer of the cabinet, and I'm pretty sure I know what Marina is thinking. The banks will get their money one way or the other, if not in cash, then with property.

They might lose the house. It's highly likely that they will lose the house. And where will they go then? Where will Dylan find shelter from his fears, if not here?

Marina is thinking precisely this. Her eyes linger on the back of her brother's head for a long time and yet she doesn't say anything. She has protected him from the beginning.

But these debts are a new revelation. A new fear for her to shield him from, like a deadly spider that she should squash before he understands the real threat. Her worried eyes, steady on her brother's future, accuse me of my past. She swallows her dread until it's deep in her stomach where Dylan won't see it.

She says, "You're right. They're not our bills. No point in worrying about it."

Sometimes we can trace the present state of our lives—no, of our loved ones' lives—all the way back to a single moment of decision made years earlier, a decision in which they had no say.

Forgive me, forgive me.

Dylan is thumbing through the drawer, everything neatly labeled, nothing in the category they seek. His medical records, insurance filings, therapy bills. Copies of utility charges, titles to the vehicles, the kids' report cards since elementary school. At the very front of the file, he finds a loose sheet of pink paper. A receipt for a work order that has been separated from the file labeled Home Improvement Receipts. He reads the sheet, figures out what it's for, and puts it back into the right hanging folder.

"Birth certificates" hang in the folder next to this one. Dylan's hand pauses there, then reaches in and pulls out the decorative papers embossed with their official seals. He reads them slowly.

I reach out, wishing I could take this load off his hands. My touch slides right through his forearm.

He flinches. The movement is like an electrical charge zapping my fingertips. Dylan glances at the place where my fingers brushed up against him. I want to hold on to him forever, but I can't even lay my hand on his arm.

I try to guide him. There's something else in the cabinet that he needs to see.

"Ow," he utters this time, grabbing his elbow.

"What?"

"Something in here keeps shocking me."

Marina gets off of the desk chair and comes to crouch next to him. Dylan slips the birth certificates under the laundry basket where she won't see them.

"Static from the carpet," Marina says. "You touched the file cabinet."

"No, I didn't."

She grabs the bottom drawer pull and isn't shocked at all. It glides open and yields its contents: a stack of thick manila envelopes, records older than Marina. She takes out the one on top and flips it over. A clap of dust rises. When she opens it, the metal brad on the back breaks. She drops the piece into a nearby trash can and withdraws a stack of papers. Real estate documents for homes bought and sold before she was born. Tax filings. Auto and property insurance policies.

"Well, maybe we'll find something in here."

She scoops up the rest of the files, hefts the bundles to the desk, and drops them onto the surface.

The boom sounds to me like an announcement. A fanfare announcing the thing I wanted Dylan to see. It's contained in a black box, satin-sleek with gold lettering embossed on the surface. I forget myself, diving for the box as if I can get to it first and show him everything myself.

"Man!" he exclaims at the shock of our shoulders passing through the same space. The corner of the metal drawer, flaking its brown paint, slices open my finger. New blood oozes from the tip, darker than the wet smudges still on my hand from the elbow cut.

Dylan lifts out the box. He runs his fingers over the scripted gold. *Sara's Sins*, it says. Back when this box was produced, Sara Rochester's company was little more than a startup. Now it's nationally known, the same name with a different look. I'm not sure if Dylan has heard of it.

As much as I want my children to know the truth, I feel sick about the way it's going to come about. A lie that is discovered hits harder than one that is confessed. This is why I had hoped Sara would be the one to break the news. But this will have to do.

The lid is hinged. Dylan flips it open and the faint scent of chocolate escapes. It was once a box of chocolates, yes, and not merely chocolates but truffles in scalloped gold-foil cups. The smell is too rich, too heady, too cloying for something almost twenty years old. Immediately I want to close the lid, put it away, shut the drawer, and forget. Just forget.

I scramble for the fresh air of the window, stumbling through Dylan, zapping him with all my failures. He staggers back from the closet, brushing down his limbs as if his skin were crawling with bugs. I cram my head out the window, drawing in the air scented with nothing but the ocean, and breathe, and breathe, and breathe.

Seven

The same air flows past the entrance to Rincon Point, which is where I find myself when I finally catch my breath. The gated community sits at the end of Bates Road. On the private side of the gate are the security guard's shack, residences, and isolated rocky beaches. On the public side are general parking and access to Rincon Park and Carpinteria State Beach.

This narrow strip of land separates the white-noise rumble of crashing waves from the perpetual hiss of traffic flying by on Highway 1. Out on Bates Road the gulls are screeching around some stinking roadkill. But the sky is blue, and I think of the time young Dylan asked Marina how heaven got its color. She told him it was because it reflected the blue water that covered most of the earth. And why was the water blue? Dylan supposed it was because everyone used blue toothpaste, and whatever they spit into their sinks drained into the sea.

The summer beachgoers are out, sauntering up the blacktop under the shade of old eucalyptus trees. Surfers mostly, headed to the beach with boards tucked under their armpits. College kids from UCSB too, the ones who stay to work through the summers. Locals from Ventura and Carpinteria. Some carry sparklers and red mesh bags stuffed with illegal fireworks. Their beachwear is red, white, and blue, and they haul heavy coolers into the park.

One group looks like trouble, three guys who probably bought the beers they carry with fake IDs. They wander the parking lot in swim trunks and graphic tees, their flimsy footwear slapping the bottoms of their heels, seeking unaccompanied girls and flashy cars. One wears an Uncle Sam top hat. Another sports sunglasses shaped like stars.

Sara pulls in as the three musketeers are crossing Bates Road from the south lot to the north. They raise their bottles in a toast, not to her—that would be like checking out their mother—but to her pretty Porsche, a glistening sapphire-blue Boxter with the top down and the silver-gray seats soaking up the sun. The custom-painted door panels advertise her success, as if the car itself fails to do that: *Sara's Sins, A Fine Chocolates Café* is scripted in white letters almost too difficult to read, though I'm sure they look good on a chocolate box. *Santa Barbara, California.* She doesn't notice the boys. Her eyes are locked onto the keypad that operates the gate.

Sara hesitates before pulling her car off to the side in a spot that's not exactly a parking space. Though no one waits behind her, she runs the risk of blocking the entrance if her old code doesn't work. She leaves the engine running and grabs her purse off the floor of the passenger seat. She hurries on light feet to the pad, fishing a scrap of paper out of her bag on the way. She consults it, bending at the waist to see the little metal buttons lined up in rows of three like the face of an old telephone. The hem of her coral-colored sundress teases the toes of her sandals.

Over the years, the code has changed as many times as Marina's hairstyle. Sara would do better if she sweet-talked a homeowner into an invitation to enter. If she's really committed she might just take one of the rentals for a week and get the code when she pays in full.

She punches the keys with her pointer finger. The gate doesn't budge.

"Help you, ma'am?"

The offer comes from the seasonal security guard, paid for by association dues, who mans the gate on peak weekends when beer-drinking patriots are more apt to cause trouble than at other times.

"Yes," she says hopefully as he steps out of his shack. She approaches the gate, which stays closed between them. Behind those vertical bars he's a zoo creature on display, a man made worse by his captivity. He's all bones and sunken cheeks except for a strange little paunch the size of a basketball sticking out over his tight belt. That might be a melanoma on his nose, shaded by the long bill of his cap.

Sara hands the paper through the bars. "Can you tell me if the Becker family still lives at this address?"

He takes the scrap, holds it at a distance from his eyes. The cap gets in the way and he lifts it an inch. "The address is still here," he says. "Can't say who lives there."

"You don't know or you're not allowed to tell me?"

"Can't say," he repeats. She sticks out her hand to take the address back. He leans in to the shack and puts the slip on the desk in there.

"Is it a rental?" she asks.

"I honestly dunno."

Sara places her palms together and tips her fingers to her lips, thinking. "If I leave a phone number where I can be reached, can you pass it along to the residents of that house? *Would* you?"

"I'm no mailman here."

"No, I just thought—"

"You seem like a nice enough gal." He pulls the bill of his cap back down. "You probably don't mean to cause any trouble, but that's not for me to say. My only job is to sort out the folks who live here from the ones who don't, and to keep this gate between the two. No point in trying to memorize which ones belong in every single house."

Sara opens her purse again and fumbles around in it. "I completely understand." It takes her only a few seconds to withdraw a business card holder and her wallet, and with a swift thumb she opens the latches on both. "My problems aren't your responsibility." She pulls out a card bearing her business number, and then a folded green bill, and she pinches them together and slips them through the gate. "I sell chocolates in Montecito," she says, holding it out. "They're high end, popular with the celebrities and politicians. The president orders boxes for the first lady on Mother's Day and her birthday." She nods at the guard's wedding ring. "Does your wife like chocolate?"

"No. Messes up her heart." But he takes her payment for the favor and tucks the bill into his back pocket.

Sara sighs and closes her bag, her money and her ideas gone for the moment. "Then maybe you can come by sometime for yourself."

He looks at the card. "Montecito's a little bit like Rincon Point, don't you think? A place for those who belong on one side of the gate and those who best stay on the other."

"There aren't any gates where my store—"

A scream of tires and a whooping of boys cut her off. The trio have commandeered her convertible, two in the front and one trying to settle in the back, having jumped in almost too late. The driver throws the car into reverse, cranking it back into the north entrance of the parking lot with force enough to throw the rear passenger onto the floor. He loses a shoe on the pavement, and his beer showers the hair of his friend in front. Their laughter is a howl.

Sara shouts and takes a step, but what else is there for her to do?

The rear tires throw up smoke as the driver crushes the accelerator to the floor and shoots out onto Bates Road. The southbound freeway on-ramp is only a few yards away, and if he had taken it, Sara might have had a chance of getting her car back. Between here and Ventura there just aren't too many places for a joyride to go. But the kids are smart fools, or maybe just lucky. They take the engine to its max and fly out to the northbound ramp, hooting all the way. The kid in the back recovers, turns around in the seat, and tips his striped top hat to Sara before the jarring left turn throws him on his face. Then they're gone.

Sara stares at the empty road, shading her eyes from the noon sun. She groans.

"You sell enough chocolates to get yourself a new one?" the guard asks.

Eight

Marina was named for the emerald blue cove where she was conceived, sheltered, and protected for such a short season of her life. But her sleeping mind recalls nothing of those promising beginnings.

In her nightmare, which recurs more frequently these days, she's abandoned on an open sea in a perfect storm. She is a child of twelve, not twenty, choking on salt spray at that bleak spot in the Pacific where North America and Asia are equally distant.

She rides a rickety raft of sticks lashed together with long strands of black hair. Between the rising and the falling, the water grabs at her hair and snakes into her throat and slaps her face sideways.

Always, I'm with her—but she's alone. I stand so close to her small body that if this wasn't a dream I could touch her. In a different dimension I could wrap my arms around her shoulders and hold her above the water, save her with whatever powers have made me impervious to the danger here. My beautiful girl. In Marina's dreams I never drown. I never even get wet.

The first time Marina experienced this night terror, the fragile ties held her float together until a rescue boat appeared behind a mountainous wave. Since then the raft has come to fall apart sooner each time, as if it doesn't get to start fresh with each recurrence. The angry ocean swoops her up and then slams her down again and again. These stomach-heaving rides on Neptune's tail don't end until Marina tumbles off her imagined raft onto the real, unyielding floor of her bedroom, drenched in the salt water of her own sweat.

The battering has had a cumulative, exhausting effect across the years since it first took her, and tonight the platform is finally brittle, and its black lashings start to break within minutes. Marina spreads her adolescent wings to their full span, stretching out to grip the sides and hold everything together with her birdlike strength. This is what she does, not only in dreams. The tallest wave tops a skyscraper's height before dropping her, and the raft bursts as it falls. Impact isn't necessary to scatter the sticks across the white-capped water.

Marina goes down only for a breath. The water swallows and then spits her out. She pops up like a resilient buoy, gasping but whole, holding something glistening in her hands—a gold orb the size of an orange. It's made of glass. It breaks in her hands and comes apart like an eggshell, and the salt water rushes over the cuts in her hands. She flinches away, blinded by water. But then we see:

The raft wasn't made of sticks, but bones. A rib, an arm, a femur, a skull no bigger than Marina's corresponding parts are grotesquely animated by the churning water. And I know—in the way one knows in dreams—that these bones belong to her brother.

The child Marina screams, and then the grown young woman wakes on the floor of her lonely room, and we sit together as far apart as the northern and southern horizons.

———

The imagined storm has broken, and sunlight is warm and red through my heavy eyelids. The breeze caresses and the gulls chatter, and it doesn't feel at all like I lie on a rickety raft that is falling from the sky. But there it is: a sudden thrust, a dreamlike spasm, and on the platform beside me Marina is saying something that I can't quite make out, something about how a power of attorney might have been handy at a time like this.

The gusts continue to stir my hair. Voices swirl around my head: Dylan's and Marina's and someone else's. Male, middle-aged, authoritative. And then we crash on the water.

"You're probably going to lose the house," the man says. I recognize his voice then: Jamie Blythe, the attorney. "Without a miracle."

The announcement takes my breath away. Me, I could live and die without this house. In so many ways I have. But my children need it.

I open my eyes. I'm sitting outside of the beach house on the wood bench on the porch, and the kids are inside. Again I am barred from the house. Their voices reach me through the open living room window. A soft mist rises from the tiles beneath my feet. I cautiously lift them up to the bench and turn sideways.

"I don't understand," says Marina.

But I do: the house will have to be sold to pay the inheritance taxes, and that isn't the worst of it. Jamie drops one shoe after another.

"Your father's debts are significant. The outstanding mortgage, the credit cards. He exhausted two lines of equity drawn before the housing collapse. Here in California, debtors have the right to collect what they can from the estate."

I wonder if Marina and Dylan know what this means.

"Dylan needs this house," Marina declares.

"Looks like we need to sell it," Dylan says. I wish I could see his face.

But I can, as if through a window in my mind: his eyebrows are high in those shaggy bangs of his, and his lips form a tight smile. He's trying to be funny because it's better than showing his fear.

The attorney's face is as coarse as a boat's barnacled hull. It tells an intriguing tale of an acne-ridden adolescence, a brief career as a street fighter before he turned to the law, and a success-induced love affair with food and drink. His unattractive mug is far more interesting than the rest of him, which is nearly a Californian cliché: the sculpted body outfitted in silk, the feet clad in Italian leather, the spine straightened by a proud reputation. From what I hear he uses his suave confidence to his clients' advantage, and I hope Dylan and Marina are no exception. Even if they have nothing to pay him.

"Unfortunately, the place is underwater," Jamie says. "That means you'll have to come up with another forty, fifty thou—"

"We know," Marina snaps.

Jamie is patient. "When I said 'lose the house', I meant the bank will step in. They'll simply take it back and ask you to leave."

"Does it matter that Dylan's underage?" Marina asks.

"Not to the mortgage holders. Am I right that you have family up in Monterey, someone who could help?"

"I'd have to look up their names. If they're still there."

"Doesn't have to be family. Good friends can help you back to your feet just as well."

Neither Marina nor Dylan respond to this.

"You're old enough to assume guardianship of your brother,

Marina, but the courts might step in if you don't have a permanent address."

"Step in?"

"Dylan is still eligible for foster care services."

Foster care—as if having to leave the home wasn't impossible enough.

The leather rocker by the fireplace, the one that we bought from the antique store in Thousand Oaks before Dylan was born, squeals as if it's going to pop apart when Jamie rises from it. How we failed to notice the noise at the store became an argument later, when it was clear the chair made too much ruckus for any nursery.

"We have some time to think this through," Jamie says. "I'll work up a plan to clear you of as much financial responsibility as possible. It's only been a month. Anything can happen."

"Thank you," Marina says.

She's old enough to know that sometimes not even qualified people can do what they promise.

Marina is ransacking the attic. It's nighttime, and I look in on her through the small dormer in the roof.

She's shuffling heavy boxes within reach of the attic's weak light, an old lamp for a child's room. Dinosaur silhouettes decorate the shade and cast prehistoric shadows on the walls.

It was a playroom once upon a time, until one of the nannies declared it unsafely stuffy and hot, even when the windows admitted the ocean breeze. Over time the toys moved downstairs into the bedrooms and living areas. Boxes of outgrown clothes and school art projects were carried upstairs. The ABC area rug became covered by a sheet of dust, and the humid air peeled back the dinosaur wallpaper and filled the beadboard grooves with grime. When the garage was cleared out to make room for Marina's new life as a licensed driver with her own car, she relocated the Christmas decorations and the winter skis and the suitcases to the short walls under the steeply pitched roof. Her prom dress came to hang on a coat rack in front of the window, and her graduation gown, and underneath these the file box containing applications and acceptances to three universities with paths to prestigious law schools.

But applying to law school was an expectation of others, not a dream of her own. The deadlines for declaring her intentions came and went, and without declaring anything at all she chose her home over a distant dorm by simply staying here. In Marina's world, it went without saying that Dylan shouldn't be alone while his father worked all day. She merely assumed it, the way she assumed the role of his mother at the age of three.

Marina attends a UCSB Extension program part-time, where she learns Spanish, French, and how to teach English to non-English speakers. She volunteers regularly for UNICEF. And at the end of most days, she stands silently at the edge of the Pacific and watches the sun set abroad. One day I expect she'll walk across the water to whatever child in whatever country needs her. If ever she's not needed here.

Right now, though, her attention is on the past rather than the future. When a ski falls over and hits the floor that is also Dylan's bedroom ceiling, a puff of dust mushrooms.

A short while later her puffy-eyed brother stomps up the narrow stairwell. His slender fingers can do nothing to smooth his crazed hair.

"Still looking?" he asks.

She glances up. "You should go back to bed."

"You go back to bed." Out of any other boy's mouth it would sound snarky. Coming from Dylan, it's somehow respectful. He wins a flicker of a smile.

He comes to the top of the stairs and the floor creaks under his slight weight. Marina is emptying a clear plastic bin full of glass Christmas balls, stacking their cardboard boxes on a child's table. Dylan pulls a miniature chair out from under it and squats to sit, blinking.

"What can't wait?" he asks. He lifts the red lid of another bin that holds decorations. "It's July. It's four in the morning."

"Mom died at Christmastime."

This is a long-established piece of family history. A senseless nonanswer.

He narrows his eyes and whispers, "The quick brown fox jumps over the lazy dog."

But Marina won't elaborate. So Dylan leans the red lid against a tower of brown boxes and begins to add to his sister's pile on the table: the tinsel, the tangled lights, the reindeer candy dish that hasn't been set out for years.

He finds an artificial plum rolled in purple glitter. "Here." He offers it up to her. "Now we can go back to sleep."

She gently pushes his hand away.

"Sometimes I think things would be different if they'd found Mom's body," Marina says.

"The ocean is a big place for a body to get lost in."

"But don't you ever wonder if finding her would have changed anything? For us, for Dad."

"No." Dylan's lie is swift, reflexive. He's not only thought about it, he's written of it—nothing Marina has ever seen. But there are things we think and never speak. For some of us, more things than others.

Unfortunately, his answer shuts her down. "Maybe," he revises. "What would be different for you?"

Marina pauses with a ceramic candy cane in her fist. "I dream about her sometimes. Being alive."

"You knew her when she was alive."

"You knew her too."

"What, for three weeks?" The silliness of it forms a *pfft* on his lips.

"I believe your subconscious remembers the important details."

"My mother killed herself after I was born. Were you referring to something that'd be more important to me than that?"

"Dylan, it wasn't your fault."

"Right."

Marina sighs. She pulls out the kiddie chair next to her brother and joins him in emptying the bin at his feet.

"I don't remember what she looked like," Marina said. "In the dream I never see her. I've had it a zillion times. I'm on a raft in the ocean, and I'm drowning, it's stormy, and she—I don't know what she's doing. Watching? She's on some kind of boat, or land maybe. The point is, she could help me but she doesn't. She just watches me go down."

"See, I don't think anything would really be different if she were alive. You think you're drowning, but you're not. Not even when she just stands there. You always survive. You don't need her help." Dylan reaches back into the bin for the closest distraction. "*We* don't need it. In fact, maybe her leaving us early was good practice for what we're going through now."

He places a red satin box on the table, smacking it down like a period at the end of their conversation. It has a hinged lid and a band of red sequins around the rim. Marina doesn't see it right away. Her eyes have welled with all the pain Dylan thinks he carries alone.

"You said Mom left us early," Marina says.

"Died young. Left at the intermission. Took her life. Any euphemism sounds better than 'committed suicide.' You know I'm right. Pick your pet phrase."

"What if she didn't die? What if she just left?"

"I thought we just established that it wouldn't matter."

"She and Dad never divorced."

"Hard to divorce someone who's dead, isn't it?"

"Maybe she could help us keep the house."

Dylan shrugs and props his elbow on his knee and his jaw on his fist. "If she wanted to help us, she's had plenty of time."

"Maybe she'd still be responsible for his debts, whether she wants to or not."

"Is that how it works?"

"Dunno. I'll have to ask Jamie." Marina picks up the red box and lifts it closer to the dinosaur lampshade that's been shoved to the edge of the table. She leans in to examine the patterns of sequins along the rim. "When I was going through Dad's stuff, I found an old brochure about bipolar research at Stanford's School of Medicine."

"And you're thinking . . ."

She shakes her head. "What if she's been there all this time? In a hospital. What if Dad put her away and just didn't want us to know she was crazy?"

"That'd be hilarious," Dylan deadpans. "Because if she *is* in a loony bin, she won't exactly be in a position to help us pay the bills, will she?"

Marina shoots him a glare. "I thought I'd call tomorrow, ask some questions."

Her brother seals his lips. There's no point in trying to talk Marina out of this line of thought. Better to help her out. That's what I would have told him anyway.

"I know it's insane, Dylan, but what else am I going to do? I have to know. There's so much Dad didn't ever explain—and by the way, I don't believe you when you say you never wonder. You sound like Dad."

Dylan doesn't argue.

Marina says, "It's a gut feeling. I don't expect you to understand."

Gut feelings are one thing Dylan understands perfectly. She'll remember this later. But he's too wise to contradict her. He tries to go in the back door of her emotional lockdown with a peace offering: "This is probably nothing, but when I was going through Dad's closet I found some pictures."

"This is what I was looking for," Marina finally says of the red box. Dylan surrenders. "It's from Mom."

She flips back the flat-topped lid and reveals a blown-glass ball cushioned by a red satin nest. Carefully she takes it out, lets it hang from her finger by its sheer gold ribbon. The opaque globe is weighty, its surface swirling with storms of gold and copper and white. The frosted exterior looks like cinnamon sugar.

The ornament has been out of its box three times since it was gifted: on Marina's fourth Christmas, on Marina's twelfth birthday, and today.

"For you?" Dylan asks.

"Christmas the year she died. I found it the year I started

decorating the tree myself, but Dad didn't like to see it so I never put it up."

This is an alarming development. Why is she showing him this when there is no similar gift for Dylan? *See what I have and you don't?* Dylan leans back in his chair as if the thing is radioactive.

"Tonight I had that dream again, and when I went under the waves this globe was down there, and I grabbed it, and it pulled me back up to the surface."

"While Mom looked on," Dylan says wryly.

"I'm just wondering why a mom would buy a present like this and then kill herself."

In the dim light it's hard for Marina to see Dylan's expression, and his tone is tightly controlled: "I wouldn't know," he says. She isn't listening to anything but her own thoughts, and she doesn't really hear what her brother is saying. *Because I completely disrupted her life. You should know something about that, Marina.*

"Now that you found what you're looking for, I'll get out of your hair," he says. "Let me know if you want help calling Stanford."

"I'll take care of it," she murmurs.

He leaves Marina crouching over the miniature table like a storybook giant with stolen treasure, while the robbed peasant slips away, hoping to escape with nothing worse than a few flesh wounds.

I want to go to Dylan and stop the bleeding, but I can do that as easily as I can keep Marina afloat on a raging sea.

Nine

From the beach house rooftop I have a clear view of the ocean waves, which aren't raging at the moment. They need winter for that. Come January the famed Rincon Classic will draw unbearable crowds to watch the surfing competition, but in summer this sea is tame, the surges mostly flat. Dylan doesn't usually go out in this—pancake sea, sunshiny morning. The sun glows in that way it does only over the California coast, like a parent over a favored child: glare-free, warm, and never blazing. But today Dylan goes out anyway, in a wetsuit and FiveFingers shoes to protect his feet from the rocky sea floor. There's enough of a wind swell to promise some atypical left-breaking waves over the point.

That and his mind is too restless for the house to contain.

Dylan rides his board the way most kids ride a bike. He doesn't even have to think about his judgment, his timing, or his balance. He's as comfortable in the water as any otter or dolphin. Again and again he predicts when each wave will crest and the precise moment when the water will fold. He breaks every ledge and catches every drop as if taking a walk down the street. And he rides every wave, even these smallish ones, all the way to its smooth and gliding end. No dramatic wipeouts, no blinding spray and reckless air time for this boy, just one graceful exit after another. Even at the high points of winter, his anxious nervous system is at peace with his environment.

But today, he's off. I blame the poor conditions. The wind is firm and would blow me off the roof like a dry leaf, so I watch from the shelter of the satellite dish.

There aren't many surfers in the water today, mostly summertime beachgoers—Boogie Boarders and body surfers complaining that there aren't any waves. Skimboarders get the best ride right on the shoreline. Some kids are talking about what they'll do come fall when the action picks up. They're planning trips to the "real" pipelines of Hawaii or Australia—which is funny if you know that come winter, surfers from all over the world will journey *here*, to surf *this* point break. Dylan avoids the big talkers. There's always plenty of personal space available during the summer for guys with the longboards, which he prefers when the waves are weak.

He's on his stomach, paddling away from shore, thinking that the ocean is a mighty big place for a body to get lost in. And what if the body he's thought of most often isn't here at all?

Dylan turns his board around and floats over a swell that doesn't interest him. He wants the surge coming behind it, and without looking, going by nothing but the sensation of water collecting beneath him and lifting him toward the sky, he paddles, pops up in the wind, and waits for the drop.

This time he gets hung up on the lip. The wave casts him off, pitching him over the back. His board launches out over the water, then comes to a sharp halt at the end of the leash attached to his ankle.

I stand up on the roof, holding on to the rim of the dish, looking for him. Dylan's head pops up behind another low swell. He coughs once. For a moment he sputters and spins, his neck twisting for sight of the beach.

On the other side of the house I see Marina returning to the house in her convertible, top down, waiting in the driveway for the garage door to open.

I know about the pictures and articles that Dylan found in that black candy box at the bottom of the file cabinet. And I know he is keeping them from Marina, wanting something of his mother for himself. Because that's what he thinks they are, something of his mother. A black satin box instead of a red one, containing a possibility that he doesn't have to share.

Dylan decides to pack it in. He carries his board out of the water and across the pebbled beach and up the old, uneven railroad-tie stairs that cut through the ice plant to the enclosed patio. I slide to the edge of the roof and jump down, weightless on the rain gutters. A burst of a breeze spins me around once as I dangle, but it's not too bad. I drop silently.

Dylan looks okay, frowning but unhurt.

"Not the best conditions today," I say.

He stands the board in the corner between the house and the windbreak, then goes to the outdoor shower behind a redwood screen. There he peels off his black suit and rinses off the sand.

Marina pops her head out the back door as he's finishing. "Help me with the groceries?" she asks nicely.

He's still wet, water seeping through the legs of his fresh shorts and dripping from the ends of his hair, when he goes to help her and leaves the back door open. I see my chance. I make a break for the door, but my luck's as bad as my son's today. Just as I pass through, the kitchen door to the garage opens and Marina comes back in, canvas grocery sacks dangling from her arms. The house becomes a wind tunnel, pulling the breeze from the wide-open mouth of the garage straight through to where I'm standing. A puff that might not even dislodge a dandelion knocks me back onto the patio.

"Towel!" Marina barks, seeing Dylan's drips on the hard-wood floor.

She sets the bags down and drops a stack of mail on the dining room table, then treks to the patio door and pulls it shut. I want to break one of the wide windows, I'm so sick of these barriers. Marina spins back toward the kitchen, brushing the tottering pile of envelopes as she passes. A little black card escapes the stack, then flutters to the floor and sticks to one of Dylan's puddles.

He finds it when he comes through with the good towels from the downstairs bathroom. The guest towels that have almost never been touched by any guests. With one he squeezes the water from his hair, and with the other he mops up the floor. He wipes the card down and turns to toss it back onto the table when he catches sight of the print. It's Sara's card, and it bears the same name as the black satin box that's up in Dylan's room, hidden high on a closet shelf. *Sara's Sins.*

"What's this?" he asks his sister.

Marina turns to look. "No idea. The security guard said some woman left it."

"Why?"

"How should I know? Maybe she came about something for Dad and she doesn't know."

"'A Fine Chocolates Café'? Dad hates chocolate."

"Just throw it away."

When Marina isn't looking, Dylan slips it into his shorts

pocket, and when he brings in all the groceries, he tries to slip up to his room.

"You could help me put it away," Marina calls out when he's halfway up the stairs. "Most of it's for you."

Dylan obediently turns around and returns to the kitchen.

"I've got the closing shift tonight so I'll be out until around one," she says.

"'Kay."

"How's the new game coming?"

He shrugs. "Maybe it's not as cool as I thought it was."

"It's tough to be creative right now. Can I try the beta?"

"Not ready."

"When will it be?"

Dylan shrugs again. He puts a box of cereal next to a cookie jar.

"You up for a drive today?" she asks too casually.

"Like, to where?"

She avoids looking at him by bending into the fridge with a bag of oranges. "Wherever you want to go."

"No."

When he's finally freed, Dylan goes up to his room. I climb the bougainvillea trellis and swing myself up on the beams, then creep along the ridge, past Marina's room and over the sloping roof to his side of the house. The breeze might as well be a gale force. It takes me forever to get to Dylan's window by belly crawl.

Dylan's bedroom is a showcase for electronics, everything from early-model Macs to huge, hot flat-screen monitors, ultra-high-speed processors, hard drives, and cables. I know more about his surfing than I do about the computer parts strewn around the room. How does he keep track of anything? Instead of sports gear and stinky shoes he has futuristic gloves wired to the elbows and headgear that can probably teleport his brain to alternative dimensions. I recognize the old black Atari box but not the camera-like device mounted atop his desktop monitor. It's a motion sensor of some kind. He owns every gaming system ever invented, though these seem to be going the way of VCRs and DVD players and DVRs. Everything's virtual now, stored remotely in some invisible space rather than in a tangible, physical piece of hardware.

Kind of like me.

The posters in his room are geeky, even by geek standards. Computer diagrams and coding cheat sheets that look like the periodic table of the elements. His favorite avatars stare down on him while he works and sleeps. I couldn't say who these guys are, or what fantasy universe they belong to, or what admirable skills they have. But they are Dylan's friends.

My favorite poster is one he made himself, a self-portrait he took with his own camera. It's a picture of the back of his head, with all that sloppy trademark hair. He's framed by a glowing computer screen, and the picture is upside down. The caption: *One does not become brilliant by mimicking a meme.* He tells Marina that the poster is the only copy of that meme. He will never post it on the web, so if she ever sees it there, she should know it was done by a mimic.

By the time I arrive, Dylan has taken the black satin box down out of his closet and is sitting on his bed, going through the contents.

A photo: a young couple stands in front of the Becker beach house shortly after the papers were signed. He holds a bottle of champagne and her waist; she seems not to know what to do with her hands. A wide wedding band on his ring finger is visible, pressed against the bottle's label. The pair stands at the front door on a day when there was only green grass and a chipped concrete stoop leading the way. The wide red-tiled porch and bougainvillea trellis came after. A laborer took that picture—the man who installed the hardwood floors in the kitchen and dining room. He captured the moment and then was gone.

Another photo: Marina, two years old. She sits in the crook of a woman's arm. Marina's cheeks were fuller then, and her black hair curly, tied up in pigtails. But her eyes are as constant as stars. She looks into the camera with the same courage that has come to mark her entire life, and I have always wondered if she knew even then, in that innocent way that observant children do, what was about to happen. Maybe an angel told her the future and prepared her for it—an angel, a fairy, or God himself. Definitely not me. Not the woman nuzzling Marina's cheek, eyes closed. Content. Happy.

Sane.

No photos of Dylan. There was only one at the time, and the police took that.

There are other papers in the box.

A formal, professionally printed invitation to the Rochester family reunion at Pebble Beach in Monterey, August 1997. No envelope.

A napkin bearing a handwritten note. It's a recipe for something called "Cha Chi Cha"—a "dancing chocolate chili candy." A few ingredients have question marks beside them. Some of the quantities have been struck and revised. On the back of the napkin a note: *For GB, because your good taste might be worth something someday, 10/97.*

There's a newspaper article turning brown, a tiny clipped

rectangle with no photos. *Presumed Suicide at Monastery Beach.*
Dylan reads:

> An abandoned car registered to a missing Marina del Rey
> woman, Misty Becker, was found yesterday on the Cabrillo
> Highway at Monastery Beach. Authorities confirm that a
> suicide or accidental death is suspected. No body has been
> recovered. The area is notorious for tragic drownings but has
> no recorded suicides. Becker was born and raised in Monterey
> and has a history of mental health issues.

There's a note, written on stationery instead of a napkin. No
date, no endearment, no signature.

> I have to go, for the kids' sake. You see the damage I've already
> done. I would take it back a thousand times if I could. Please
> let me go so you can heal. So all of you can heal. In time you'll
> forgive me.

Dylan holds the note up next to the candy recipe. The writing
is similar. Maybe the same.

He has folded the birth certificates he found and tucked them
in here as well. He opens his and smooths it out on the bed. Father,
Garrett John Becker. Mother, Misty Rochester Becker. Until Dylan
found the box I'm not sure he ever knew the Rochester part. His
sister's is the same.

Dylan holds the business card up and compares the names.
Sara Rochester. Misty Rochester.

He puts the birth certificate back in the box and taps the card
on the flat of his bent knee, thinking, but not for too long. Soon

enough he goes to his computer and maps the Montecito address. The shop isn't so far away. Ten, fifteen minutes depending on the traffic.

A gust of wind kicks sand up into my eyes. I rub it out, squinting. When my eyes clear, I see I'm no longer gripping the open frame of Dylan's window, but Marina's.

Ten

Marina is making a call. She sits at a white desk under a white lamp, her dark brows pinched as she listens to the receiver at her ear. Old, yellowed brochures from the Stanford University School of Medicine are spread out on the desk in front of her. The pencil she holds hovers over a white scrap pad monogrammed with a hot pink *M*—last year's stocking stuffer from Dylan.

The room's windows overlook the bougainvillea trellis that covers the front porch, and the raspberry color of those tissue-thin petals seems to have blown inside through the French-paned window. The white-on-white room has dark-pink accents: a pillow, a reading chair, a picture frame, the case she chose for her cell phone. A pink rack holds the remotes for the flat-screen TV mounted on the wall. Accessories hang neatly from a pink tree that grows atop a dust-free nightstand. Books she's reading are stacked on the nightstand. All her clothes and shoes are out of sight, in the closet, where they are stored in bins and folded on shelves and ironed and hung and labeled. The recently vacuumed carpet shows off neat footprints.

Her friend Jade lies on the bed, a foot crossed on one knee, clashing with Marina's controlled environment in a red tank top and turquoise shorts. Her fluorescent-green electronic tablet keeps her entertained. Jade's floppy purse has spilled open on the floor, and Marina's eyes keep darting to it while she talks on the phone.

"So you don't treat patients?" Marina asks. "I thought you were a hospital."

The answer is muffled.

"I see. Outpatient only. How long are— Yes, I can hold."

She says to Jade, "They're developing treatments for bipolar disorder and schizophrenia, that sort of thing. Clinical trials."

Jade sits up and swings her legs off the bed. "So does that make sense? Is that what your mom had?"

"I told you, I don't know."

"But don't people have to volunteer for the studies?"

"Not for years at a time, locked up in a padded room some-where. Is that what you meant, that my mom might be their hostage?"

Jade rolls her eyes and falls back onto the bed. "I'm only saying what you've been thinking."

My daughter looks embarrassed. She hangs up before the person on the other end returns.

Jade turns onto her side and props her head on her fist. "This whole rabbit trail about finding your mom is a distraction, Marina. What you need is a way to earn some cash."

My daughter presses her lips together. Jade's theatrical head wobbling and hand motions underline just how out of whack her compassion-meter is.

"Let's take a good look at the fantasy playground you've been playing on for the last twenty-four hours: you think your suicidal mom might actually be alive, and although she's probably mental she must still be clearheaded enough to take responsibility for you and your brother. Or, in a different scenario, she might be too unstable to hold a job but rich enough to save this beachfront property. And she hasn't sent you a birthday card for seventeen years, but when you show up she'll care enough to kiss all your tears away. Do I have that right?"

By the time she's done, her glossy blond hair is swishing around her goosey neck.

Marina is staring at her, strong as a sea wall. "Sometimes I wonder why I call you my friend."

"Because I say it like it is. You used to do it too. C'mon, Marina—you know you're chasing a ghost."

"I'm trying to save this house for Dylan."

"Well, maybe you can't."

Marina shakes her head. "If he has to leave it's going to set him back. Maybe years. Maybe forever. There should be limits on how much stress a person has to face in a lifetime."

"But it won't kill him, right? Has anyone ever actually *died* of a panic attack?"

"Probably. In fact, maybe I'll look into that, scare myself just a little bit more."

Jade's impatience comes out like a growl. "Leave it to the therapist—which I'm sure you can *qualify* for with some special program for low-income families."

"Jade—"

"No, no." Jade shushes Marina by sitting up again and scootching to the edge of the mattress. She leans forward and cranes her neck so she's right in Marina's face. "Here, listen to me, I know what you have to do. You have to start making some money, hard and fast. No more of this UNICEF-volunteer-dreamer stuff for you, Marina, not for a while. All your free hours—you work, you save. And Dylan had better start thinking about getting his high-functioning self out there to pull a paycheck too."

"Says the slacker who wants a husband who can fly her to New York for weekend shopping trips."

Jade grins at that. "But we're talking about *you*." She stands up and lays down a new track of flip-flop prints in the clean carpet. She paces around the back of Marina's desk chair. "Look: remember my next-door neighbor? The one I used to go to elementary school with?"

"The family that lost their home?"

"That one. They stopped paying the mortgage eighteen months before they had to leave. My mom used to go on and on about that—"

"You're saying you think we could stay here for a while." Marina's mind is already running with this possibility, or maybe tripping over the question of why she didn't think of it herself.

"Until they throw you out. Your attorney said you had some time, didn't he? Might take years. And by then you strike gold, Dylan gets better, who knows? Remember I told you I met a guy who has the body shop in Goleta?"

"Waiting tables pays better. The tips alone. All I have to do is pick up a few more shifts."

Jade's earnest face melts into a sly grin. She reaches into the back pocket of those turquoise shorts and pulls out a dollar bill folded twice. Then she waves it in front of Marina's eyes before unfolding it and flattening it out on that tidy, white desk. Money truly is a dirty-gray shade of green.

It's not one bill but two. And each isn't worth one dollar, but a hundred.

"For two hours' work," Jade announces. "You can't make that in restaurant tips."

Disgust wrinkles Marina's mouth. She pushes back from the desk and stands up. "I don't know what kind of body shop you're talking about, but I won't *ever*—"

"Chillax!" Jade laughs. "Seriously, it's an *auto* body shop. And I assure you, I did this work with all my clothes on. Shoes too." She puts a scandalous purr in her throat. "Even a jacket."

"Forget it, Jade. I have trouble getting the hood of my own car unlatched. I can't do that kind of work."

"You can do *this* kind."

Marina sighs and goes to her closet in the corner of the bedroom. "Tell me it's legal and I'll listen." She pulls open the single door and reaches inside for some shoes.

"What kind of work is actually one hundred percent aboveboard these days, huh?"

Marina looks at Jade sternly while she leans against the closet's doorframe and tugs on a pair of strappy sandals. "You forget I almost went to law school."

"Well *that* opportunity's gone, isn't it?"

The girls are silent until both of Marina's feet have shoes. I don't like the whirling going on behind my daughter's eyes. The anxiety, the sadness, the recalculating of her moral code. I know how the mind contorts until it can finally justify the choice it wants. The inconsequential choices and the life-changing ones sometimes look identical before they're made, but the life-changing ones can't be called back.

"Are you going to tell me or what?" Marina asks.

Jade perks up, energized by the chance that her friend might approve.

"He's got us all over town, anywhere we might catch a sneak peek at a car's registration—the car wash, the valet—there's even someone at one of the lube shops who feeds him owners' addresses. He has needs for certain cars, certain parts. He gives us a list, and if we find him a match, all we have to do is get him the owner's address. Twenty per car, fifty if you're willing to play with the big boys."

"The big boys. Is that how they talk?"

"The repo team—"

"Are we talking about car theft?"

"It is *such* a rush, Marina."

"Which part? Rifling through someone's glove box for the registration? Please tell me that's the only team you're on. There's a million ways to find out a person's address. I could excuse you for just being nosy."

Jade lifts her eyebrows, smiles, and tilts her head to one side.

"I don't believe this. Do you know how dangerous that is?"

Her friend groans and rolls her eyes. "You're supposed to be my friend, not my mom."

"I'm sure your mom doesn't know what you're up to."

"Exactly! And now I'm finally going to have enough money to get my own place, besides!"

"Maybe I should report you both."

"Oh, stop pretending you're better than me." Jade stands up and starts scooping her phone, a pen, a lipstick tube, her car keys all back into the purse that has spilled out over the floor. "I'll tell you why we're friends, Marina. It's because we know how to survive while the people who call themselves our parents stumble around like zombies."

"What does that have to do with stealing cars for a chop shop?"

Jade slings the long strap of her bag over her shoulder, and the bag smacks the side of her bare leg.

"This: I've always known that I never had anyone to count on but myself. But you, Marina—you're only just finding out that you never did either."

That's totally false, of course. So why does this mouthy girl fill me with shame?

Oh, my beautiful girl. Please don't.

Marina follows Jade out of the bedroom. *Please don't.* Almost a prayer. I can't remember the last time I prayed.

Eleven

A blink, and the window separates me from a different scene.

I've never been into Sara's Sins Café before, though I know enough about her rising-star career. I'm on the inside looking out for once, standing in front of a classy wood-and-glass door. The sign hanging right before my eyes says *Open*, which means the side facing the public says *Closed*.

Someone in the kitchen behind the shimmering glass display cases is humming.

It's cold in here. Summer's warmth is locked out to protect the sweets, even though I can tell by the angle of the sun that it's early morning. The shop's candy odor is pleasing and overwhelming at the same time.

My cut fingertip throbs. My bloody elbow feels bruised. They won't heal or clean up, so I try to ignore them.

Montecito is an understated village version of Beverly Hills. I recognize the narrow street outside the shop. A quaint row of storefronts lines this swooping, little road that eventually waltzes downhill to the beach. Ancient eucalyptus and olive trees shade the low rooflines.

A car door slams shut and draws my attention. Marina's white convertible is parked behind a flowering brick planter in one of the slots lining the sidewalk. Its vinyl top and windows are sealed up tight, and no one could be more stunned than I am to see Dylan standing on the asphalt, leaning against the driver's side door as if that's all that's holding him up. His face is flushed and he's sweating again. He's looking up at the sign hanging over the door—*Sara's Sins, A Fine-Chocolates Café*—and cramming keys into the pocket of his threadbare jeans.

How did Dylan get here without his sister? He's had a handful of online driver's ed sessions, but next to nothing on the road, not nearly enough hours to qualify for his license even if he aced the required exams. Climbing into a small box with closed doors and a stranger is just too much for him.

But here he is, alone and unlicensed, hugging Sara's black-satin chocolate box. A terrified mummy holding on to the suitcase of stuff he'll need in the afterlife. But he's alive. He talks to himself. His lips move with words I can't hear but assume are a calming mantra that might or might not pull him through.

When he finishes, he takes a deep breath. The tightness over his cheekbones passes and he comes toward the shop.

His fear and his courage grapple in a deadlocked arm-wrestling match. Years of therapy push against years of entrenched bio-logical response to fear. Fight or flight.

My children fight. They want to live.

Dylan raises a fist to the locked door. He pounds on the glass. His energy vibrates through the palms of my hands with so much force that I have to step back.

The humming in the kitchen stops to listen.

Dylan rattles the door again. His eyes are on the light in the back.

After a few seconds of this, Sara Rochester sticks her head

out of the kitchen. "We open at seven," she calls cheerfully. She sounds lighter than she did the day her car was stolen. Maybe she has it back.

A flash image comes to me: a different car parked in the rear of the shop. Apparently she's driving a rental, a sporty two-seater, also a convertible, though not quite as high end as her Porsche.

Even in the morning dimness of the unlit café, I'm struck by the fact that she and Dylan have the same coarse hair, cut to show off its natural thickness. They have the same deep complexion, the same sun-kissed youthfulness, though they live a generation apart.

Sara ducks back into the kitchen, clueless that Dylan can't wait until seven. Thirty minutes of waiting for the unknown might lead to a full-scale crisis.

In the kitchen Sara's voice mingles with someone else's. Glass dishes tap each other and make their own chatter as they're placed on a counter, and tissue-paper wrappers rustle as sweets are transferred to plates. Dylan's boldness falters, then he draws a full breath and leans in. His hands form a shade between his eyes and the glass so he can see.

The café is cozy, so unlike the more common chocolatiers with their sterile black-and-white decor that brings to mind a hospital. The low ceilings and rustic brick walls surround the space like a comforting blanket. At the bright windows, a counter and tall café chairs look out onto the tree-canopied street. Seven round tables fill the space in what might be a feng shui design, each having enough elbow room to feel private. Eleven tables could comfortably fit here, but Sara has left room for built-in bookcases and love seats that frame coffee tables. On the walls are simple photographs of candied flowers—violets, roses, orchids dusted with sugar.

A handwritten menu on a triptych of blackboards offers chocolate crepes and chocolate croissants and chocolate-raspberry tarts and chocolate pastries. There is a list of suggested coffee and truffle pairings, wine-cellar style. A long list of drinking chocolates gets its own board. Beneath these, the ordering counter is topped with a display case that is presently empty, except for rectangular crystal serving plates and the tented labels that hold the name, description, and price of each chocolate that will soon fill it.

Sara brings two filled plates out of the kitchen and slides them into the case.

When Dylan sees her, he pounds again, then smacks the door with the flat of his hand, and Sara lifts her eyes. He's holding a picture pressed down against the glass.

With his other hand Dylan presses the black box next to the photo. The gilded shop name catches the distant kitchen light. Sara is frozen, except for her eyes. They move from the box to the photo, the one of the couple standing in front of the beach house's front door, and then finally to Dylan's flushed face.

"I'm looking for someone," he shouts. Then as an afterthought, "I'm Dylan Becker." He licks his lips, and his eyes plead with hers for long seconds before she comes unthawed. She closes the temperature-controlled case and opens a drawer under the register and fumbles for the key inside of it, then comes around the counter, moving like someone shaken awake from a troubled sleep.

She recovers by the time she reaches the front. She fits the key into the lock and turns it and opens the door in a practiced move. She's so swift that it's possible she's angry. Dylan seems surprised that she's done this. The photograph flutters to her feet and he almost drops the box, saving it on juggler's luck. He takes a step back and loses his voice. She might go after him. She might take our history out on my son, though he's a head taller than she is.

His mouth forms words that don't come out.

Sara bends down to pick up the photograph. Dylan pulls the box to his heart like a shield. She looks at the image for a long time, still holding the door open.

"Garrett Becker," she finally says. Her voice is kind, friendly even.

"Dylan."

"I meant in the picture."

"Yeah. My dad."

"I can see the resemblance."

The silence stretches out.

Dylan lifts his chin toward the picture. "That's you." It's half question, half announcement. A thing for her to contradict.

Her nod is minute.

He says, "This is weirder than I thought it would be. You look like my sister. Sort of." He looks away from her, down the street. "I didn't think you'd actually be here. I wasn't even sure . . . I mean, it could have been just a box."

Sara steps back to make room for him. "Why don't you come in."

His phobia won't let him. In a blink he measures the confines of her shop, calculates that the exit is too easily blocked, that the unknowns are too threatening.

"You must have a lot of questions. I'll make you a hot chocolate."

He just doesn't have enough air in his chest to laugh full out and tell her he hasn't had a sip of hot chocolate since he was eleven years old—though he'll eat a bag of marshmallows straight up if given the chance.

The strongest objection he can manage is, "It's July."

"The expiration date isn't until October," Sara says good-naturedly, and when a smile catches a corner of Dylan's mouth, I know that they get each other.

"Thanks anyway."

But she's still studying the picture, holding it close, and though he's standing sideways now, leaning toward Marina's car, it's clear he won't leave without that snapshot.

"I heard about your dad's accident," she says. "I'm so sorry."

He nods, a quick bob. His eyes keep darting to the picture.

"I've been thinking about you and your sister, but I didn't know how—"

"Did you come by?"

"I tried. Didn't know the secret handshake. Did you get my card?"

"Yeah."

"Please come in," she says again. "We'll talk."

Dylan can't come or go. It's Sara who finally moves, so cautiously. She reaches out toward him like a rescuer approaching a wounded animal. He's still clutching the black box with both hands. Her touch lands on his wrist.

For someone like Dylan a kind hand can be as threatening as a knife at the throat, and Sara is asking him to come farther away from all his safety nets—home, sister, car—into a dim café surrounded by brick walls.

Dylan looks at Sara's fingers lying on his arm and lowers the box-shield to his side. And when she lets go, he grasps for her hand, a boyish gesture that looks like an awkward but sincere handshake.

I feel a surge of hope.

"Are you—?" What he wants to say catches in his throat and his flush comes back. "I guess you're Misty."

She squeezes his hand before releasing it. "Sara Rochester," she says gently.

He nods as if that changes nothing. What's in a name, after all? We can change our names but not who we are.

"Come in."

He needs no further reassurance. There's a trash bin near the exit, and I see him glance at it. If possible he'll pull it over and use it to prop open the door. He'll take the nearest tall chair at the window counter so he can make a quick getaway if needed. He'll turn the seat around so that he's facing the room with his back protected. This is what Dylan does even in those few places where he is at ease.

"No hot chocolate, you're sure?" she asks as she moves across the room.

"Just coffee."

"Any special kind?"

"The black kind."

She glances back at him and her warmth alone pulls him in. I wouldn't believe it if I wasn't watching it myself: he forgets the trash can, his need for escape hatches, and follows her all the way into the shop, all the way from the door to the opposite corner, where an overstuffed chair sits facing the copper espresso machine. He drops himself into it, easy as a baseball into a glove. I am stunned. Sara places the photo on the coffee table before him. He stays. I approach.

Invisible sea monsters stir in the hopeful pit of my dead stomach. This is it: the truth is about to come out.

Sara is grinding beans, then measuring and tamping and brewing in quick, fluid motions. She glances at the black box Dylan has set on the table next to the photo, unaware that he is not himself.

"That's a rare edition," she says of the box. "I thought I'd like the black satin in the beginning, when I was just working out of my kitchen. But they're too stiff. Formality doesn't really whet the appetite. I want people to relax. Loosen their belt buckles." She nods at an antique china cabinet that displays gift boxes of brown corrugated paper ribboned with raffia. The red straw-like bows match the bricks' color. "Brown paper packages tied up with string. You know."

I don't think he does. Dylan slouches in his chair with his hands on his thighs and his mind on other topics.

"I never believed you killed yourself," he says. Sara looks up at him over the coffee machine. "Even though everyone says that's what happened. I've just always sensed . . . I don't know."

Her silence is thoughtful, her sigh weighty. She waits for the coffee to fill the glass mug.

He raises his eyebrows and shakes his head. "Marina isn't going to believe—" Dylan cuts himself off. "Well. She will eventually."

Sara brings the black coffee around and sets it in front of him, then lowers herself to the edge of the love seat opposite him. She leans forward.

"Dylan, I'm not your mother."

He shifts in the deep seat, looks down at the picture beside the steaming mug. "I get it if you don't want us to call you that," he says. "I mean—duh, right? Almost seventeen years. I'm sure you have your reasons. We're all adults."

He's a terrible liar. Hasn't had any reason to master that yet.

"Your dad and I were friends."

He reaches for the box and lifts the hinged lid, then withdraws the picture of Marina. He hands it to Sara. With the exception of the hairstyle and the clothes, Sara looks as if she could be the woman holding the toddler, aged by twenty or so years. Sara stays where she is, lips pressed tightly together.

Dylan says, "Marina's the one who really needs you. Especially now, with Dad . . ." He clears his throat. "I don't know if that makes sense. She's got herself together, I don't mean like she's falling apart or anything. It's just there's some things that maybe you could help with. The way she's helped me."

Sara puts the picture of Marina back on the table.

He scoops the birth certificates out and unfolds them. "Misty Rochester Becker," Dylan says, laying them out in front of her. He points to both lines as if this evidence of their mother's name will make Sara wilt. I notice a tiny tremble in his hand. This isn't how I thought this would unfold. My son doesn't understand. "You said you're a Rochester. I heard that much right."

Sara clears her throat and picks up the invitation. "I met your dad at this reunion—"

"Why would he be there, if he wasn't family?"

"Misty was a Rochester too, as you've pointed out."

"So are you a friend of Dad's, or are you family too?"

An answer to this pointed question eludes her.

Very slowly—maybe to give Sara that time he thinks she needs, maybe to hide his mounting stress—Dylan takes the paper napkin bearing the candy recipe out of the bottom of the box and sets it on the table. Sara's eyes linger on it. Then he takes out the folded note. He returns the birth certificates one at a time to their container but leaves the pictures on the table to stare at her.

"These are the first pictures I've ever seen of you. Did you know my dad would do that? Bury you in a file cabinet?"

"He probably recalled that I once said the box looked like a coffin."

Really, Sara? That's what you'll choose for this moment? I can't tell if she's angry, ashamed, or trying to break the tension.

He spreads his hands wide, palms up, indicating the sum total of his family knowledge there on the table. "He told us you committed suicide, swam out into the ocean up there at Mortuary Beach and kept on swimming. They believed it too." He points to the newspaper clipping. "I think that was the easier story to tell. Easier than saying you just took off." He starts to bounce his right knee under his hand. But he forgets to take calming breaths.

"I always thought there was something about the house—that you were still there with us. Close somehow. I didn't ever guess it was like this, though. Fifteen minutes away. Fifteen minutes." He laughs and his voice breaks. "It took me an hour and a half to get here. That's how messed up I am."

"You're not messed up."

"What do you know?" he says. Dylan, my quiet child, the one who never gets angry. "And I don't believe you're Dad's friend. What kind of friend lives fifteen minutes away and never even visits? And what kind of friend shares my mom's name but can't be bothered to get to know her family, unless she *is* family, and she just doesn't want to be associated with us at all?"

Sara's hand goes to her mouth. She's shaking her head. "You were just a baby," Sara finally says. "You didn't deserve what happened."

He shrugs and takes awhile to answer. His eyes are on the handwritten blackboards, absorbing every detail.

"You didn't even stay long enough for a picture."

There was a picture. One. Time only for one. I wonder if Sara is thinking of it. That season passed more quickly than a Southern California snow, though it felt like a million years.

Dylan picks up the stationery and unfolds it. A simple red line frames the neat handwriting. He glances at the blackboards again, then looks at her.

She stares into his eyes as if she doesn't see what's in his hands.

"Read this," he says.

She refuses by holding her tongue.

"Then I will." He holds the note with two hands right in front of his face.

"Dylan, stop. This is between you and your father."

"You think he's going to explain this to me now?"

Blood rushes to Sara's face. Dylan lifts the page. It is practically fluttering in his quivering fingers.

"'I have to go, for the kids' sake. You see the damage I've already done. I would take it back a thousand times if I could. Please let me go so you can heal. So all of you can heal. In time you'll forgive me.'"

Sara is pinching her hands between her knees.

"Well, it's not poetry," Dylan says. He swipes at a sheen of sweat above his eyebrows.

"Your mother was *sick*."

He stares at Sara with a new kind of scrutiny. He refolds the paper, pinching the creases. "Sick, like, in the head? Like multiple personality disorder or something? Like"—he waves a hand in the air—"she might forget who she was?"

"No, not that."

"Because this sounds like a suicide note to me. But maybe it isn't."

"I'm saying the whole thing was tragic."

Dylan glances again at the three blackboards. "Whoever wrote those menus wrote this letter."

Sara catches his drift right away. She objects with her whole body. She stands, she plants her hands on her hips, she frowns. "I'm not your mother."

The swift movement threatens Dylan. He cracks then, a seashell hit by one too many waves.

"I have to go." The note crumples when he grabs it and the black box together, the lid still flapping open. "I have to go," he repeats, and this time Sara doesn't try to stop him. Not very hard, anyway.

"Please let me explain."

He's panting more than breathing. His short breaths take on a wheeze. He bangs his shin on the edge of the coffee table as he rushes off, staggering for a safe place where no one has any secrets to hide, if such a place exists. And he says, "I don't want to hear any more lies."

———

Miraculously, I manage to get out the door when Dylan passes through it. I slip into the car the same way, tumbling into the passenger seat. I plead with Dylan to call and wake Marina before he kills himself driving home. He doesn't, but he has the common sense to stay put for a bit. He sits in the driver's seat in the safety of the closed-up car, and I barely get in before he closes the door. His breathing is so shallow that I worry he might faint—which would be one way of overcoming the present crisis, but it's not ideal.

"Steering wheel, sidewalk, flowers, dress shop, tree," he whispers. "Birds, traffic, breathing, voice, truck." He's working on a 5–4–3–2–1 exercise that breaks the snowball effect of panic by bringing his mind back in touch with his surroundings. He'll name five things he can see, five things he can hear, five things he can touch. Then four, then three, and so on. "Jeans, hair, upholstery"—he touches each one in turn—"dashboard, steering wheel."

I join him in the exercise. Four items per category now. "Glove box," I say over his own observations. "Kleenex, sunglasses, cyclist."

He swiftly moves to the auditory: "Wind, heartbeat." The keys jingle as he puts them into the ignition and a satellite station kicks in through the speakers. "Car keys, radio."

Already Dylan's breathing has come down a few notches. It's deeper. "Black box," he says, running his fingertips over the satin container that still sits on his lap.

"I would have picked something else," I say.

He opens the lid. "Crumpled paper, glossy photo." He caresses both. "Pseudo-suicide note."

He stops there, lost in the unpleasant revelations of the morning. He has it all wrong. I touch his hand and he flinches as if from a shock, as before.

"Montecito!" I shout at the top of my lungs, though he can't hear a thing. "Pretty girls! Ugly seagulls!"

Dylan looks up, straight through the windshield and into the front of Sara's Sins. "Sara," he says. And there she is, standing on the other side of the glass, watching him. The morning light on the window makes her face unreadable. "Misty." Then, "Mom."

"You ought to hear her out," I say. "Go back in there and give her a chance."

He turns the key all the way over in the ignition, and when the engine catches, he pushes the button that releases the convertible's roof. He stares at Sara while the mechanism whines and whines until it has fully retracted the soft top into the compartment above the trunk.

What on earth?

Sara bears the weight of his glare. Then he puts the car in drive and pulls out onto the road, and like an old man on a Sunday drive he cruises on down the hill and finds the 101 headed south. He drives by the book. He uses his blinkers and everything. We pick up speed.

The noise of freeway winds whipping round the passenger seats doesn't faze him. But his calm completely unnerves me. As does his pace. He's easy on his sister's car. There's no gunning the engine or burning rubber or peeling across the lanes, but he steadily accelerates until we've passed sixty-five and seventy and smoothly sail right on past seventy-five. In no time at all we've left the lush Santa Barbara scene and found the Pacific again, where he flies down the curvy highway so fast that it seems we're skimming the water. When he tops eighty-five, I can't look anymore. It might seem like I have nothing to lose, but there's Dylan, see? And there's nothing I can do to help him get back home in one piece. I try to stay calm.

Things I can smell: salt, humidity, seaweed, sunscreen, sweat.

Things I can hear: gulls crying, waves breaking, an engine straining, my heart throbbing, a woman speaking:

"Why do we lie?"

It's Sara. She's leaning into my ear, so close that she must be in the backseat, pushing against the winds to speak to me without shouting. The wind sits on my eyelids and I can't look for her.

"Why do we lie to the kids?"

Her voice has the power of Jesus calming the storm. All around me, the clatter is silenced. No more screeching birds, no more crashing surf, no more zooming car, no more racing pulse beating against my ears. Just the even-keeled voice of a woman who hasn't spoken to me for years and years, and her voice restores peace. The car vibrates gently beneath my body, letting me know it's still flying. But I can't see a thing. The whole world is dark, tires on asphalt, shadows running over a long road.

"We lie because the truth would kill them," I say. And then I wait for her to respond. Agree, disagree, offer her own theory.

She gives me nothing but lonely silence, because the truth is, she isn't really with me. I am utterly alone.

Twelve

This isn't Marina's convertible anymore, the one Dylan pinched, the one that smells like suntan lotion and fresh strawberries. Sara's rental car smells like vanilla-scented carpet shampoo, and the fresh air coming in through the open windows can't blow the artificial odor away even at top speeds. She isn't sitting behind me anymore; now she's beside me, in the driver's seat. She's racing away from her shop, from her past, from the possibility that Dylan might come back before she knows what to do about him.

It's easier to watch her drive than Dylan, though she might be as distracted as he is inexperienced. The odd sight granted to me in my present state confirms that he made it home safely without me, but the sight of him bent over the computer in his bedroom tells me nothing about the condition of his heart after his encounter with the woman he thinks is his mom.

Sara looks out the windshield without seeing anything. She points her car out of Montecito and descends the low hills to the oceanfront streets. The sun is a philosopher's stone dropping into the ocean, turning the water to gold. A stoplight changes to yellow, then red, and she slows. She stops, then doesn't notice when the light clicks back to green. The driver behind her honks. She flinches, then moves on.

She rolls up the windows and gives her voice-activated cell phone the command to place a call to "the vineyard." When nothing happens, she remembers that she isn't in her own car. Her cell phone is on the console. She fishes it out and dials the old-fashioned way.

"Karen, it's Sara Rochester," she says when her call is answered. "Well, I've been better. I really need to get away. Is there any chance Ian has a vacancy tonight at the B&B?"

Ian McCleary's success with the bed-and-breakfast side of his business surprised some folks around here. Most tourists think "wine country" exists only farther north: Sonoma County, Napa Valley. Fewer visitors come as far south as San Luis Obispo and Santa Barbara Counties. The scenery isn't as spectacular, and the name dropping not quite as potent.

But not even someone like me can pretend that acres and acres of vines bowed with purple grapes against a backdrop of blue sky and golden grass aren't eye-catching. The foothills are low, smooth, soft, the ocher yellow of a dun horse that lay down to soak up the sun. Pluck a person out of the congested Southern California hubbub and drop her into a landscape that's quiet, orderly, and scented with salt air even though the ocean isn't in sight. The chaos swirling within the heart, the brain, the stomach will take on the nature of its surroundings. At least for a little while.

I gather from the phone conversation that Sara goes there often for this effect.

Karen, the B&B manager, has good news. There was a cancellation the day before, so Sara's in luck. Her new plans reanimate her. She calls her head confectioner and makes sure Sara's Sins will be in good hands the following day. She drives home and packs a small bag with a change of clothes and sturdy walking shoes. She leaves a message for Ian announcing her spontaneous visit.

It takes her a full five minutes to figure out how to put the convertible's top down. And then she's off, unaware that she's not traveling alone.

With the Pacific at her back she heads up into the Los Padres National Forest along the San Marcos Pass, along the inky waters of Lake Cachuma, and down into Santa Ynez, home to old Ford pickup trucks and roadside fruit and vegetable stands. All it lacks today is John Steinbeck sitting under a shady oak tree writing a new novel. The journey from beach to vineyard takes less than forty-five minutes.

Ian isn't there when she arrives and settles in for the night. He won't return until quite late, Karen says, plump-cheeked and smiling and rosy as if she's already had a few glasses of something red. In fact, the manager offers, Sara probably passed him on the highway without realizing it. He's with Denica, gone to fetch her brother, Gabe, from the Santa Barbara airport.

Of course. Of course. Now Sara remembers Gabe's long-anticipated visit. Ian has mentioned it several times, but she never noted the specific dates.

Sara veils her disappointment with cheerful gratitude. She knows the way to her room. She walks there alone, her floral-print overnight bag knocking against her leg. Her wedged sandals make soft noise on the stamped concrete path. A breeze swirls her summer skirt around her knees and blows the silver eucalyptus leaves across her way like apologetic rose petals. The resort house on the north end of the estate is booked, but as she makes her way there, it seems she is the only one in this whole small world, the universe gone out to dinner or over to the beach she has just left behind.

She slips her modern plastic key card into the slot in an ancient-looking wood door, which swings on iron hinges into the well-appointed room. The guest rooms are named—tongue-in-cheek—after what Ian calls "the first vineyards": Noah's Acre, Solomon's Song, Heaven's Parable. The little getaway that is Sara's for the evening is called Eden's Garden.

Out of the hearing of guests, Denica refers to the room as the Serpent's Lair. On Sara's first visit to the B&B, during a rare late-spring cold snap, she was welcomed by a garden snake with a fine taste for warm floors. It found the room's subfloor heating system when it came in through a tear in the sliding screen door. Eventually the greedy little snake curled up in her warm slippers, where Sara's toes found the tiny reptile the following morning.

Ian quickly repaired the screen. Sara paid for the ceramic vase that broke after she kicked off her horrifying slipper, and she apologized to the guests she woke with her ear-splitting shriek. So each time Sara enters the room and sees that the glass slider is closed, she feels a little relief.

Her overnight bag sinks deep into the feather duvet. A lamp in the corner of the room casts light and shadows across the mission-style furniture: the plump pillows, the wide picture windows, the complimentary bottle of red wine standing on the dresser with a vase of roses. A small box containing four of her very own confections sits between the bottle and the roses. Her spicy dark chocolates and red wine don't really pair well, she keeps telling Ian, and he keeps saying that it doesn't matter. Visitors receiving the gifts hardly care what the critics say.

I know a few things about the appeal of a tightly controlled environment.

Everything is beautiful, private. Perfectly staged. Empty.

Exactly what she would've got if she'd stayed home.

The coffee-brightened voices of other guests slip under the door of Sara's room and wake her. They're already eating breakfast on the enclosed patio.

In the light of morning Sara is more inclined to think that her chance for redemption has come. She showers, she dresses, then she steps out of her room via the sliding glass door so she can avoid conversation with strangers and walk toward the house with the vineyard in view.

I have waited outside through the night, thoughts heavy with Marina and Dylan, feeling no urge to leave. The powers that be allowed me to stay.

The rows of grapevines are alive with hushed movement. It's veraison time—red wine grapes are turning purple, white wine grapes become more yellow than green. Harvest is about a month away, and Ian still does his by hand. Workers in bandanas or wide-brimmed hats are moving among the rows of vines, tying holographic foil bird tape to the trellis wires. The iridescent streamers glitter in the sun and make metallic noises in the wind, frightening off starlings and robins. Other employees are draping the vines with nets to protect the rich fruits from hungry squirrels.

At the private residence where Ian and Denica live, Sara passes by the gate beside the vegetable garden. The vineyard's pervasive peacefulness makes it easier for me to hear her thoughts. She's happy that Ian is comfortable entering her home through the back way, but when she's here, she prefers to use the massive entry at the front of the swooping driveway. It might be different if he lived alone, but he has family. Sara has never met Ian's son. He attends the university in Edinburgh, and she hates the idea of intruding on them. Also, although she likes Denica, she fears the young woman a little bit. Denica's love for her father is fiercely protective, and she watches Sara with a wary eye. It seems she sees more than she ought to.

Sara rounds the garden fence and passes under the kitchen window, then pauses. Sounds spill out: a whisk beating eggs in a bowl, a gurgling coffeepot, a family enjoying being together again. The view through the glass is almost Rockwellian. Tall Denica, slim as a model, chops onions and uses the knife to instruct her brother on where he'll find a frying pan.

"It's not that long since you've been here," she says.

"But you wouldn't allow me to cook last time." Also tall, Gabe has a high brow and a nose made crooked by rugby. Together these give him an open, approachable demeanor. Gabe bends to look into a cabinet. "What happened to your vegan phase? What—raw foods, no honey? Now you want me to scramble eggs? You're asking me to keep up with a lot!"

"Not so much. I'm a flexitarian. It's all about balance, harmony. Everyone says they want it but hardly anyone goes out and gets it."

Ian enters the kitchen, and Sara finds herself admiring the deep lines of his happy face, the curve of his contented smile. He heads directly for the coffeepot in front of the window where she stands. "Better make sure those eggs are free range," their father advises Gabe. "And local. Or next time you come she'll have talked me into a hen house of our own."

Denica puts a hand on her hip. "That would defeat the purpose of supporting our community farms."

Ian winks at her and she softens. Gabe lifts the egg carton and examines a broken eggshell with unnecessary attention. Denica pokes him with the butt of the knife. Sara smiles. This, after all, is what she really came for: the confirmation that this kind of scene exists in the real world. A brother and sister getting along, a single parent enjoying his children. It used to be my scene, and I'm filled with yearning.

Ian knocks on the window and holds up the coffee mug he has just filled. "You coming in or will you take your breakfast outside today?"

Sara blushes on the spot.

Gabe cranes his neck. "Who's that?" he asks.

Sara retraces her steps to the garden gate and lifts the latch as Ian comes out to meet her. I don't try to follow but wait under the open window.

"You caught me peeping," she says.

Ian lowers his voice and hands the coffee to Sara, then holds the screen door open. "If you tell Denica there's a box of microwavable popcorn in my wine cellar I'm going to have to ask you to stop dropping in unannounced."

"Popcorn?" Sara whispers back, wrapping her fingers around the cup. "That's serious. Is it organic?"

"Artificially buttered."

"Genetically modified?"

"No doubt."

Sara shakes her head gravely and the two go into the kitchen.

"Hey, Sara!" Gabe waves the skillet at her as if he's known her for years, though Denica has just clued him in. "Top o' the morning to you!" He makes more than needed of the accent she likes so much and puts the pan on the stove.

"And the rest o' the day to yourself," she replies in kind, butchering the brogue.

"Ah, she's a keeper, Da."

"She's a *colleague*," Denica corrects. At the butcher block, Denica gives Sara a weak wave and a dim smile that might meet her father's lowest expectations of courtesy. Ian draws Sara into the large kitchen and pulls out a stool at the center island.

"If you're the one who made those sweets I found in my room last night, I'll place a standing order," Gabe says. "Do you ship?"

"For free to Ian's family."

"Take care where those chocolates come from," Denica tells her brother. Sara smiles fully and doesn't take the bait.

"I didn't mean to intrude," she says to all, but to Denica especially. The girl pours olive oil into the skillet.

"Never," Ian says. "In fact, I have to keep reminding you that we have space for friends in the house."

"That would have been awkward, coming home to find Sara in Gabe's bed last night."

Gabe laughs, but Sara is feeling every bit the interloper, even more when Ian hushes his daughter with one flicker of his eyebrow. Denica extends a peace offering: "Make you some breakfast?"

The temptation is there, but the moment is gone. Her craving to be with this family can't be sated with one meal. She has never been more aware of it than she is now, sitting outside the circle. She and I will always be sitting outside.

Sara shakes her head and lies. How easily they come these days. "Just the coffee. I need to leave soon. Appointments in Solvang today." Ian gives her the same eyebrow that was a warning to his daughter. He doesn't believe her. "How long are you here, Gabe?"

"Six weeks, until the fall term kicks off," he says. "Thought I'd come to warmer climates for a bit, help get the harvest started."

"The three of you should come down for dinner next week. Pick a day, we'll go out before things get too busy around here. There's a new seafood place on State Street that I hear is five stars."

"Brilliant," Gabe says.

"Mercury." Denica throws the onions into the hot oil and they sizzle. Gabe swats her on the back of the head. The gesture might mean *Don't be rude*, or *I agree with you but at least I'm not rude*.

"I'm sure they have vegetarian options," Ian says.

"I'll dig up some reviews," Sara says, standing. Steam is still rising off her coffee. "It's nice to meet you, Gabe. I hope the jet lag's not too bad."

"It's easier to come than go," he says.

He speaks more truth than he knows. Ian walks Sara outside.

The sun is already warm and glancing off the estate's clay-red stucco. A basket holding a pair of gloves and clippers sits ready to collect zucchini and tomatoes from the yard. It would have been a nice way to spend the morning, in different circumstances.

"Denica gives it to all of us," Ian says. "Please stay."

"It's right for a girl to want her dad and big brother all to herself for a while."

"She'll want to boot him back to university soon enough."

"I mistimed my visit."

"Was there something you wanted to talk about?"

She grins. "Even now, Denica is racing to cook those eggs and drag you back in to eat them."

"I never minded my eggs cold. Now out with it, before I force you to come on back in and eat with us too."

"Garrett Becker's son came to see me. He thinks I'm his mother."

"Ah. That's a tricky one. Did you explain?"

"He couldn't hear it. He's so young still, Ian. He needs a mother—or at least a parent."

"So be his friend."

"I think that might be difficult. For them. And okay, for me too. I wouldn't know the first thing about what to do."

"No parent does, no matter what they say. You learn as you go."

"I always thought someone should offer training first. Parenting certification."

Ian laughs. "Yes, that would have been helpful for me when Gemina died."

"I can only imagine," she says gently. "But you're a natural."

"No one's a natural, but some of us manage to find our way. You don't need training, Sara. You have a good heart."

"I can't really be their mom, of course. Not at their ages. But how can I help? If they know I'm the one who destroyed their family, they'll never speak to me."

"My children speak to me," Ian says.

"You have a different story," she says.

"Do I? Listen, Sara, you can't force anyone to accept help. You can only offer it."

Denica's shout from the kitchen cuts in. "Food's hot!"

"Right there," Ian says over his shoulder. "If you want to help, treat them with respect. That's how you earn trust. Then, when they trust you, they'll tell you what else they need."

"Dylan couldn't even accept me saying that I wasn't his mom."

"Nothing you can do about that."

"I wish there were."

"See—you're a natural. All mams and das wish our kids would just listen to what we say."

Sara laughs and shakes her head. He nods and crosses his arms. A breeze lifts his graying hair off his forehead. His brow is raised.

"I'll send Denica a link to the menu at the fish place," she says. "Then let me know if you can come."

"Oh, we can come," Ian says.

They wave good-bye and she makes her way back to her room, where she hastily prepares to leave even though she doesn't need to drive to Solvang and won't be missed at her shop. When she finishes, she sinks onto the bed and holds her stomach, clutching anxiety.

My plea comes out in a rush.

"There is a way to help them," I say to her. "There's a way you can do it, a way they'll let you. Even Marina will. You don't know her yet, but she'll remember how good you are. She'll remember."

An image of Marina, just three years old and running to Sara with outstretched arms, comes to mind. Christmas lights in the background.

I cross the warm floor and kneel down in front of her, so that I look up into her bowed face.

"They need your help, Sara. There's no one else."

I can't hold her hand and I can't wrap her in a hug. Instead, I place my palm over her heart and let my hand go straight into her chest. Right through her blouse and her skin and her ribs and her lungs. I can feel her life beating in the palm of my hand. It's healthy and strong and good. Marina and Dylan need that so much. She shudders, and I ask her a question.

"Do you still love my kids?"

I'm thinking of Marina, barely twenty, still a child to me.

"If you ever loved them, protect them, Sara. Protect my little girl and—"

Thirteen

*Sara vanishes midsentence. The room disappears, the vine-*yard is swept away. Still holding an image of my daughter at the front of my mind, I find myself suddenly outdoors on dry ground, standing next to the skeleton frame of a small car.

This scenery is familiar. I'm surrounded by oak trees that aren't as mighty as the ones poets like to worship. These California live oaks that cover the foothills are scrubby and scrappy. They survive the rainless summers on their store of coastal fog. Through the twisted branches I see blue—not the sky or the sea but Lake Cachuma, the freshwater reservoir for Santa Barbara County. Sara and I passed it when she drove to the vineyard.

The car carcass matches the sapphire blue of the lake.

Pieces of the Porsche litter the ground. And by pieces I mean everything but the frame itself: the tires, their flashy wheels, the platinum-gray seats, the sleek blue door panels, the retractable black top. The lights, the stereo, the filters, the belts, the hoses. The engine, hanging from a portable hoist. Two of the men who disassembled the convertible are lifting it into the back of a nearby truck. I recognize them. They were the passengers who rode away in Sara's car. A third has just placed something behind the driver's seat and shut the door, summoning me with that slam. One more is scooping up fenders in his arms to load alongside the engine.

It's a stretch to call them men, these four kids who have only a few years on Dylan, if that. One might even be younger, with a shadow of baby fat rather than hair on his cheeks. And they're idiots too, doing this work when the sun is up. Road noises from the nearby highway float in through the trees. We're hidden by a few short hills and not much else. I scan the area, and my eyes land on a third vehicle parked beside an oak.

It's an old four-door sedan, and Jade is at the wheel. My daughter sits on the passenger seat. It doesn't matter that her dark features are darker today, that they tell me with a glance she'd rather be anywhere but here. She's frowning. She's slouched and shrunken in the seat. She's checking her watch. I don't care. She's *here*, with *her*, and I go ballistic.

"What the heck?" I shout and rush the car. "Are you out of your mind? Did you get stupid overnight?"

I smack the fender with both hands. "Marina! What are you *thinking*?"

She doesn't hear a word of it. I hate this. I hate it, hate it, hate it. I grab the door handle and try to shake it in my impotent grip, but the only thing I rattle is my own teeth.

"How much longer?" she asks.

"Long as it takes," Jade says. She puts a hand on the door. "If we help it'll go faster."

"I'm not a part of this."

"You're here, you're a part of it."

"Not a chance. You didn't tell me what we were doing."

"You just needed to see how *easy* it is." Jade swings the door open and steps out. "Ditch the car, take it apart, leave the area, let someone else find the remains."

"Five more minutes and I'm out of here."

"Sure, you just go ahead and walk home. But me and two of those guys need a ride."

"Maybe I'll steal *this* car."

"You're funny, Miss Model Citizen." But she leans in to take the keys out of the ignition before she goes.

"Never again," Marina says. "Don't you dare bring me up here ever again."

That's my beautiful girl.

"Cross my heart and hope to die," Jade says in a baby voice, dragging her finger in an *X* across her sternum. "Trust me—they never chop a car in the same place twice."

Marina glares at her, and I feel my blood pressure drop just enough to quiet the pounding in my ears. But the danger is far from over. My child needs help, however adult she may be. And I'm not *completely* powerless.

Jade slams her door and heads off for her twisted sense of adventure.

———————

As it turns out I can't fly, though I try, because it would be convenient. The good news is that I don't have to worry up here in these oak-studded foothills about barriers like walls and doors to keep me from getting where I want to go. I find my bearings quickly enough. The blue lake is to my north. The road noises are to my south. This means the highway that I hear is the one Sara will use to drive home, if she didn't already drive home this morning, or yesterday, or a week ago.

The chop-shop crew has brought their operation about a quarter mile off the nearest one-lane dirt road, which might be some kind of private reservoir access, and another quarter mile from the highway. When I reach it, I am strangely composed, not even breathless. My heart rate is easily lower than when I discovered Marina.

But it jumps at the sight of Sara's rental car, which comes into view from the west not two deep breaths after I step out onto the road. The convertible's top is still retracted. I take long strides to the center line.

She's going to be on me in five, four, three seconds. There's no time to plot. I'm thinking of electricity, of startling shocks, of tilting silver trays and throbbing hearts.

The car flies by, and I reach out to touch her without being struck by the windshield, the mirror, the headrest. I can't close my eyes. I can't afford to miss. I have to touch *her*. I aim for her brain and come in a bit low. My palm passes right through flesh, muscle, nerves, bone as if it's nothing more than water. I feel the gasp in her windpipe, the stiffening in her spine, the electric messages roaring up into the base of her skull. Then I'm through, and my fingertips clip the metal rods of her headrest and I go spinning.

Just like Sara's car. When my eyes come around to her again, I see she's got the wheel in a death grip and both feet on the brakes, and she's flung the tail of the convertible wide, counterclockwise in a corkscrew that spirals over the oncoming lane.

No, no, no.

The road is clear of cars. The steep rise on the north shoulder puts an end to the spinout. The passenger side of the convertible hits flat and hard, and the airbags deploy. They don't hide the sight of her head flopping side to side. For long seconds after everything comes to rest, the still air is filled with the hissing of a deflating tire.

The airbags sag and Sara raises both hands to her ears.

My own head is still vibrating with the impossibility of the moment. It worked. I didn't think it would.

Now what?

My body behaves like it still moves among the living. I shout her name. I run to her car. I stare at her lovely face. The bridge of her nose is flaming red where the airbag struck. Slowly, she takes her hands off her head and takes the wheel in her grip again. Her breath is ragged and her arms are visibly trembling.

"Are you okay?"

Her inability to hear my voice pains me.

I look back at the short stretch where the shoulder widens and the dirt access road emerges from behind the hill. Sara's spinout has turned her to face it directly.

Her rental is still running. The engine sounds like it came through okay. But she's still getting her bearings and the airbag is in her way. The car sits lopsided on the uneven ground.

A lone car flies by and doesn't notice her trouble. Jerk. Wish I could reach through windows and zap him out of his air-conditioned oblivion.

I'm still looking after the bad Samaritan when the convertible lurches forward and comes away from the hillside with a crude scraping sound. The front fender knocks me aside, and I drop to my knees.

"You've got a flat," I try to tell her, but it takes twenty yards of telltale thumping for her to realize this herself. This time she puts the car into park and shuts off the engine. She exits the car and circles it until she sees the flat, and the worse damage to the side panels.

"Maybe it's time to hire a driver," she mutters.

She has pulled her purse off the backseat and set it on the

trunk, and now she's digging through it all, looking for her phone. A mist of sweat glows at her hairline. She swipes at her temple with still-quivering fingers.

"I'm sorry for doing that," I say. "But my daughter needs you *right now.*"

She's scrolling through her contacts, zipping all the way up to the top, when the truck carrying her Porsche in pieces noses out from the dirt road. A tarp covers the heaping mound of parts. It flaps around as carelessly as they secured it. Sara glances up, and her finger hesitates over the link to AAA Road Service as her eyes process the sight.

The truck turns left in front of her as she stares, as invisible to Jade's friends as another rock in the dirt.

A gust lifts the tarp one more time and reveals the door that Sara herself has opened hundreds of times. The custom-designed advertisement painted on the panel in delicate white lettering is the irrefutable proof: *Sara's Sins, A Fine-Chocolates Café, Santa Barbara.*

She thinks to turn on the phone's camera and snap a photo. It's blurry and of questionable value. But her quick mind catches what the camera couldn't. She repeats aloud the numbers and letters of the truck's California plates until she can type them into her phone's notes screen.

As Sara toggles back to her dial screen and hits the number nine, Jade's car appears on the dirt road, but this time Marina's the one driving. Jade's beside her, and the other two mechanics, if that's what they are, are in the back. One of the Boxter's bumpers sticks out of the trunk between the elastic of some bungee cords.

My take-charge girl probably thinks driving is the best way to get straight home without further detours. I doubt she's considered that transporting three criminals from the scene of the crime might make her even more of an accomplice than she was before.

She signals a left turn and looks left, right, left before pulling out. As the sedan rolls into the road, Sara and Marina notice each other the way a person catches sight of herself in a mirror she didn't know was there.

I believe the similarities these two see in each other have little to do with their physical appearances. More than the intractable but naturally pretty black hair, more than the right-sided dimple in their smiles, more than the elegant fingers and dense Audrey Hepburn brows, they recognize the history that ties them together. The tangled ropes of family history.

Well, in a poem it might be that way. In a ballad.

Silently I beg Marina to pull over and get out of that car. Let Jade take the wheel again. Let Sara take the load off her shoulders. Maybe I should have screamed.

They both blink and the moment passes.

"They were young, early twenties," Sara says to the police officer who found the discarded skeleton frame of her Porsche not far from the road. He's hardly old enough to grow a beard himself. "One of them might have been a teenager." She shakes her head, doubting her memory. "I've never been good at guessing ages."

"You didn't get the plates for the car?" he asks for the third or fourth time.

Sara crosses her arms protectively. "Just the truck, sorry. I guess I was distracted—my car in pieces, you know."

He raises an eyebrow at the broken-down rental behind her. "Not a good day for you."

She twists to look at it. "Not all bad. What are the chances I'd blow a tire right *here*, right where my stolen car would be found?"

"If there was more of your car to find, I would call you lucky." This deflates Sara a little bit.

He gives her a card. "You can call this number if you have questions or think of other details. We'll find the truck, but I don't know if we'll find anything in it."

Sara studies the card and shakes her head. "They're just kids. Aren't they supposed to be toilet-papering houses and sleeping until noon, that kind of thing?"

The young officer tries to hide his amusement. "That what you did when you were a kid?"

"I attended more classes outdoors than in, if that's what you mean."

"My job would be easier if that's the worst they did."

"What do you mean—this is normal?"

"The average age of first-time felons has been dropping since you were a teenager," he says.

"Well, that's just wrong. Where are their parents?"

"That's the million-dollar question." He looks at his watch. "It's eleven o'clock—do you know where your kids are?"

Sara laughs uneasily. "I don't have any. How do you think I could afford that Porsche?"

"See, there's our answer: all the great parents never had children."

"You're a cynical one."

"Kids left to their own devices can find trouble faster than water runs downhill. I'm experienced, not cynical." He nods a good-bye to her. "Hope this all works out for you."

He returns to his squad car with his report, and Sara bends his card into a gentle arch between her fingers as she waits for the roadside service to finish changing her tire. I see her mind racing away while her body is parked, speeding downhill, chasing water, running after my daughter and son, who've been left to their own devices. And I know she won't stop until she catches them.

I go to them too. I run.

Fourteen

Dylan and his sister are in the garage. He's standing in the doorframe that leads into the kitchen. She's two steps below him on the concrete floor, pointing at her convertible and yelling at him.

"You *drove*? You took my car?"

"And I brought it back safe and sound, all in one piece."

"When were you planning to tell me?"

Dylan answers with a victorious grin.

"Do you *want* to be arrested? Is that it? Do you want to wreck my only way to get to my only job—"

"Overreacting!" Dylan pronounces.

"There is no such thing as an overreaction to that kind of moronic behavior."

"I didn't get arrested. I didn't even get pulled over. Nothing got wrecked."

Marina and Dylan hold their words for a time. He kicks at the metal threshold beneath his feet. She paces to the workbench.

"Why did you do it?" she asks. "*How* did you do it?"

"It doesn't take a genius to put your foot on the gas and turn the wheel."

"You just walked on out here and drove away."

"It was like catching a wave."

"Liar."

He doesn't contradict her.

She continues, "How many times?"

"Just once."

"When?"

"Last week."

Last week? Seriously? It took me how many days to get here?

"C'mon, let it go," he says. Her questions are starting to irritate him.

"Where did you need to go that was so important?"

"Where did you go with Jade?" he challenges.

"Is it illegal all of a sudden to go out with my friends?"

"I don't know, is it?"

His tone has changed. His words are little shoves instead of light volleys. Is he angry at Sara? Marina? At the anxiety that governs his life? Me? He's sixteen—probably all of the above and more.

Marina hears the change and knows what do to. She has always known what to do.

"Jade had a job she thought I'd be interested in. Something that pays more than the waitressing."

"What kind of job?"

"Stealing cars and hawking off the parts."

Dylan's eyes go wide and he gives off a hoot. "So it *is* illegal."

"Like driving without a license, yeah."

"Oh, not even close! I yield this contest to you, dear sister." He folds an arm across his waist and bows.

"You've been spending too much time in that fantasy gaming world of yours, little brother."

"Name your prize," he says with exaggerated drama. "What would you have me surrender?"

"I'm going to see Dad. I want you to come with me." Her face is straight.

A visit to a grave site. Now there's a ritual that I've never completely understood or been inclined to embrace, though it has been forced upon me the way Marina forces it on her brother now. I don't wish this on him, and I question her method.

"You were supposed to make me tell you where I went," Dylan says.

"I want *this*. You'll brag to me about your little adventure all by yourself someday."

"I won't go. I can't."

"Apparently you can get out of the house when it's important enough. This is important, Dylan."

Dylan swears. "You go. That place freaks me out."

"Says the guy who spends hours creating digitized zombie lands."

"Key word: digitized. Not real. Therefore, not freaky."

"I've gone alone too many times." She approaches him at the steps and looks up at him. "First Mom, then Dad . . . if you quit on me too I might start thinking Jade is my only real friend."

"And then you're going to blame me for your downward spiral into a life of crime."

"You can bet on it. Next thing you know, I'll be in jail and they'll impound my car and foreclose on the house and you'll be living on the streets."

Dylan rolls his eyes, but she has succeeded in easing his mood. "It doesn't make any difference to anything if I go or not."

"How would you know? It isn't about you."

"Yes, it is."

"We're going," Marina says, extending a hand as if to help him down the steps.

I watch him for signs of panic. They aren't immediately apparent.

Frowning, Dylan kicks the threshold one last time, then stoops to pick up the shoes he's kicked off beside the door. He doesn't take her hand, but he follows her down into the garage.

"The least you could do is let me drive."

———

This time I make no effort to follow them. I stand in the garage as the double-wide door goes down, hoping Sara will finally decide to take care of them in ways I can't.

After a few seconds the overhead light automatically blinks out and the world goes black. Well, that was stupid. Even if I could find the light switch I wouldn't be able to move it.

My blindness makes the garage seem larger than it is. I seek the boundaries of the space like a mime, both hands up in front of me, palms flat against empty space, shuffling to the wall, the door, the steps. They're gone. I can't find the edges of this blank universe. I can't even find a toolbox to trip over or a volleyball to sit on.

But I'm not alone.

"Why do we lie to the kids?" Sara asks me again, picking up the conversation she so suddenly abandoned days ago. Or was it only hours? Seconds? I go still in the blackness.

"We lie to protect them," I say. "They don't need to know everything, even when we wish they did."

"I'll probably call them children forever." Her words have smiles in them. "They'll be eighty and I'll be on my deathbed, and I'll say, 'How'd you spend your day, kids?'"

Maybe she didn't hear me. "We always want to protect them."

"They don't know I'm here, and that seems like a lie too," she says. "Lying by omission, isn't that what it's called? I don't know why I'm so scared."

"What do you mean they don't know? Where is *here*?"

"I think we lie because we're afraid, don't you?"

This conversation confuses me. "Afraid of what?"

We're both silent for a while. She says, "Do you think it's possible to redeem one lie by telling another?"

"No. I've tried it. No matter how many lies you tell, they each just make the first lie wor—"

"I just wonder." Is she even listening to me? "The world looks different at forty-three than it did at twenty-three. I'm not as dogmatic as I used to be." She lets that thought sit there before she says, "I bet you're not either."

I twist around in the blackness, a spinning dog chasing an invisible tail, but I can't find her. I can't see anything at all.

"I'm sorry for what I did," she says. "I'm sorry about everything I thought was right that turned out to be so, so wrong. Do you think we ever get it right?" She has drifted to a distance. She's leaving me. "I'm not sure we can. But I promise you, I will try."

"Sara," I plead.

There is no answer but the sound of a door opening: a hand depressing the lever, releasing the latch, letting loose a puff of air as the seal breaks open.

———

A stale breath of recycled air flows over my face, and I blink. Above my head, an air conditioner exhales through a vent.

I'm standing outside a closed door, certain I'll encounter something bad if it opens. Something that will overcome every good thing in the world if it's turned loose.

But I can't leave the door either. I'm stuck here, straining my senses for a clue to what's here, and then maybe permission to leave it: voices, music, scents, a sudden chill.

I hear Musak. I smell disinfectant. I see stiff carpet under my feet. It's brown like the door, utilitarian. Come or go, it seems to say. Whatever you do, don't hang around here.

I hear footsteps coming from the left and turn my neck to look. My children are headed toward me: Marina wears a sundress that is effortless and classy at the same time. Sunglasses on her head, car keys clutched in one hand, she walks like a woman on a mission. Dylan lags behind, looking around for monsters that might be trailing him. The anxiety has kicked in now. His hands are shoved into his pockets. I see all his courage, his body a tough container for all that thrashing fear. Marina shouldn't have made him come here.

Here? Where have we gathered? What is this place, if not a cemetery? A mortuary, I guess and then reject. The place looks more like a hospital than a church. A morgue, then. A medical examiner's domain.

After all this time? But what do I know about how long it's really been?

My thoughts distract me, and I don't move out of the way in time to avoid Marina. She plows through me and shivers. Goose bumps run down her arms and up the back of her neck. She looks up at the air conditioner for a second and then leans into the door.

Her hand depresses the lever, releases the latch, lets loose a puff of air as the seal breaks open.

I take several steps backward into the opposite side of the hall.

"C'mon," she tells Dylan as she stands in the white mouth of the room, which sucks at me like a black hole. She waits for her brother and pushes the door all the way open, dragging me toward her without knowing what she's doing. Dylan neither rushes nor slows. The rhythm of his steps—*right, left, right, left*—is all that's carrying him right now.

Marina is patient, eyes on him. So I'm the first one to notice that someone else is already in the room. A slender silhouette of a woman backlit by the noontime sun coming in through the window. Her arms are crossed easily across her ribs, and she turns toward the open door like someone who has been expecting company.

Dylan finally enters the room and is the second to notice her. He loses track of his measured pace and the toe of his shoe trips on the carpet. Like a speck sucked into a vacuum cleaner, I can't resist tumbling in to join the meeting. I go against my will.

The bad thing happens.

Marina asks Dylan to help her find something, but I can't make out the word because my eyes are locked on myself, lying right there in the center of the room, not atop a silver table or inside a silk-lined casket, but on a fully equipped hospital bed, chained to the earth by tubes and cords and machines.

I'm at the center of this bizarre universe, both parts of me; I'm both the living sun and the most distant, dead rock of a planet. Lightweight blankets cover that bony body. A squishy pillow cradles the head. Even as I stand at the foot of the bed, I can feel the softness of it at the back of my neck. The face is bruised and broken almost beyond recognition. The skin is unnaturally color-ful, purple and green and sickly yellow. The cheekbones seem higher and the hollows underneath deeper, the eyes sinking under a quicksand of skin. Every cell weak and dying.

But these foreign parts are me. *My* bones, my eyes, my skin. The pain pulsing behind my shattered cheeks and crushed ribs is suddenly, tangibly real. My arms and legs are casted. My hands are wired to receive food, my chest to give information to the noisy monitors in the wall above my head and on rolling pedestals by my side. A machine is pumping me with oxygen that makes me light-headed.

The heart monitor claims that I'm far more alive than I under-stood. Alive and angry. The chirping pulse rate picks up its pace. What kind of deception is this? I worked so hard to reach my kids one last time. The long walks, the electric encounters, the tum-bling through time and space—do those amount to nothing more than a neat little near-death trick?

Someone ought to have told me the rules.

In spite of the mechanical assistance I struggle to breathe. The weight of the broken bones in my chest is unbearable. I've never noticed them before this moment, when they have finally become incapacitating. My heart is in a vise. I couldn't take two steps if I tried.

Marina shoves a doorstop under the hospital room door to hold it open for Dylan. He presses his back to the wall, eyes locked on the woman at the window.

My daughter goes to my side, disapproving of my matted hair. She tries to flatten it without pressing on my skull, which is both a wasted effort and the most healing touch I've ever experienced, living or . . . or whatever this state of being is. I don't deserve her kindness, but I need it more than I need that ventilator to pump air into my deflated lungs. My throat is tight and my eyes burn. There is a bloody bandage on my elbow. My hand is wrapped in gauze.

"These wounds just won't heal," she says. Her fingers flit to the cut I thought I received from Ian's winery, the finger I clipped on my own file cabinet.

"How is he today?" Marina asks.

The woman we all think is a nurse steps away from the glare and approaches the bed, standing opposite Marina. As she does, the solid black mass becomes a person with all her own features. Sara. I'm surprised all over again. I glance at Dylan and see that he recognized her before I did. But he comes no farther into the room.

"He's about the same," Sara says.

"But the nurse who called me said—"

"I never said I was a nurse, Marina."

Marina takes my hand. The softness of her fingers, the warmth and strength of her gentle grip flow all the way up my arm. "Yes, you did. You said there were some new developments in Dad's situation."

"I did. But *he's* the same." She looks apologetic. "I was a little vague. Maybe I wanted you to make assumptions."

Marina takes a fresh look at Sara and loses her tongue. I can see my beautiful girl trying to assess her. Dylan hasn't looked at me in the bed since he entered the room. He has eyes only for Sara, eyes that are both wishful and guarded.

His laugh is tight. "You guys look more alike together than you do apart," he says.

It's true, glaringly obvious. This is what scares Marina the most. I see the fear in the glance she sends Dylan's way, their roles suddenly reversed. He removes his hands from his pockets. He takes only one breath for every two of hers.

"What new developments?" she asks Sara. And then Dylan: "What do you mean 'apart'?"

"This is Misty," Dylan tells his sister. "Misty. Rochester. Becker." He annunciates each name plainly, and his calm demeanor is as unexpected as Marina's nervousness.

Sara extends her hand to Marina. "I'm Sara," she corrects. "Sara Rochester." Marina doesn't take Sara's hand, but Dylan reaches out tentatively.

"I found our mom," he says. "Right? You decided to own up to it?"

Marina's face is stone. Her fist tightens around the keys she carries.

Sara squeezes Dylan's fingers and nods. They release each other quickly. "I'm your mother."

Fifteen

My name is Garrett Becker and I should be dead. I thought I was dead, believed it with all my unbeating heart. I remember the plunge, the involuntary scream that came from my throat the moment the fence yielded to my Chevy. I remember the drop and then a jarring opposition, the cold wind streaking over my skin. I was flying through the air, I was straining for something to hold on to. The fence was still humming when I grabbed it. The links bit my fingers and buzzed through my bones. The ring Misty gave me snagged one of the wires. When I opened my eyes, the world was still except for that truck, falling like a feather from a robin's nest after the cat has pounced. And I was no longer inside of it.

I can't explain what separated me from my physical body and threw me out of that pit. Until now I thought it was mercy, an opportunity to tell my children the truth: I had an affair with Sara Rochester, and when their mother found out she went crazy. That's why she took her own life, because of me. It's my fault, and I'm sorry, I'm so very sorry.

But now I wonder: If a man can't even tell when he is dead, how can he know what else is not true?

Truth might sometimes be in the eye of the beholder—I'm undecided about that—but not on these two points: number one,

I am Marina and Dylan's father, and number two, Sara Rochester is not their mother.

"Why do we lie to the children?" she asked me.

"To protect them," I answered.

How terrible it is that they need protection from us.

Sixteen

My mind's reunion with my body changes everything. They've always had a strange relationship, the mind and the body, not only in my case, but across humanity in general. What the mind believes is power. Belief is a force that can dominate the physical self. For better or worse.

Belief is not the same as truth. It can be, but often it's not. Every once in a while the truth finds a way in. It chips away at false belief steadily, like surf that changes the shape of a shoreline over thousands of years. Sometimes truth arrives as a merciful deluge that rinses all the choking grit of deception away, and sometimes it's a flood that drowns the known world. The truth can kill.

Sara and the kids leave me alone at Marina's command: there will be no distressing discussions in front of her father that might adversely affect his condition.

Marina is more upset than any of us. I want to tell her everything will be okay, even though I'm not sure it will.

When they go, I try to follow. The door to my hospital room is still propped open wide. There's nothing to stop me except these tons of life-supporting equipment that pin me down. I don't know that I've sunk into the bed until I try to get out of it and my physical limitations become clear. All the forces that brought me, finally, to this dim place will not let me leave it. This coma holds me in its tight grip. This is my new truth—not death, but some altered state of life.

The voices of Dylan and Sara grow fainter as they walk away, following the brisk clicks of Marina's shoes in the hall.

I don't like hospital rooms. I don't like the false optimism that floats around on the grim scents of cafeteria food, though I understand it. All anybody wants is comfort. To make it through the day, the lifetime, with as little pain as possible, inflicting as little pain as possible on the people we love.

This is all I wanted for Marina and Dylan. It's the reason I didn't tell them about the affair that drove their mother to her grave.

I shut my eyes and make a last-ditch effort to go with them. I focus my mind on their faces. I wait to be transported, to be tossed back into the air, weighing nothing. Instead, I grow heavier, until I can't even open my eyes anymore. No more sunny panoramas of vineyards or shorelines for me. No more desperate darting around.

A flicker of resentment flares in my mind, then dies.

At the moment, my mind is an empty theater. I've come in alone and taken the center seat in the center row. The narrow venue has just one sloping section of seats and no stairs, no balcony for throwing popcorn down onto moviegoers' heads, no gaping cup holders for supersized, superpriced sodas. The armrests under my palms are threadbare.

My heart is oddly full of anticipation, something like relief that I got here before the feature left town. For a faltering second I wonder if the theater might not show the film with only one man here to see it. I didn't even buy any concessions. Maybe I should go do that. I feel a little hungry.

The lights dim and the trailers begin, but I have trouble focusing on the images. They're blurry, indistinct, and silent. There are voices out in the hall, faint and garbled and fluctuating. Someone laughs, a pleasant sound. The fading light shifts as the door opens to let others in. Bodies shift and bustle and bump into the theater's springy seats. The dark silhouette of an overweight woman moves through my row. She brushes against my legs and jars my toes, then to my surprise turns around and places her hand on my knee. She apologizes. I wonder why she chose this row when every other one is empty, but my mouth can't form the question.

I smell food and wish it was for me.

Someone takes a seat behind and just to the right of me as the previews end and the screen blinks to black. The dim lights fade out completely.

It stays black. The darkness is so thick that my eyes can't adjust. It's easy to imagine some old guy upstairs, sleeping on a tilting chair in the projection room, the way it was back when movies were fed one reel to another. Is that the whisper of misthreaded film forming a pile on a distant floor? Has silence swallowed all those other people who came in? There are no throat-clearing, bum-shifting, child-inquiring noises to hold the terrors of darkness at the margins of the room. Anything can happen in such a place where the few exits are hidden, where there is no life but yours for the monsters to target.

Restlessness rouses my heart. I sit forward in this old, creaking seat and put my hands on the armrests, bracing for the unexpected. Already I feel wary of another unpleasant revelation. A large hand comes down on my shoulder. A firm hand, warm and broad at the palm, powerful but gentle. Not a monster's claw.

"Be still," the man instructs. I freeze. He laughs kindly but fails to put me at ease.

"It's not a light story, but it should end well," he says.

His fingers tighten over my collarbone.

"What's going on?"

"You're dying."

Yes. I saw myself lying on the bed, alive only in a technical sense. But this theater setup—it's not what I expected. Nothing so far is what I expected. That flicker of anger in my heart flares into a steady flame.

"I thought I already died."

"Jim Davis died. Crushed by your truck. You're still working on getting there."

City planners expect the fatality to delay the project . . . Not my fatality, someone else's.

"But I believed—"

"In your lifetime you've believed a lot of lies, and disbelieved a lot of truths," the voice says.

"Whose fault is that?"

"We're going to get that sorted out now."

"I'm not stupid," I insist.

"No, you're not. So try to relax, Garrett."

His announcement fills me with dread.

The movie starts, and the lights that bounce across the velveteen chairs—they might be red, already I've forgotten—cast more shadows than assurances. I look back to see who has spoken, but my mind plays more tricks. I feel no hand, I see no man.

The mind is powerful, I tell you.

Seventeen

Dinner is a disaster. Sara has been at it all day. But the grill is too hot when she puts down the halibut, and the fillets become a flaky patchwork of charred and white meats. About a quarter of it ends up in the gas flames. The spinach salad is wilting into a bog of dressing, and the heavy multigrain rolls have gone cold and dry.

This is nothing like the easy collaboration that Ian, Denica, and Gabe shared around the McCleary kitchen. At Sara's house the kids wait to be served, and Sara's only aide is Pandora, summoned to the vast kitchen by the seafood temptation. The cat weaves itself around Sara's ankles, purring and leaning into her. I half worry that it's a ruse, that the cat plots to trip her into the flames of the gas grill, then steal the fish. Sara doesn't often cook for herself when she's alone, and preparing a meal for three is about as foreign an experience as she's had. The home of her childhood had a private cook.

She sets plates on the dining table in front of Dylan and Marina, in the room she has never used for anything but paperwork that needed to be spread out. There's a bottle of white wine on the sideboard, left unopened when Marina declined Sara's offer, and damp spots on the cloth where Sara slopped the ice water she served instead. Dylan watches with more sympathy than amusement. I don't think he's ever been in a situation where someone is more nervous than he is. Sara goes back for the bread. Marina sits stiffly in her high-backed Spanish chair and, opposite her, Dylan's shoulders are hunched over his plate. He isn't slouching exactly, but he's drawing impressions on the linen tablecloth with the handle of his spoon.

"Sit up." Marina's discrete tone is more bossy than usual.

Dylan straightens his spine.

"Elbows."

A stony roll tumbles out of Sara's basket as she sets it next to the salad bowl. Sara leans across Dylan to retrieve it.

"You have *got* to stop," Dylan mutters to his sister behind Sara's outstretched arms.

Marina does, even though he leaves his arms on the table.

Sara is finally ready to sit. She forgets to take off her apron and fumbles with the heavy chair, its legs entrenched in the carpet. Her skirt gets hung up on the arm as she sits. She unhooks the fabric. "As much as I know about confectionery—that's how *little* I know about cooking." She laughs nervously and finally settles in. "If it tastes as bad as it looks we'll move straight to dessert."

Pandora sits in the passage to the kitchen, no longer purring. The very tip of her dark tail twitches. Her crossed eye gives her the look of a pirate plotting to board a ship and steal the booty.

Marina is waiting for Sara to eat first, but Dylan beats them both to it, filling his mouth with fish instead of words. The inside of the fillet looks suspiciously like a piece of sushi. This doesn't seem to bother him.

"You must have a lot of questions," Sara says.

Dylan looks to his sister, who's dishing up her salad and trying to let the heavy dressing drip back into the bowl before she puts it on her plate. She says nothing.

"I'm sorry you've had to deal with your dad's condition all alone," Sara says.

"We've dealt with a lot more than that alone," Marina says.

Sara nods agreeably.

"And we'll keep doing it. Dad's not going to recover."

"We should be optimistic, don't you think?" Sara asks.

Marina picks up a roll. "Why?"

Sara blinks. Dylan attacks his salad. "I guess because anything can happen."

"Like mothers being raised from the dead, you mean? Maybe."

"Does Dad hate chocolate because you ruined his taste for it?" Dylan asks with his cheeks stuffed.

"He hates chocolate?"

"And Chinese food," Dylan says.

Sara frowns.

"Didn't you know that?" Marina says. "You were married for—how long?"

"Five years," she says.

"Twenty-two. I'm pretty sure it takes two to divorce."

Sara takes a deep breath and looks down at her unappetizing plate. "I guess I thought . . . There are abandonment laws—"

"Not for kids there aren't," Marina says. She keeps her eyes locked on Sara. "I can't believe you've been right here the whole time."

"Marina, I was so sick. I didn't know what I was doing."

"Sick with what?" Dylan asks at the same time Marina says, "Are you still sick?"

"I had just had you, Dylan. I was so depressed—it wasn't your fault, it's just a thing that happens sometimes, nothing to do with the baby. You were so perfect."

"Still am." Dylan's joke takes no weight off the topic.

"There's medicine for depression," Marina said.

"Doctors knew less then about what to do," Sara says.

I want to join this conversation in the worst way. I'm leaning forward on the edge of my seat, flabbergasted by the size of Sara's lies. At the same time, she's wrong to understate how bad everything was.

Sara goes on. "But I had it in the worst way, and Garrett . . . your father . . ." I know what she's going to say, and I'm filled with shame. "Your dad was having an affair."

Dylan stops chewing for a beat, as if the noise in his mouth will cause him to miss some of what Sara says.

"That's hard to believe," Marina says.

"Is it?"

"Considering he never even *dated* after you died?" She doesn't correct herself. "Yeah."

"Maybe he felt guilty about it," my perceptive son offers to his sister. Marina ignores this possibility, which I've often wondered about myself. Yes. Yes, that was probably the reason. Guilt is a powerful motivation. I hated what that affair did to my wife.

"Then you should have confronted him." Marina's tone is flat. Not even I can read her. "And besides, whatever Dad did doesn't explain why you left us."

"Marina, I'm so, so sorry. I was such a mess. I couldn't care for myself, let alone a preschooler and a newborn."

"I understand. It was all you could do to launch your new business and make it a raving success."

Dylan pulls a fishbone out of his mouth and sets it on the rim of his white plate.

"That came much later."

"Not so much later, right? Your website says Sara's Sins opened its first store in 1998. I like the name, by the way."

Sara doesn't reply.

"I mean, Dylan was born in November of 1997. So what I don't understand is why you didn't come back, even if it took you a whole year to work through your issues."

Marina and Sara haven't touched their food. Dylan is having trouble tearing into one of the rolls.

"I made such a wreck of everything," Sara whispers. She's staring at the uneaten dinner, but everyone knows that's not what she's talking about.

"Suicide is *so* selfish." Marina's anger is much more clear now.

Sara stays calm. "Yes. It is. I'm a coward, Marina. That pretty much sums it up. I intended to die, but I couldn't go through with it. I couldn't face your father. I couldn't get the help I needed for a long time. The most I could do was fake my death and then hide. I had no shortage of money. If you know my family—"

"We don't. Dad says they blamed him for your *death*."

Sara clears her throat. "They're wealthy. I had money to vanish."

"Are you saying they knew you were alive?" Marina looks about ready to launch off her chair and attack the conspiracy. "And they blamed Dad? Do you know what that did to—"

"No." Sara raises a hand. "No one knew."

"I don't get it. You changed your first name but not your last? You hid in plain sight."

"The best place to hide, especially if no one's looking for you."

"Have you been here the whole time?"

"I wanted to keep an eye on you both."

Marina shakes her head. "I'm not buying it."

"I do," Dylan says. The women look at him. He washes his dry roll down with a sip of water. "I've kind of always had this *sense*, you know? Kind of like Spider-Man when danger is near. Only not danger. Something else. Like everything is really okay, even when it's not." His plate is clean already. He forks a strawberry from the bowl of wilted salad. "Like right now."

The conversation stalls.

"What did you get me for Christmas the year you left?" Marina asks.

Sara coughs into her napkin. "An ornament," she says. "A blown-glass Christmas ball."

Marina blinks. She wasn't expecting this answer. Sara seems to be holding her breath.

"Are you still rich?" Dylan asks.

Marina warns him to stop with her widening eyes and pressed lips.

"What?" he defends. "We could use the help. You said so yourself."

"Anything you need," Sara says. "I mean that. Bills, insurance, groceries—"

"What does Dylan like to do?" Marina swivels her attention back to Sara.

Sara doesn't seem to understand the question.

"How does he spend his time? What are his hobbies? Since you've been keeping an eye on us."

"I didn't mean—"

"Where do I work?" Marina quizzes.

Sara stares.

"Too hard? Maybe you could just guess at the general *type* of work I do."

"You take very good care of your father and brother," Sara says firmly.

"I'm a waitress. At Longboard's."

"The one on Sterns Wharf?"

"The only one in Santa Barbara."

"They have good oysters," Sara says lamely.

"Where does Dylan go to high school?" Marina's voice seems to be getting louder. She doesn't give Sara the chance to answer or look away. "He *doesn't*. He's agoraphobic. He's had panic attacks since he was four years old. Because of *you*."

Dylan withdraws from his plate and looks at his hands in his lap, visibly uncomfortable for the first time since entering Sara's house.

"He does school online and tutors come to our house, and he's a brilliant gaming programmer, and he surfs. He's placed in his category in the Rincon Classic every year since he was eleven."

"Those are great accomplishments," Sara says to Dylan.

"You don't know anything about us," Marina says.

"I know much less than I want to. I'd like the chance to change that."

"It's a really bad time," Marina says. She pushes her plate away. "Besides, how can I trust anything you say?"

Pandora has been forgotten, which fuels her desire for that fish and gives her the edge of surprise. From the shadows of the curtain behind Sara's chair, the cat leaps onto the table and attacks Marina's full plate. Sara cries out, Marina almost tips her chair over backward, and Dylan watches, eyes wide and then smiling, as Pandora manages to drag the bulk of his sister's halibut off the table, thanks to the skin and undercooked center that hold it together.

Dylan holds in his laughter, waiting for Sara's reaction. Pandora has escaped to parts unknown, leaving a haphazard trail of flaking white fish on the tile. Sara puts her napkin on the table and scoots her seat away.

"I'll be right back," she tells them, then she stacks the two full plates onto Dylan's empty one and heads back into the kitchen.

"You're doing a really great job building bridges," Dylan says.

Marina glares.

"Sara seems nice. She could help us if you don't run her off."

"If she's our mother, I hate her for what she put us through. If she's not, I can't stand the lies."

"She knows about your ornament. Maybe she really couldn't help it."

Marina looks around at the pretty house, all the comforts of Sara's successful life. "Yeah, she couldn't help it."

"I can understand, if I got the anxiety from her, maybe she—"

"You have anxiety because she abandoned us, Dylan, not because there's some psycho disorder in your genes."

"I think she's telling the truth."

"Why? She lied to you the first time."

"I don't know. It's just, I feel a connection. Actually, I feel fine for the first time in a long time."

"Quit defending her."

Dylan squints at his sister and shakes his head, as if she's the one being bullheaded. Which she is, apart from whether she's got the truth or not.

Sara returns to the room with a squat stainless steel stand, a small candle, and a match. She places the stand between Marina and Dylan, lights the tea candle, and places it inside the open cavity. Then she leaves again.

Marina whispers, "If she was really keeping an eye on us, she would have seen how much Dad loved her. How much we needed her. She would have come back."

"She did come back," Dylan points out.

Marina shakes her head.

This time Sara brings a stainless steel fondue pot to the table, along with a plate heaping with fruits, cookies, pretzel rods, cubed cake, and homemade marshmallows. The pot is already warm and filled with creamy chocolate. Dylan leans in to examine it.

"Have you ever done a chocolate fondue?" she asks, handing them each two fondue forks. The handles are fashioned into distinctive mermaids and mermen, each one unique and with a tail of colored cut glass. Three women: emerald, sapphire, amethyst. Two males: gold and ruby. Sara keeps the amethyst female.

"It doesn't look too hard," Dylan says. But he holds up a crunchy cookie next to the fork and raises his eyebrows.

"If you can do chips and dip, you can do fondue." Sara picks up a pretzel rod with her fingers and dips it into the silky, warm chocolate, then twists it to catch the drips and takes a bite. "Use the forks for the soft stuff. This one's pretty basic," she says. "A chocolate turtle: milk chocolate, caramel, chopped pecans. I like the salty pretzel with it."

Dylan dives in with an apple slice and brushes his knuckles on the lip of the pot.

"Ow. It's hot."

Sara smiles at him, then turns to Marina. "You're right, you can't trust anything I say. You don't know me at all, and I don't know you like a mother should."

Marina puts a piece of cake on the end of her fork, maybe so she doesn't have to answer.

Sara says, "But we all know your father. He's brainy and private and generous and extraordinarily kind. He works hard and he loves the Dodgers even when they're at their worst."

"One of his more embarrassing traits," Dylan says before catching a dripping chocolate marshmallow on his lips.

"He always hopes for the best in people, doesn't he? He loves poetry and only told a handful of people that, because baseball and poetry together don't make sense to just anyone. He used to carry you on his shoulders, Marina, and take you for walks on the beach."

Marina's dark eyes well up. She concentrates on putting the cake in the chocolate.

"He loved you even before you were born," Sara says to Dylan. "He bought your first surfboard when he bought that beach house, and swore he'd teach you to float on a board just as soon as you could hold your head up."

"We still have that little thing somewhere," Marina says quietly. The fork she pulls out of the pot has no cake on it. Dylan sees it sinking, stabs it with his own utensil, and immerses it before lifting it out and stretching across the table to drop it on Marina's plate. Chocolate dribbles on the white tablecloth.

In the same gentle tone she's been using, Sara says, "Your father is brain-dead. Machines are keeping him alive because he doesn't have a living will. Even if he could breathe on his own he'll never return to you. You understand that a person can survive in this state for years."

Marina puts her fork down, as weary as an old woman.

"He'll draw disability for a time from his employer. And then what will you do?"

"We'll figure out something," Marina says.

"So how about this?" Sara picks up her purple fork and twirls it horizontally between her hands, the pronged end biting into her forefinger. "Until you figure out something, let me help. Just for a little while. Let's say three months, and then I'll do whatever you want. I'll leave town if you can't stand to have me here. I'll move my headquarters. Or I'll keep helping. Maybe in three months' time we'll all be able to make better decisions about everything."

Marina pushes her chair back from the table. "If you're trying to ease your guilty conscience, we don't owe you that."

"That's not what I'm trying to do."

"I don't want anything to do with you."

"That's not what you said a few weeks ago," Dylan observes.

"It doesn't have to be money," Sara says. "It can be with, with . . . moral support. I've been visiting your father. I'll keep that up. I can give you rides places. If Dylan has to be somewhere while you're working? I can clean, I can cook . . ."

Dylan looks doubtful.

"Right," she says. "I can hire someone to cook."

Marina stands.

"Or it can just be money," Sara says quickly, standing up too. "You don't even have to talk to me. I'll make regular deposits in your bank account. You can do the rest."

"C'mon, Dylan," Marina says.

Sara clasps her hands in front of her. Dylan looks at his sister and puts a forkful of bananas in the chocolate.

"Let's go."

"I'm gonna stay here," Dylan says.

"What? Why?"

"Because this chocolate is amazing. Have some."

"He's welcome to stay here if he wants," Sara says. "Both of you. Here, I just remembered"—she jumps up and runs to her little kitchen-alcove desk, fetches a new key attached to a leather tassel, then rushes back—"I had a spare made for you. Come whenever you like. My home is yours." She extends it to Marina, who won't take it.

"Do you have a guest room?" Dylan asks around the bananas.

"Dylan! That's crazy. You need to be home."

"If her help's not good enough for you we'll lose the house sooner or later. And this place sure isn't beneath me." He fingers the items on the dessert plate in search of another cookie. "You're being rude," he says. "Dad would be embarrassed."

"Dad would be angry," she says, glancing briefly at Sara. "But not at me."

The truth is, I'm neither of those things.

"You'll change your mind after I leave," Marina pronounces.

"Sara, if I change my mind will you take me home?"

Sara, who has no experience mediating sibling arguments, nods as if she doubts she answered the question correctly. She sets the key down next to Dylan's plate.

"I'll see you tomorrow then," Dylan says, feeding the fondue pot with more sweets.

Marina dashes away before Sara can offer to walk her out. She snatches her purse off of the sofa and runs to the door. She throws it open and flies out into the summer dusk.

Eighteen

The first time I ever saw Sara, in August 1997, was above the jagged bluffs and rocky shores of Stillwater Cove. I sat in a wide patio chair outside the Beach Club at Pebble Beach, drawing pictures on my sweating glass of iced tea, watching my daughter swim and waiting for the call to dinner. It had been postponed while the Rochester lords took their time completing a round of golf. They were delayed, it was said, by Aunt Judy, the family's beloved alcoholic. Apparently she had brought a fifth of Scotch for each player and insisted that each man get his shot at each hole, even though this mythical bit of Scottish lore had long been debunked and the Pebble Beach rules strictly prohibited it. The Rochesters weren't even Scots. Whether the bit about Aunt Judy was true, the number of men playing had turned a three-hour event into six so far. My stomach growled. A few mints and Spanish peanuts couldn't relieve it.

I was one of the few men not on the course, preferring the tight boundaries of a basketball court to the loosey-goosey meandering fairways. Some seventy or eighty others mingled as they do at family reunions where the relationships are strained by success and money and distance. They drank alcohol and wore masks with wide smiles and amused eyes. This was Misty's domain, not mine, though I was happy to bring her to see family. We didn't live so far away, but the six-hour drive from Marina del Rey to Monterey was no pleasure cruise with a preschooler in the backseat. So we didn't make the trip often.

Marina was my excuse for not joining in. At age three she was already a fish and wanted to spend the whole day in the wading pool, conveniently located (as far as I was concerned) at the far end of the bustle. We even had the buffer of a larger pool between us and the outdoor bar. The rambunctious older kids splashed in the deeper waters, sent cannonball splashes onto the deck, and raised a general ruckus. While Marina's mother and grandmother went off to gossip with distant relatives, I watched our daughter play with her cousins, fetched the beach ball when it escaped, and reffed their disputes. It was an approved reason not to socialize too much. I was a Rochester insider by marriage and an outsider by trade, a young and unproven architectural engineer among real estate movers and shakers in one of California's highest-priced regions.

In front of the outdoor fireplace a live band played jazz covers by the Rippingtons. Potted palms wrapped in rope lights glowed brighter as the sun began to turn the ocean pink and orange. The rope lights caught my eye. Misty wanted to use some at the beach house we were about to buy. She had remodeling plans, ideas she'd seen in a magazine for using rope lights and molding to illuminate high ceilings.

Sara Rochester came onto this scene alone. She arrived late. She stepped out onto the deck from the Beach Club's foyer holding a little black box tied at the corners with gold elastic. Her boxy business suit and shoulder pads, already a few years tired, were clean and well fitted but hit the wrong note here in the glitter of imminent sunset and Rolex watches and crushed-velvet fabrics. Still, my eyes went to her throat. A crisp abalone-blue blouse turned her long neck into a plunging dagger. Her fine collarbones formed a dip exactly like Misty's in the center where they met, a line my fingers had traced many times. She looked like my wife's twin.

Sara looked around as if trying to locate someone she knew, clutching that box. When no one noticed or acknowledged her, I stood.

"Marina, I'll be right over there." I pointed to Sara.

There were at least four other women by the wading pool, sipping their rum and Coke or whatever the trend was at the time. I had eye contact with them too, and they nodded at me. One even waved. *Go on, we got it.*

Sara had heard me, and though she didn't know me she reached for my hand in greeting while I was still out of range, as though I'd thrown her a lifesaving ring. She shifted the box to her left hand, and I could smell the chocolate.

"Sara Rochester," she said.

"Garrett Becker."

Her handshake was too firm, overcompensating for nervousness.

"You must be related to Misty," I said.

"A cousin, yes. I didn't think we'd still look so much alike, after all this time."

Misty had never mentioned Sara to me, so I wasn't sure what she meant about the time.

"If I wasn't married to her I'd have done a double take. Your hair's cut different."

"I missed your wedding, sorry."

I could barely remember the faces of those who *did* attend. "We've had several years to get over it."

She smiled. It was the same smile that had made me fall in love with Misty, the coy smile of a secret-keeper. Now Misty, she had secrets to keep, and if I'd known them from the beginning I might have done a better job of eluding her. But by the time I learned the whole truth I was already committed for the long haul. And I loved her. I was as madly in love with my wife as any husband could be.

On Sara, the half smile looked guileless. Almost naive. Even now when I see it here, thrown up larger than life on this movie screen of memory, I can see the reason I wanted to take her by the hand and make sure she got through this reunion unscathed. She was like the other Rochesters in appearance only. Beneath the pretty face was an outsider like me. She clutched her box of chocolates as if they might steal it from her and fling it into the bay.

"Misty's in the Club Room, or maybe changing for dinner if you didn't see her when you came in."

But Sara made no move to find my wife. She was looking past me at my daughter, who was emitting ear-piercing squeaks. "Is that your little girl?"

"Marina, yes. She thinks she's a dolphin."

"She's gorgeous. All that thick hair."

"Your side of the family." I gestured to my fine brown cap, which was lightweight in those years even before it started to thin.

"May I meet her?"

I failed to hide my surprise.

"The kids are always so much nicer than the grown-ups," she whispered. "Though you seem decent." She didn't wait for me, but headed straight for the wading pool, away from the entertainment. The chatter of the partygoers was rising as the sun fell. I don't know why that is, whether it's the alcohol or the music or something atmospheric about the outdoors, but the volume of a party seems to go up in direct correlation to how dark it is.

As we approached the table where melting ice cubes were diluting my iced tea, Marina stepped out of the pool and marched over to us, her feet slapping the concrete like the flippers of a wet seal. Goose bumps rippled down her arms. Sara put the chocolates on the table next to my glass and removed her suit jacket. The brilliance of the blue blouse brightened her face.

I threw a towel over my daughter's shoulders. She ignored it, lifting her hands to the satin box. I deflected her sopping wet grasp.

"Is that mine?" Marina asked, looking hurt.

"No," I said. "That's Miss Sara's. Don't grab."

"Do you like chocolate?" Sara asked her, throwing the jacket over the back of the chair.

"Yeah!"

"I think I can find a piece in there for you if your daddy says it's okay."

Marina flew into me, soaking the legs of my pants with her hug and staring up the tall length of my body with those eyes of hers. She didn't even have to say anything.

"A little piece," I agreed.

When Sara lifted the lid, the rush of spice that came out with the chocolate surprised me.

"Let's see," she said, "a lot of these are dark. In my experience the kiddos prefer the milk."

Marina immediately stuck her finger onto a heart-shaped piece with a dusting of sugar on the top.

"Don't touch," I reminded her. But I lifted the tainted piece out.

"Hmm," Sara said. "You can try that one, but I was thinking

this might be more your speed." She picked out a truffle-shaped ball of milk chocolate topped with a caramel drizzle.

"I like the heart," Marina announced, and faster than a hummingbird sipping nectar she pinched the sweet and popped it into her mouth. It was too big a bite, and the moment she chomped down on it her face registered shock. A tiny dribble of chocolate saliva escaped the corner of her little mouth. She stopped chewing as if unsure what to do.

Sara looked at me apologetically. "I made it a heart shape because it's my favorite. Dark chocolate around a cayenne ganache."

"Cayenne?" I felt alarmed. "You mean the pepper?"

"Not enough to hurt her, but I'm sure it wasn't what she was expecting."

Marina was looking at me for direction, unable to speak around the mound in her mouth. It was difficult not to laugh. "Swallow it up, that's what you picked."

Frankly, I was just glad she didn't spit it out.

"I don't like it," she said when she finally swallowed. "It's salty."

"Yeah, that wasn't sugar on top. Try this one." Sara held out the lighter-colored globe. "I promise it's much sweeter. This one has a clove-caramel filling."

Marina distrusted the offering.

"Want Daddy to test it for you?" Sara held it out to me.

I bit down on half of it, cupping my hand underneath to catch bits of chocolate that might break off. But none did. I expected the caramel to be thick, like the stuff in grocery stores' candy bins, and I expected the cloves to be pungent, like the twiggy spices stuck into orange balls and hung in closets until everything rotted. But I was so surprised by the blend that I didn't know what to say right away. Everything was smooth as the meat of a ripe peach and so harmonious that I couldn't tell where the caramel ended and the cloves began.

"It's terrible," I told my daughter. "You'd hate it."

Marina scooped the other half out of the paper and popped it into her mouth.

"Mmmmm," she said, nodding. She reached for the box again, and I saved it from being dragged over the edge of the table. I suspected she was looking for a duplicate. She brushed a wet strand of hair off her jawline, leaving a chocolate smudge behind.

"That was the only one," Sara said, fishing through the box for something else. "But you might like—"

"Is that chocolate?" It was Misty who demanded to know, and she asked the question while she was still twenty-five feet away. My wife was striding down the deck like a mama bear, pregnant with Dylan. Pregnancy was Misty's great beauty secret. It made her hair and nails thicker and her skin smoother and her breasts fuller. Her complexion took on a glow that made the finger-width scar on her left cheek nearly invisible. I didn't especially like the sequined dinner dress—it was just a few too many inches of sparkle for my taste—but everything else was magnificent.

Everything but the fact that she had discontinued her medications. I understood the reasons why. I wanted no risk to our unborn child either. But I had lost the argument that her wild mood swings—I preferred to say *good days and bad days*—were equally risky for the baby. The doctor agreed with me, but neither of us could force her to swallow, especially when Misty pointed out that Marina had turned out perfectly, and I couldn't contradict that. But those nine months had been the longest of my life, until these six.

"Seriously? Are you feeding her *chocolate* right before dinner?"

"It was a taste," I defended. "A half a piece."

I stood up, practiced at handling these outbursts. Misty didn't mean any harm, not really. She was full of love and fierce protectiveness that took over now and then. Occasionally I was a casualty of her passions, but Marina never was, and that was what counted. I saw my mother-in-law coming from a distance and knew she'd help keep Misty calm. Lena Rochester tempered my wife's temper, so to speak.

Misty said, "Sometimes you don't have a brain, Garrett. I swear. We're going to be eating in five minutes."

I doubted it, as the golfing crew hadn't even appeared at the seventeenth hole yet.

Marina seized a chocolate in her fist and held it up to her mom. "This one's yours," she announced.

"Oh, thank you, sweetness," Misty cooed. She didn't take the chocolate but instead squatted to wipe Marina's face clean with her fingers. The candy quickly softened and oozed in my girl's hand. "Where did these goodies come from?"

I could see her casting about for a paper napkin. Sara presented her with a tissue from her purse.

"Perfect," Misty said and she glanced up. Then she stood quickly and I had to grab her arm to steady her. "Sara? Oh my gosh, is that you? Sara!"

Dodging her daughter's chocolaty fist, Misty gripped Sara in a squeeze so tight Sara couldn't raise her arms from her sides. That was my initial interpretation of Sara's stiffness; I didn't see the truth until later.

"I can't believe you *came*!" Misty squealed. "This is wonderful! When did you get in?"

"Just a few minutes ago."

"And you haven't even had time to change. Mom, look—Sara! Did you ever think she'd come?"

My mother-in-law gave Sara a curt nod. "Sara."

"Good to see you, Aunt Lena."

"Still making candy, I see."

Sara's lips flattened into a tight line, but Misty didn't notice. Lena frowned. Marina started licking at the mess in her palm.

"How many years has it been? Eight? Nine? Garrett, she walked off into the sunset without even saying good-bye and now here she is, just popping up like she never left. I shouldn't forgive you for that," Misty announced, but she was smiling so broadly. She swung around so that she was standing right at Sara's side, then linked her arm in Sara's and held on. "Have you seen everyone? Who'll be first? Does your mom know you're here? Mom, go tell Aunt Barb."

"I was just in town on business and thought—"

"Aunt Barb!" Misty shrieked, having spotted Sara's mother across both pools by the entrance to the massive dining room. "Look who's here!"

Aunt Barb wasn't the only one who looked. But she was the first to turn away after seeing who Misty was screaming about. Sara looked out across the ocean.

"I don't like this one either," Marina told me, holding up her goopy fingers. A tissue wasn't going to be strong enough for this kind of mess. I used Marina's beach towel.

"Stop! Stop!" Misty freed Sara when she yanked the towel away from me. "That'll stain. I'll never get it out." She wiped Marina fairly clean with the tissue, which immediately disintegrated. "Time to change for dinner," she said to our daughter. Then to Sara, "You *have* to sit with us."

"No, no. I never RSVP'd. I was just in the neighborhood."

Aunt Lena wrapped Marina in the towel and deftly tucked her filthy hand inside where my daughter couldn't smear it on her dinner dress.

"No excuses," Misty said. "There's enough food in there to feed three times the number of people who actually came. You *must* eat."

"I'm not dressed for the occasion."

"Who cares? But if it matters that much I've got an outfit you can borrow." I wondered if Misty noticed that her cousin wasn't six months pregnant, but she raved on. "Isn't that crazy? Remember how we used to always share—"

"I'm staying in Monterey. At the Bay Lodge. I'll go change."

"Okay, suit yourself. I'll get to work on Marina. This child is so sure of what she wants to wear that it'll take me longer to wrangle her into the right clothes than it'll take you to drive there and back." She dropped a huge kiss on Sara's cheek. "I just can't believe this. What a treat. See you soon."

The whirlwind of women moved off, and Sara had her jacket shrugged and her purse shouldered before I even realized it.

"I'll walk you to your car," I offered, closing the lid on the chocolates. I left the gold band on the table. Never knew what to do with those things.

"No need."

"But I have to look busy or one of your great-great-aunts will insist I dance with her."

Sara didn't smile at that, but she didn't object further. We walked back the way she'd come just a short time ago.

"Misty seems . . . happier than she was the last time I saw her."

I wasn't sure what kind of condition Misty had been in eight or nine years earlier. Her official diagnosis of bipolar disorder hadn't been made until after we were married, though I saw the signs while we were dating. They must have come on the scene long before that. Her family seemed to think there was some stigma with this condition and came up with a million euphemisms to avoid speaking of it directly: "fragile" or "temperamental" or even "a tortured artist." Because Misty was an amazing dancer. If I'd known that Sara was no stranger to Misty's episodes, I would have answered her more completely. But in that first hour of our meeting I said only, "Pregnancy suits her. She's a good mom." Both of which were true.

Sara nodded.

"Sara's Sins," I said, noticing the embossing on the top of the candy box for the first time. "These are sinful, to be sure."

"It's just a prototype. A joke, actually. The chocolatier who apprenticed me, he used to call my mistakes 'Sara's sins.' I told him that one day my 'mistakes' would be trendsetters. So it's the name I picked." She seemed suddenly embarrassed.

I held the door open for her, and we passed through the club's short foyer.

"Cayenne pepper?" I put a lot of doubt in my voice, but secretly I wished I could have tasted it.

"And chilies like pasillas and anchos. I'm even working on one with habarñeros, but it's not quite right yet."

"I'm not a connoisseur, but that sounds just weird."

We pushed out through the double doors onto the sidewalk. The gardens were in full bloom, and the heady scents mixed with the chocolate.

"That's what a lot of people say. They like their nuts and fruits, their commercial Cadburys."

"Are you a snob?" I asked with mock offense.

Her laugh set a bird flapping out of a nearby tree. "Yes, in fact I am. I predict the future of chocolate is going to go all the way back to the beginning. Did you know that the ancient Latin Americans consumed their cocoa spicy and bitter? No sugar, thank you very much."

"That takes all the fun out of it."

"Chilies are my thing. I don't care what anyone else says about it. Except today"—her sigh was happy, contented—"today was a good day."

"And what happened today?" We reached her car, an old Volkswagen bug that had seen its best years.

"Today, every shop I visited in Monterey placed a holiday order for my confections. Not for the products my employer sells, but for my very own stuff."

"Congratulations."

"Thank you. I'm afraid I let it go to my head, though. It wasn't the best idea to show up here unannounced."

I couldn't offer an opinion on that point. "I thought the clove thing was a winner."

She opened her car door and threw her purse down on the seat. "That's my safety net. You have to try this one."

While I held the box, she lifted the lid and quickly pulled out a little square topped with a simple green dot of icing.

"Sweet lime-infused ganache enrobed in dark chocolate with pasillas," she announced.

"You need a shorter name."

"Yeah, that was a pretty consistent opinion. Similar to the one Marina ate, but more complex with the citrus."

I decided to eat this one the way Marina did. I put the whole square in my mouth and bit down.

Like I said, I'm no connoisseur, and Dylan has turned out to be the one who writes poetry. I just like to read it. So how could

I adequately describe the flavor combination of limes and chilies and chocolate? My mouth was too moist to whistle.

"Wow. That is better than a margarita with a chimichanga."

"Don't say that in a room full of guys."

Her eyes sparkled under the lot's lamps. Something told me she didn't expect the praise. That's all I saw at the moment, gratitude. But now I'm older, and as I watch the screen, I notice how her eyes dart toward the Beach Club and back again, fast as pain can run along a nerve. No gushing praise from an outsider can ever make up for the pride withheld by loved ones.

"You have any more of these with you?" I asked, holding up the box.

"No, that's my last one. Keep it." She dropped onto the seat, closed the door, and rolled down the window.

"I'll buy them from you."

"My gift."

"Then where can I buy more?"

"Little chocolate shop called Allegro, in Santa Barbara. State Street."

"Santa Barbara? Misty and I are buying a place down on Rincon Point."

"Ah. Not far, then," she says, turning the key in her ignition and dropping the stick into reverse. "You'll have to tell me more at dinner."

I closed the lid. "Not gonna happen," I said. "Who in his right mind would sit down at a crowded, gaudy table when he could walk the beach with these all to himself?"

"Right," she said.

But I was half serious, because I knew she wouldn't be coming back.

Nineteen

Back at the beach house, empty of everyone she has ever loved, Marina allows herself a breakdown. She doesn't turn on the lights tonight, inside or out. In her pristine bedroom with the pretty pink accents, she falls on her bed and cries.

She thinks she's angry. She can't figure out how a mother can walk away from her new precious, helpless infant, or how that child, once grown, can return to her so easily and without the least bit of resentment. Dylan has never had such low expectations of anyone.

I watch my beautiful girl, knowing something that might take her years to see for herself: that it's easier to be offended for someone else than it is to be grieved for our own pain. What Marina really wants to know is what her mother was thinking when she loaded up her three-year-old with adult responsibilities. How is a preschooler supposed to take care of a needy baby and a sad daddy when the grown-up mommy can't cope with them herself? And yet she did it. So Sara's offer to pay the bills is more an insult than a miracle. It's an indictment of Marina's competence, because—and this is how my high achiever thinks—if she was able to do the impossible in one area, she should be able to do it in every area.

This wasn't how she thought it would be when she hoped to find her mom alive. The truth is, Marina's heartbroken. After a lifetime of caring for others she has no one to care for but herself tonight. She doesn't know how to do it and doesn't know how to let anyone do it for her.

In time her tears cut a path through her anger, like a river through a canyon. The river can lead lost wanderers to safety. It can show the desperate the way out of a ravine.

She blots her puffy face with a tissue and then goes directly to my bedroom. She begins her second search through all my personal belongings. The first time she was looking for legal documents— a will, insurance papers, a journal—anything to help her brace for my slow-motion plunge into death. That search turned up nothing, but now she is looking for something different: evidence of Sara's place in our lives.

If I could, I'd tell her she won't find anything again, but that wouldn't matter. She needs to see for herself. She goes through every dresser drawer, every nightstand cabinet, every closet box. She has seen the photos that Dylan discovered, the only kept mementos of my affair with Sara. He shared these in exchange for supporting Sara's claim. But he's kept the box and its other contents secret. The affair was the only secret I kept from my children. Well, the affair and the debts. But Marina's investigation sets me on edge.

My phone is on the dresser top, returned with my wedding ring, which they cut off of my finger, my wallet, and the woven leather belt that was holding up my jeans. That was all they could salvage from the wreck. My clothes went straight to the trash. The phone is long out of juice, so Marina plugs it in and scrolls through every contact, searching for Rochester. Then for Sara, or Sarah, or Sara's Sins.

She scrolls through the photos, which are far too recent to be of help. She picks up my broken wedding ring and holds it under a light, reading the inscription: *Garrett & Misty Forever, 6-27-92.* Marina stares at the ring for a long time.

She carries it with her back into her room, where she finds her phone and calls her brother, hoping he won't ignore her.

Dylan answers right away. "Yeah."

"Ask Sara where she and Dad were married."

"Wasn't it, like, San Francisco or something?"

"Just ask."

Dylan delivers the question and the answer is quick in coming, even though Sara wasn't there. The Rochester family is pretty tight.

"Monterey," Dylan repeats.

"Where in Monterey?"

This time Sara's answer falters a little bit. Misty's frame of mind at the time was expansive and happy; Sara probably received a wedding invitation, though I can't say for sure. She and I might have mentioned it to Sara in passing during our short time together. But it's not the kind of detail a person would remember if they didn't attend and were invited only because custom dictated they should be.

"The Pasadera Country Club," Dylan says for Sara. Marina writes this down.

That was the place Misty's father would have chosen—he was a member—but she wanted the Monterey Plaza Hotel and eventually won that battle.

"Did she grow up in Monterey?"

"Do you want to talk to her yourself?"

"No."

Dylan is the go-between once more.

"Yes," he says. "She grew up in Monterey."

"Where'd she go to high school?"

This time there's a brief pause as Sara suggests she take Dylan's phone. He willingly gives it up.

"Marina, you can ask me anything."

"I just want to know where you went to high school."

Sara hesitates. "The Stevenson School. In Pebble Beach. Why don't you come back over? I can pull out some pictures. I was just showing Dylan—"

"That's all for now."

Marina ends the call and heads to the computer in her pink bedroom where she sits down and begins a new search. For several hours she finds a way to quiet this strange, restless state in which it seems like no one needs her. A lengthy search—she hardly knows where to begin searching for a copy of her parents' marriage license—takes her to the Monterey Clerk and Recorder's Office, where she prints an application. It must be notarized before she mails it in. Tomorrow she'll call Jamie to find out what that means.

She fills out a web form at the Pasadera Country Club and asks if they can confirm a Rochester-Becker wedding that took place there in 1992.

At the Stevenson School she sends an inquiry to the alumni office—and this e-mail takes her a very long time because Marina is unaccustomed to lying to anyone, even a stranger, though it helps that she is typing a letter to a nameless person whom she doesn't know, has never seen, and might never meet.

I'm making a surprise scrapbook for my family and am collecting memories from everyone's school years. I'm looking

for pictures and information about your former student Sara
Rochester (she might have gone by Misty Rochester then), who
would have gone to Stevenson

—Marina does some math in her head—

in the mid to late '80s. Please write back to tell me if you have
any information about her extracurricular activities, report
cards, or other interests. Maybe you have an old yearbook that
I could buy? Thank you.

And after a little more thinking Marina decides to sign her
name

Marina Rochester Becker, daughter

Then she adds her phone number, just in case, and sends off the
request, feeling vaguely criminal. She goes to the Monterey *Herald*
next, thinking to search engagement and wedding announce-
ments, but that visit is a short one. The newspaper's online archives
go back only as far as 2002.

She wonders how to get her hands on Sara's Social Security
number. Is it possible for a private citizen to find out all the names
a person has been known by?

She wonders if she should repeat her searches in Marina del
Rey, down near Los Angeles, which is where the birth certificates
say she and her brother were born.

The night turns into morning as Marina fills her empty heart
and the empty house with the glowing distractions of the wide,
wide world behind her computer screen, where people robbed of

purpose can always find something to do. She is doing something important, she believes.

The odd thought that she has traded places with her brother comes and goes with the click of the mouse.

In the black pit of two a.m. my son awakens and can't remember where he is. Everything about Sara's guest room is wrong: the texture of the sheets, the faint chocolate scent, the moon-cast shadows on the wall. The atmosphere is silent and sounds like death to Dylan. Ocean noises that rumble outside his window every day of the year, as much a part of him as the sounds of his own heartbeat, aren't loud enough to reach the foothills of Santa Barbara.

For a terrifying moment he knows it all: this is not his home, Sara is not his mother, he hurt his sister. He's alone and can't survive the solitude. But these aren't conscious thoughts. The facts are nothing more than emotions charging the walls of his brain, desperate to get out. He couldn't name them if I asked.

Though the evening air has cooled, he's unbearably hot under the sheet. He kicks it off, but his heart is racing already and thin sweat coats every inch of his skin.

Breathe, I whisper. *Deep breaths.*

His fingers and toes are tingling. He curls himself into a tight ball, trying to hold the panic down. His whole body is coiling for action. There's only one way this is going to go. Still, he boldly resists it. He takes a deep breath, not because I told him to, but because that's always the first thing to do. Get oxygen to the brain that thinks it doesn't have enough.

Count to five, I remind him. He only makes it to four. It's impossible to breathe deeply in that position.

Try again.

His next breath is a wheeze and not half as deep as the first.

Focus on your toes. Your big toe. Wiggle it. Now all of them—flex, release. Right, left. Together.

Maybe he doesn't remember that exercise, or maybe it doesn't work for him as well as others. He starts rattling off a list aloud, taking a sharp breath between each name.

"Washington, Adams, Jefferson, Madison, Monroe, Adams, Jackson, Van Buren . . ." He has done this often enough that he can name all forty-four US presidents while chewing gum and playing a video game, but that's when he's showing off. In serious situations his breathing often returns to normal by the time he reaches Kennedy.

At Harding he rolls out of bed and is barely able to support himself on hands and knees. His trembling is visible and frightening. Worse, he sees the scrollwork of wrought-iron bars outside his window, the decorative Spanish accent that confirms he is trapped and will die if he can't get out. And he can't get out. This is his tipping point.

Get Sara, I order him. *Shout for her.*

He won't, of course. He couldn't survive being seen like this by a stranger, because that's exactly what Dylan and Sara are at this moment. He gives up the list at Truman and fumbles for the clothes he left in a heap on the floor. Though he tries to concentrate, the T-shirt goes on backward. And if the cargo shorts didn't have a drawstring he might not have been able to don pants at all. His quaking fingers couldn't lift a zipper or put a button through a button hole.

His foot catches inside the leg and he stumbles, his shoulder hits the wall. He knocks a book from the carefully arranged nightstand onto the floor. Then he's upright again and groping for the doorknob in the darkness, and he's anything but stealthy. The hardware rattles. When the latch finally releases the door, he all but falls out of the room.

Sara is already in the hall, cinching a robe at the waist. A little book is tucked under her arm. She was awake and he interrupted her reading. Or reflecting. It's a small photo book, the cheap plastic kind that could be purchased at a Longs Drug in the days before we stopped printing photographs and started storing them on digital drives.

"Dylan?"

He grimaces to see her and leans against the wall for support, hands on his knees.

"Are you okay?"

Clearly he's not.

"Panic attack? Is this what Marina was talking about?"

He nods this time. He's hyperventilating now, which puts him at a pretty fair risk of passing out. And Sara is clueless. She sets the photo book on the ledge that overlooks the lower level.

"Okay. Okay. Just calm down. Everything's going to be okay." She raises her hand as though to rub his bent back, then decides not to. "There's nothing to be afraid of. You're in my house, that's all. I know it's different from what you're used to, but it's safe here."

"I need to get outside." He heads for the door, one hand staying in contact with the wall.

"You can't go outside, it's two in the morning. I'll open a window."

She slips past him in the hall and goes to the window at the end, then raises the sash. Her refusal to let him out only makes his need worse.

"Outside," he repeats, heading for the stairs.

"Dylan, you're overreacting. Let's talk this through. There's nothing to be afraid of."

He is right to ignore her. In thirty seconds she's said just about every wrong thing that can be said to a person having a panic attack. Dylan knows the fear rattling his body isn't rational. There's no point in talking about it. But it's still very real, so real that he can barely descend the spiral staircase in his bare feet with both hands on the iron rail. Sara turns on the light as if that will help. "Please stop," she begs, as if his condition is a switch he can flip. She stays at the top of the curving flight, one hand over her mouth.

Don't leave him alone, I instruct her.

But she doesn't move until his foot slips off the bottom step and he goes down, finally too oxygen deprived to stay upright. He blacks out. Just for a few seconds, but he's out nonetheless.

Sara gets her own taste of panic then as she flies down to him, too late to cushion his fall. She's thinking of how ill equipped she is for this role, and what Marina will think when she learns what happened.

Dylan is conscious before Sara arrives. She takes his hand and he grabs it.

"I'm going to take you home," she says. "I'm going to call your sister."

He won't let her rise, though. He holds her next to him until the terror finally passes and his lungs relax and a goose egg has risen under his left eyebrow and he can form a sentence, a request.

"Please don't tell."

"I don't like where this is going," I say to the invisible man sitting behind me in the theater.

"What don't you like?" the voice says.

Light from the projected film flickers across my body. The images from the world on-screen batter me, but I can't feel a thing.

"My kids are coming apart. I didn't think Sara would lie to them. Not like that. Why did you take me out of their world?"

"I didn't take you out. You've been here ever since the accident."

I twist in my seat. I still can't make out the speaker, but I see a form, a black shape on a blacker backdrop. "No, I was there. I could . . . influence them still."

"That was all illusion."

"It wasn't—I showed Dylan the black box. I freaked out Sara's cat. The accident on the highway!"

"There was static in the closet. The cat was startled by Ian. And Sara's tire took a bolt."

This is ridiculous. "I made Sara drop the tray."

"The weight of the candy shifted when she wasn't paying attention."

"Outside the hospital door"—I point to one of the theater's emergency exits—"Marina knew I was there!"

"The air-conditioning gave her a chill."

"You're telling me it was all coincidental."

"No."

"Then explain it to me."

"As I've said, you were here. You have been here the whole time. But you didn't want to believe it. You didn't believe it until you saw it."

"Believe *what*? I thought I was *dead*."

The man doesn't answer. A fleeting, bright image flashes across the scene and, for just a moment, illuminates my companion. He's thin and long, folded into his seat. His age is difficult to guess. He nods at me and tips his maroon-colored beret, then returns his attention to the screen.

Twenty

In the beginning, I didn't see myself as creating a problem. I thought I was helping. I convinced myself that I was doing more good than harm—until the damage was done and I realized, too late, that I was the one who'd caused it.

Misty was crushed that Sara didn't return to eat with us that night of the reunion. In the banquet hall turned golden by candlelight and sunset, she refused to give up the empty seat next to her at the big, round table. I knew my wife hoped Sara would walk in late, but Misty insisted she held the chair for Aunt Judy, who'd imbibed too much Scotch on the golf cart to have an appetite. (She reclined—passed out, I thought—in a lounge in front of the fireplace.) Little Marina wobbled on a booster seat between us; my parents-in-law, Lena and Lionel, and Sara's parents also shared our table under the expansive vaulted roof. The older generation spent the entirety of the main course consoling Misty by itemizing Sara's bad character.

I was glad to have seized the bay-view seats for Misty and me, gladder still to have a fidgeting preschooler who needed my attention. The rest sat with their backs to Stillwater Bay, so focused on Sara's perceived flaws that they would have been blind to the view anyway.

As it turned out, Sara's great sin was her decision to make her own way in the world.

This small bit of history might help explain their attitude, one that I thought had died out somewhere around the Civil War, but no. The Rochester family dates its roots in Monterey back some twenty-five years before Robert Louis Stevenson's short stay there in 1879. The city's popular association with the writer who wasn't a Californian, wasn't an American, in fact wasn't even an actual *resident* of Monterey causes the Rochesters no end of irritability. Their patriarch, Andrew Rochester, came to the bay as a fighter in the Mexican-American War and stayed as a fisherman. When the fishing industry collapsed, his great-grandchildren solidified the family's security by pouring all their sweat equity into real estate investments. The generations-long commitment to hearth and home and the family name became a sacred part of their identity. To such a family, celebrities like Stevenson are mere interlopers. They leave a mark on history just by passing through and consuming resources. (Adding insult to injury, Stevenson was at death's door during his brief stay in the seaside city; the Californians nursed him back to health and he moved on.)

What do Sara Rochester and Robert Louis Stevenson have in common? Her parents didn't hesitate to say that she, too, devalued tradition and social hierarchies. She demanded too much attention for her lack of contribution. She was selfish in her need to feed her creative spirit rather than the family's security. She was recklessly carefree, care*less* with the lives of others. *Just look at poor Misty here, wounded by her cousin's broken promise!*

After high school Sara turned down a Stanford education in exchange for an apprenticeship with a local pastry chef. She was the first Rochester in seventy-five years to turn her back on Stanford.

Her father tried "tough love" and pressured the chef to withdraw his job offer. He succeeded in that much, which prompted Sara to leave Monterey. She "abandoned" the family and, according to those folks who shared the table with me, hadn't made any appearance of any kind until that evening.

I didn't point out that surely Andrew Rochester had been led west by an adventurous spirit like Sara's. When he left Massachusetts in the mid-nineteenth century, what did he leave behind? Who raged at his departure? The questions stayed in my head. For this tough cypress-tree family, a century and a half of West Coast living has yet to soften the stiffest genes in their East Coast DNA.

In the weeks following the reunion, Misty's gloom persisted, but I don't believe it was all because of Sara. For people with bipolar disorder, it's difficult to blame depressive episodes on only one cause. In Misty's case, her refusal to take her medications was the largest factor in her rapid destabilization, and no amount of cajoling on my part could change her mind.

It's a terrible thing to watch someone you love suffer and not be able to help them in the way they need.

That September, I made an effort to cheer up Misty by inviting Sara to dinner at our new vacation home. I drove up from Marina del Rey on a Thursday evening with plans to oversee the installation of the TV cable, phone, and a new kitchen floor, all of which would go in Friday. Misty and Marina would come up Friday night, and I planned to grill kebabs out on the back patio.

All went as planned until the new phone rang at six thirty.

"I just can't do it," Misty said, so softly I almost couldn't hear her. "I can't face the drive, the traffic. And Marina's being so crabby today. Please tell Sara I'm sorry. Can we reschedule?"

"Of course. I'll call her. You rest."

The floor installation had taken longer than expected. Though the laborers were collecting their tools and tossing remnants of the hardwood flooring into the back of their truck, the kitchen and dining room were too cluttered for dinner company anyway. Maybe it was for the best.

I tried calling Sara at the chocolate shop, which was the only number I had for her. They'd closed for the evening.

At six forty-five she knocked on the front door, holding a bottle of champagne in one hand and a wrapped gift in the other.

"What a pretty neighborhood," she said. "Every house is unique. I've never been in here before."

I stepped down onto the tiny concrete block that was our stoop and took the package.

"Happy housewarming," she said.

"Thank you."

She looked to the west, where the sun was beginning its descent. "Can't complain about the view."

The property had a southerly view from the enclosed patio out back, front-row seats on the surfing season, but the front of the house was where to watch the sunset. "We want to put a big porch right here. The whole length of the garage. Red tile, red-wood trellis"—I lifted my arm to indicate a canopy—"some kind of climbing flower, benches."

"Oh, I can see that. Very nice. Bougainvillea would be nice."

"I'll file for the permit next week. Hopefully we'll have it all in before winter."

"Where are Misty and Marina?"

"Just called—I tried to reach you. Traffic, see? I didn't even think of it on a Friday night. They turned back, couldn't make it up before Marina starved."

The lie was spontaneous, but I would be compounding it if I claimed to know whether I was trying to protect my wife or protect her cousin. Even now, I can't say. If Sara was wounded, if she wondered, as I did, whether Misty was paying her back for the disappearing act at the reunion, she didn't show it. She was about to say something when the kitchen installer came out through the front door, which I'd left open, and said, "That'll do it, then." He held out a clipboard for me to sign, which I did quickly.

"Do you have half a minute to take a picture for us?" I asked him, and when he agreed, I dashed into the house, set down the gift inside, and returned with my camera. I set it up for him. "You can be in the before-and-after," I told Sara. "Over here." I pulled the front door closed and motioned her to come stand on the step next to me. I took the champagne bottle. The step was narrow then, and I put my arm around her waist as easily as if it had been Misty standing there.

After the camera clicked she pulled away quickly. I thought I'd offended her, though I meant nothing by my touch but the kindness of a family member. I wondered when any of her family members had last shown her kindness.

"I'm so sorry they couldn't get here," she said. "We'll do this another time."

"You don't have to run off. At least let me show you the house."

I held the door open and she agreed to that much. She followed me through the living room and then upstairs, tipping her head into each of the empty bedrooms. She admired the view from the master and suggested we install a window seat. Downstairs she ignored the clutter and dust and was polite about everything. She praised the craftsmanship that had just gone down on the kitchen floor.

I found a corkscrew and opened the champagne.

"You shouldn't leave without having some," I insisted. "Look— we won't have the feast Misty planned, but I did put all the kebabs together earlier, before the floor guys came." I opened the fridge to prove it. A dozen skewers loaded with marinated beef and peppers and onions formed a pyramid on a platter. "They'll go to waste if you don't help me eat them. *And*," I said with all the theatrics I could muster, "I spent all afternoon putting together that table on the patio so we'd have a place to eat. Don't let it be for nothing."

Maybe I was trying to prove that I wasn't like the rest of Sara's family. I was unreasonably worried about her leaving early and feeling as rejected by Misty and me as by her own parents.

"I'll stay, then. I don't want to eat the dessert that I have in the car all by myself."

———

The reason I couldn't remember this scene clearly before now, when it's being replayed for me in high-definition clarity, was because Sara and I polished off that bottle of champagne all by ourselves. I see, on this larger-than-life screen, that she ate two of the kebabs and I devoured four, not quite enough to offset the effects of the bubbly.

I had planned to leave the gift for Misty to open, but the dessert Sara brought required it: a chocolate-fondue pot with flashy glass handles, mermaids and mermen.

"Misty's going to love this," I said after Sara taught me how to use it and I took my first bite. "But I don't think the chocolate will make it back home."

"Did she get to taste any that I took to the reunion?"

"Are you kidding? I finished those off before they served the appetizers."

This made her laugh.

The sun was long set. The lights of the oil derricks out on the horizon winked like Christmas come early. I hadn't known before then that one of the outdoor floodlights was burned out, so, lacking a spare bulb, we sat half in shadow at the outdoor table I had assembled, sheltered from the offshore breeze by the acrylic enclosure. We lost track of time talking about Sara's newest chocolate "sins." We talked about her plans to open a chocolate café, a concept that was way ahead of its time. We talked about the culture of Santa Barbara, where she'd lived for almost nine years. She told me where Misty and I would find the best restaurants and antique furniture stores, where we should go for walks and hikes, which art and music and wine festivals were most worth it, and how to avoid the party scenes created by students from the notorious university. We compared life in Marina del Rey to the promise of a quieter life on the Rincon.

Though single and childless, Sara let me talk and talk and talk about Marina, about her stunning list of three-year-old accomplishments and my hopes for her future. I pointed out the star that I'd told Marina could be hers. We talked about what a good big sister she'd make for her baby brother, due at the end of November. Dylan, we'd call him. I'd bought his first surfboard already and pointed to it leaning against the side of the house. Sara found this hugely funny.

"Good water names," she said. "Marina and Dylan."

"Misty thought of that."

We talked about what a good mother Misty was, in spite of her . . . and here my thoughts skipped.

"I know about Misty," Sara said gently. "I understand."

So few people did. It was 1997, and bipolar disorder had been recognized—by various names—as a mental illness for more than a hundred years, but those who hadn't experienced it firsthand still tended to look on the diagnosis with suspicion or, as the Rochesters did, with denial.

"Misty never mentioned you," I said with intoxicated negligence. "Until the reunion I never heard your name. Why?"

Sara was unfazed. "I don't really know. We were close as kids, because our parents were. It was expected, I guess—we're the same age, we look like sisters. They sent us to Stevenson together, starting in the third grade. In high school, though, she changed." Sara leaned back into the cushioned chair. "One day we were tanning at the beach and swapping dreams about the future, the next she blamed me for starting a rumor that she snorted cocaine. Personally, I think she started that rumor, but who can really say? A week later we went shopping together for sundresses in Carmel as if nothing had ever happened. Then a month after that Misty read *The Bell Jar* and attempted to follow Plath's example, but she didn't know she needed a gas range for that, so she didn't succeed in anything but getting a burn on her cheek."

There was nothing funny in the way Sara told the story or in the way I heard it. "She told me that scar was from a tree branch."

Sara nodded. "It's important that you give what she says more weight than what I say."

Of course in this situation I couldn't. "It's faded. She covers it up with makeup."

"Her doctor said she was just depressed. Prescribed sunshine and fun and vacations. She said she was depressed because I was dating the only boy she'd ever loved, that I'd stolen him from her. I can't guess what she meant by that. I don't know what she said to her parents, or to the boy, but within two weeks he'd broken up with me and started dating her, and she was happy again. That was the beginning of my fall from grace." Sara shrugged. "Her parents thought I wasn't sensitive to her issues. They even accused me of making it worse, if I ever did something without her, for example. She was always the extrovert, except for a few times when she completely disappeared into her shell. Her parents were looking for a reason for all this, something to blame, or someone. I was convenient. In some ways she made it easier for me to leave. I'm not bitter toward her, you understand that."

"You're understandably cautious," I said.

She nodded again.

"The medications have helped. She's a different person when she's on them—I mean, more truly her real self."

"I'm surprised Aunt Lena admitted she needed that kind of help."

"She didn't. I insisted on it."

"Brave man," she said.

"Was it bravery or self-preservation?"

Sara's eyebrows went up. "She's violent?"

"No, I didn't mean that." I finished off the bottom of my last glass. "But she can be desperate. I love her, you know. The worst thing in the world that I can think of would be the possibility that she would hurt herself." Sara watched me closely. "Even burning herself on the cheek. And now that we have kids . . ."

"She's a blue-ringed octopus," Sara said. I didn't have a clue what she meant, but it sounded funny, so I laughed. It was the first time I noticed we might have been under the influence. I clasped my hands and leaned forward on the table.

"A what?"

"There was this special on TV—a blue-ringed octopus. One of the most beautiful creatures in the Pacific. Australia, if I remember it right. It's little, and it spends a lot of time being this drab gray color. But when it's agitated, it starts to glow with all these luminous blue rings. They pulsate. Mesmerizing. So pretty."

I waited for more, but Sara bit her lip.

"I just thought of Misty when I saw that," Sara said. "She'll be okay."

"She's gone off her meds during the pregnancy. One day to the next, I hardly know what to expect. I'm holding my breath all the time."

It was the first time I'd spoken those words to anyone. It might have been the first time I admitted the truth of it to myself.

Sara sighed and swiveled her chair to face the dark water, then she reached across the table sideways and put one of her hands over my two.

I accepted her sympathy for the gift that it was. I felt tired all of a sudden and turned my chair like hers, so we were both pointed at the ocean, holding hands like a comfortable old couple who'd been married for years and years. And when I closed my eyes, it was easy to imagine I was holding on to Misty, that we were both strong and whole and completely reliable.

We sat that way for a long time.

———

That night I woke from a nightmare. I was diving and found a dead octopus on the bottom of the ocean floor. The limp creature balanced on the edge of a sheer drop-off that plunged down into places that the sun couldn't reach. Its flesh was the sad, dingy color of concrete freshly poured, but I knew it should have been blue. A glowing, brilliant blue. Overhead, a muted storm stirred the waters, and the octopus slipped off the shelf into the blackness.

I couldn't go back to sleep. I crawled off the mattress that still awaited its box springs and went down to the living room, where I booted up my laptop, pulled up AltaVista, and told it to search for blue-ringed octopus.

The octopus was listed in a catalog of deadly but beautiful animals. It's loaded with neurotoxins. One bite can kill an adult human. And something else that Sara decided not to tell me: the female carries her fertilized eggs in her arms until the eggs hatch. And then the mother dies.

Twenty-One

The story Sara and Dylan agree to tell is that Pandora tripped Dylan on the stairs and his eyebrow hit the railing. Sara isn't sure whether Marina believes it, probably because Marina hasn't decided yet.

Sara frets about the incident as she drives over to Rincon Point three days later. There's an odd bag of groceries from Trader Joe's market on Sara's passenger seat. It contains several boxes of organic frozen dinners, a half dozen bags of spicy trail mixes and nuts and dried fruits, a clear plastic container full of meringue cookies, trays full of chunky vegetables ready to be skewered and grilled, some salsa, a boxed banana-bread mix, and a red-mesh bag of Valencia oranges, the best variety for juicing. Sara's doubtful of all of it, not sure what Dylan and Marina like to eat and afraid to ask, because she thinks a good mother would know these things intuitively. So she based her choices on what she thought Denica might approve of. Organic stuff. Vegetarian. Fair trade. Mercury free. At the last minute she threw in a box of her very own chocolate turtles, even though Denica would have rejected that choice, because Dylan had devoured the fondue version. Sara's most worried about the oranges. Dylan mentioned the evening of the dinner disaster that Marina loves Cara Caras, but they're not in season and Sara couldn't find any.

Sara has the gate code now, having taken Dylan home at the crack of dawn after his visit. She lets herself in, drives straight to the beach house, and parks in front of the garage. It's closed today, and Marina isn't there to meet her this time.

She hesitates at the porch, the reusable grocery sack weighing down her right side. It's the first time she's seen the house in the daylight.

"This turned out nice," she says aloud. I think she's talking to me. Then she steps up onto it and approaches the front door.

Dylan opens the door. The bump over his eye has turned dramatic colors that she can see even through his bangs, and Sara can't keep her eyes off of it.

"You don't do anything halfway, do you?"

He puts his fingers to the bump and smiles. "Ready?" he asks, staying inside the house.

"I thought Marina was coming."

"Had to take a last-minute shift," he says.

"Oh." Sara looks at the heavy bag, tossed into uncertainty by the change of plans. "Should we go another day?"

"If I have fun today, sure." He tosses his bangs out of his eyes.

"You're not worried that—"

"I'm not."

Sara takes a good look at him, sees no signs of nervousness. She's read up a little on agoraphobia since the incident at her house. Though she isn't all that clear on how to help a person having a panic attack, she has a much better sense now of what *not* to do.

"You seem strangely excited to pick grapes with a group of complete strangers."

"I decided I need to get out more." His eyes flit past her to the length of the tile porch.

Sara lifts the groceries. "Some of this needs the freezer."

He swoops down to take it before she can enter the house. "I got it. I'll lock up from inside and go out through the garage."

Something about Dylan's behavior strikes her as off, but her only real exposure to this age group is Denica McCleary, and Ian's daughter isn't a good reference for this young man. And she's twenty-one, closer to Marina's age. But I think I know what's bothering Sara. Her intuition is on the alert. It senses the fact that Marina isn't working an early shift, she's out taking a walk on the beach. It's that Marina would have argued about this outing if she'd known of it, and so Dylan didn't tell her. And it's that Marina is about to return to an empty house, a vague note from her brother, and a bag of random groceries thawing on the kitchen counter.

But all Sara has is a sense, not specifics.

There's something else on Sara's mind, a detail so insignificant that it passes through and then is gone. In what universe is it simpler to secure the house by going through the garage than out the front door?

Well, who can fathom the mind of a sixteen-year-old boy? Maybe he just doesn't want the terrible burden of carrying his key.

By the time they reach McCleary Vineyards all the way out in the Santa Ynez Valley, she's forgotten it entirely.

"You told them you're their *mother*?" Ian is shocked, and Sara doesn't have time to justify herself. Ian impresses me with this response. Already I like him more for voicing what I cannot. Dylan and Gabe are nearly back in earshot, having fetched the tractor Ian needs. The boys have turned onto the wide lane between the garages and a stately windbreak of eucalyptus trees. Gabe has let Dylan take the wheel.

"I should have explained when I asked if they could come." She and Ian are standing in front of the winery, Sara shielding her eyes from the sun and Ian squinting. The morning fog has burned off and given way to a warm afternoon. Seasonal workers are hammering together wood pallets that will be laden with bins full of grapes in just a few weeks' time—or sooner, if the heat persists and the grapes' sugar and acid levels reach the ideal before expected.

Ian is shaking his head.

"I didn't think you'd have such a strong opinion about it," Sara says.

"If I were a psychologist I'd say that's exactly why you didn't tell me before now."

"Just don't say anything to give the wrong idea," she whispers.

"I'm not the one giving the wrong idea, am I?"

She frowns at him. "What is so wrong with wanting to help? I have money, I have love—"

"You have guilt," Ian says.

"Haven't you ever lied to your kids about anything?"

"Aye—about what they'd be getting for Christmas. But Marina and Dylan aren't your kids. How do you think this is going to end, Sara?"

To the side of the winery, Denica emerges from the storage sheds with a short stack of picking bins in her slim arms. She drops them onto the flatbed of another tractor that will haul them to the fields and deposit them throughout when Ian gives the go-ahead. Her flannel shirt is covered with dusty purple smudges from the bins, and the gloves she wears are too big for her hands. She goes back for more.

Ian's also decked out in his work attire, tough canvas pants and a blue chamois shirt, sturdy work boots. He's got a picking knife with its short, curved blade in one hand and a refractometer in the other. When Gabe and Dylan arrive with the tractor, everyone will go out to the vines to take random samplings of the grapes and test their sugar content. Sara had feared that Dylan might not consider a winery to be interesting at all, but good-natured Gabe snatched him away from Sara's side so fast that he hasn't had the time to ponder boredom. It didn't take more than three minutes for Gabe and Dylan to find a common ground in their passion for gaming, and the two have been talking a streak.

Ian says to Sara, "When their mother died, they heard it from me. And when they were old enough to know how it happened, I didn't lie about that either."

"Didn't you worry they'd hate you?"

"They did for a while."

Ian's transparency, which I applauded only moments ago, strikes a wrong note now—the kind that causes wincing. What kind of man is okay with his kids' resentment?

Denica emerges from the storage shed again with her arms full, Gabe hops off the tractor to take her load, and Sara is watching the scene as I am, trying to fathom how the McCleary family made the journey from hate to this. Dylan waits behind the wheel, and Gabe introduces him to his self-assured sister. Dylan runs his hand through his hair before taking Denica's in greeting. His grin is sweet, but after a cursory "nice to meet you" his next words get stuck in his throat. Denica seems used to this kind of reaction. She turns back to fetch more bins. The boys follow her.

"When did they stop hating you?" Sara asks.

"I don't know. One day the love was stronger than anything else. They chose to forgive me, and that's something I can't explain or take credit for."

"You must have made it easy for them to do that."

"Forgiveness is never easy. They picked that path all on their own."

"But you had to be a certain way. As their father. Maybe parents can't make it easy to forgive, but I know they can make it harder."

Ian tucks the picking knife into a sheath on his waistband. "Possibly."

"So what did you do? How did you win them over?"

"You don't want to know what I did—you want to know what you should do."

"You can be exasperating."

"It's something you're destined to learn about me."

"All right, then, maybe that's exactly what I want. Tell me, what should I do?"

"I have no idea. Your situation isn't even remotely like mine—except these kids might be about to hate you in ways you didn't think possible."

Sara crosses her arms across her belly and holds her elbows. "There must be something." She is less confident than she was.

"Just something, that it? Aye. Then I say don't lie. And don't ask me to lie for you."

"I tried to tell Dylan, but he wanted it so badly to be true."

In that moment I think I understand my son more than ever before.

Ian shakes his head and takes a step toward the tractor. "I doubt he wants *this*."

———

Marina enters the house upset even before she discovers Dylan's trick. I want to forewarn her, ease the blow of each discovery about to come. She slides the patio door open and comes in from the beach, her head still bowed over the e-mail app on her cell phone and the reply from the Stevenson School.

> Ms. Becker, thank you for your inquiry. According to our records Sara Rochester was a student here from 1985 to 1989. Yearbooks from those years are available in our library, but not for purchase. If you find anything in the annuals that are relevant to your project, we might be able to find original prints in our archives or could grant you permission to scan the images directly.
>
> In my search for your mother's records I discovered that a Misty Rochester also attended the Stevenson School during the same years. I wasn't here during that time and can't confirm their relationship, but I thought it was a coincidence worth mentioning in light of your message.
>
> Please call to set up an appointment. We're happy to assist you.

Sara and Misty, not one woman but two. The discovery is hardly coincidental from Marina's point of view.

"Dylan!" she calls out, directing her voice toward the stairs. She puts her phone down on the kitchen counter, on top of a note.

Went out with Sara. Back at dinner.

It tells her everything but what she most needs to know. Went *where*? Why? What will you do if you panic? She picks up her phone again and tries to call him.

This time he answers with a recorded voice. "S'Dylan. You know what to do."

Marina in fact doesn't know what to do. This is a new circumstance. She thinks, she decides. She goes upstairs in search of Sara's cell phone number, which Sara wrote on the back of a business card of all things, as if Marina would ever have business at a place like Sara's Sins. I always told them I hated chocolate and right now Marina is thinking she knows why. The association with Sara is only partly right. The more compelling reason is that the scent of chocolate fills me with an inexplicable grief.

Marina thinks she put Sara's card in the desk drawer, but when she rifles through the contents, so organized that nothing in it is out of place, she can't find it. It would stick out if it were here, so out of the ordinary is a business card among her drawer bins that keep pens and clips and pushpins rigidly contained. Frustrated with her own forgetfulness as much as with Dylan's disappearance, Marina tries Dylan again.

Across the hall, a phone rings. Marina's attention turns toward Dylan's closed bedroom door, then she stalks the ringing phone into his personal space. He has left it behind, smack in the middle of the bed as if he didn't want to annoy her further by making her look for it.

She thinks to check for Sara's number in his contacts list. She sees several calls between them. Marina rings through and gets no answer there either. She wants to leave a nasty message. For half a second she wonders if she can threaten Sara with kidnapping charges, running off with a minor without the guardian's permission, but she's not sure if she could get away with that. She doesn't know Sara or the law well enough. And besides, Marina isn't technically Dylan's legal guardian. Not yet.

"Hi, Sara, this is Marina. Just wondering where you and Dylan are. Please call back."

Her own voice sounds funny to her ears. Without Dylan the room is wrong. Marina can't think if she's ever been in here when he wasn't. Probably, but she can't call up a memory of it. She looks at Dylan's belongings the way she sometimes looks at a fixture so much a part of her life that she takes it for granted. The clock on the living room wall, say, or the antique rocker in front of the fireplace. If she stares long enough, as she has from time to time, they begin to look out of place, as if their very existence is an illusion. Dylan's room, without Dylan, looks to Marina like the private quarters of a man who doesn't actually exist.

A single key on a ring lies on Dylan's nightstand among candy wrappers and earbuds and loose change. It has a decorative leather tassel on it—the key Sara gave them at dinner.

Marina takes the key and Dylan's phone and shuts the door snugly behind her. Then from her own phone she places another call.

"I need your help with something," she says to her friend Jade. "You free?"

———

Dylan's hands are shaking, and because his assignment is to help Denica collect grape samples to take back for Brix testing, there's no way to hide the trembling.

"It's okay," I say aloud. "There's nothing to be ashamed of."

Except maybe trying to parent after it's too late.

He concentrates on the scheme Gabe explained: Pick from every fourth vine in every fourth row. From each cluster pick four grapes, from the top, bottom, front, and back. Two hundred grapes in a gallon-size bag—this is what Ian requires for a fair measure of the block's sugar content.

Denica stands on the other side of the vine, taking a sample from the other side. Her practiced movements cause the grape leaves to quake like his own arms and hands.

He counts grapes. *One. Two.* The third one falls into the dirt. *Three again. Four.* It's not quite as helpful as the sensory counting, but so far it has tamped the panic down. Dylan hates this disorder, hates the way it owns him. He has never wanted to kick it in the teeth as badly as he does right now, with Denica so close, right *there*, watching him through the shivering leaves. He knows she's watching, even though he can't catch her in the act.

"Don't forget to eat some," Denica orders. "Best part of this job." He likes her accent because it sounds happy and reminds him of what it feels like to ride an awesome wave. He wonders if she's putting it on.

"They're so sweet. If I eat too many I'll hurl."

Denica laughs. "Not sweet enough yet. I'm guessing"—she pops a red berry into her mouth, and Dylan can hear it crunch when she bites down—"that we're still not going to break twenty percent Brix this week."

"Whatever that means." He ducks under the trellis wires, and together they cut across the dense rows to the next fourth, careful not to dislodge any clusters. The aisles are thick with clover, planted to reduce soil erosion. Once arrived, he counts up four more vines. His mind is a fraction on Denica, mainly on trying not to embarrass himself in front of her, such as by dropping the bag. But the whopping majority of his thoughts are dedicated to the trembling in his fingers and the telltale pounding that's picking up in the blood vessels behind his eyes. He looks down the row for Sara. She was supposed to be with them, but she followed Ian in some conversation. Sara and Ian are in the same block of vines counting four and four from the opposite direction, so that eventually the two pairs will make an *X* across the plot.

"Do you like her?" Denica asks.

"Who?"

"Sara."

"Yes."

"Why?"

Dylan drops another grape. The third? Or the fourth? It's lost instantly in the clover. "I just do. She's my mom." He steals a look at Denica, and in that instant I understand that the real reason he likes Sara is because in her presence, his panic has no power over him. He noticed it the first time he went into her shop. It wasn't the milky chocolate scents that soothed him. And at her house, he was fine once she stopped trying to order him into calmness. By the time she had thrown on a sweatshirt to drive him home, he was perfectly fine, just fine.

"Do you like her?" he asks.

"She's all right. My da fancies her, though."

This makes Dylan grin. "It's a terrible thing, being *fancied*." He tries to say it like she did.

"'Tis, so she'd better not return the favor, if you know what I'm saying."

He didn't, exactly.

"My ma was all about the poor," Denica said. "Sara likes her profits too much."

"It's not really fair to compare Sara to your mom, though."

"Not if she's yours—right. I didn't even know she had kids before today. Don't think Da knew either."

"Might put a damper on his fancies."

Denica grins at that.

"I bet your dad likes his profits." Dylan can't help it.

"Not at the expense of poor farmers in third world countries."

"What?"

"Chocolate slaves. They use child slaves to fill our candy baskets, you know."

"Are we talking about Sara?"

"Her sins," Denica says firmly.

"So your dad prefers to use migrant workers in our first world country?"

Denica's eyes scold him. "Everyone here is legal. And they get more than minimum wage. He was an immigrant himself once upon a time."

Dylan nods. She's not offended, just passionate. He cares, but not as much as he cares about Sara coming into his line of sight again. He wonders what it's going to take to get her and Marina on better terms.

"You known Sara long?" he asks.

"Nearly two years."

"Then you know her better than I do."

"True. And you don't mind my saying that's odd."

Dylan shrugs. "I guess we all want what we didn't get to have, and don't want to ruin what we thought we had."

That thought made sense in his head, but once out, it sounds like gibberish. Denica drops a grape into her bag. "Deep thoughts, by Dylan Becker."

He can't tell if she's mocking or admiring. He takes a deep breath. She glances at him, seems to size him up in one second as if she might have got something wrong the first time she looked and needs to double-check her impressions.

"Your hands are shaking," she says. They're done with this vine, and Dylan wants to move on but lacks the confidence to step out ahead of her.

"My fingers are just counting to four, over and over and over." He curses himself silently. Her noticing is going to be an accelerant. He braces himself.

"Panic attacks?" she asks.

He tries to think of something else, anything else that will make him seem less pathetic. Because it doesn't really matter what the doctors say, or what Marina says—Dylan knows that until he can get out of the tight spaces of his mind with his body firmly under his control, he will always wish to be more than he thinks he is.

Denica is looking at him, chewing on a grape, eyes raised. She looks skeptical and he's not sure why.

His sigh is shaky, disappointed in himself. "For as long as I can remember."

"Sucky issue to have. Sorry it's yours."

"We all have our stuff, don't we? What did you get saddled with?"

She ducks through the next row and answers as she's walking away.

"Thinking I'm right all the time."

Dylan's laugh bursts out of him. He folds himself through the row. "So I guess you don't have many friends, do you?"

He meant it as a joke, because surely she was joking too, wasn't she? But she stops abruptly and turns back, crushing the clover under her shoes. He comes into her space too quickly. There's a V between her brows, and she's leaning into a confrontation. But when he pulls up short, startled, so does she.

She blinks. "That's right," she says slowly. "*You're* right." She crosses her arms, then uncrosses them. Her bag of grapes swings from the end of her fist.

He tries to think of something to say. Gets nothing.

"Though you're the first with the guts to say so."

Dylan is trying hard to figure out what just happened.

"Truth feels good," she says. "Or maybe it depends on the messenger." She turns back and resumes her walk, counting grapevines with one hand, swinging the bag of grapes with the other.

He watches her go and notices that the space behind his eyes isn't throbbing anymore. His arms aren't vibrating. He could carry a full pot of water to the end of the lane without spilling it. But at the moment, his heart is racing.

"Hey," he shouts out. He's louder than he thought he'd be, drawing from the bottom of open lungs. Dylan starts to jog. "Hey, Denica. Do you know how to surf?"

Twenty-Two

*Pandora follows the girls around Sara's house, her dark-*brown paws padding silently and her tail erect. In Sara's bedroom she rubs her fawn-colored flank against the leg of a dressing table and mews.

Jade sits down on the unmade bed to rub the cat's ears. When she sits, the bedspread shifts and reveals the corner of a book forgotten under the sheets.

"She's a chocolate-point Siamese," Jade says of the cat. "My grandpa used to have one."

"That figures," Marina mutters. She has pushed aside a mirrored closet door and is scanning the stacked shelves for a place to begin. "She's completely chocaholic. Check the drawers."

"What am I looking for again?" Jade's long blond hair falls over one shoulder as she stoops to pull open the slim drawers in the vanity.

"I don't know. Anything that looks old."

"Everything looks old. *She's* old."

"Think sentimental, then. Pictures from a long time ago, letters, birthday cards, scrapbooks. Anything that might tell us something about her past."

Jade starts sifting through the contents aloud. "Lipstick, brushes, a million tubes of hand lotion, nail polish—"

"I don't need a list."

They ransack quietly for a few moments. Most of the boxes in Sara's closet hold various pairs of shoes.

"Oh. My. Gosh." Jade finds a snapshot jutting from the mirror frame. She lifts it out and slowly turns to Marina. "That's the car."

Marina turns around, holding a dusty handbag. "What car?"

The photo is of Sara sitting in the driver's seat of her Porsche. Ian is in the passenger seat, and they're grinning at the photographer. Denica, I'd guess.

"We chopped your mom's car."

"I told you, she's not my mom." But Marina comes over to get a closer look.

"Why didn't you say anything?"

"I'd never seen it, never seen her. Of course she's got something else now."

She stares at the image for a while, though, and her caramel complexion pales a little.

"What are the chances?" Marina says.

"I am so out of here." Jade hands over the photo and picks up the floppy purse she had tossed on the bed. "If she comes home—"

"It's nothing." Marina puts the picture back in the mirror. "Why do you think we're starting in the bedroom?"

"Because that's where most people keep their personal stuff, genius. Have fun!"

"Also because we'll be finished in here long before she gets home." Marina steps into the bedroom doorway to plead with Jade not to leave. "I have a key, she invited me to be here, and I doubt she'll complain about me bringing a friend. By the time she walks in the door we'll be kicking back on the sofas reading her magazines and eating her food. Her kitchen's bigger than your entire apartment."

Jade crosses her arms, then throws her hands in the air. "Fine." She keeps her bag on her shoulder, though. "What about the guy in the picture? Who's he?"

"Doesn't matter. I'm looking for something older than Sara's Porsche."

Pandora leaps onto the bed and finds a sparkling tube of lip gloss that has fallen out of Jade's bag. She bats at it and it rolls onto the floor.

"It's too much stuff to go through," Jade complains.

Marina has pulled down an old stationery tin and lifted the lid. The container holds a mismatched bunch of spare envelopes and loose notepapers. "Help me think. When Jesse broke up with you, what did you do with all your stuff from him? The pictures, the notes?"

"I *deleted* them," Jade says, waggling her phone in front of Marina's face.

"What about presents?"

"Gave 'em away." Jade gives up on the vanity and goes to the nightstand.

"No, you didn't—I just saw you wearing those earrings last week, the big hoops he gave you for Christmas."

"So I keep those in my jewelry box. Are you trying to get me to think like a forty-year-old? Because it's not going to happen. We're not even as old as the stuff you're trying to find."

"Then think like a secret, special hiding place. If you were a hiding place, where would you be?"

"You are *so* whacked."

"A pillow. A mattress. A book. A safe—"

"We're the criminals in this kooky little scenario, Marina. It's not like she robbed a bank and needed a place to stash a million bucks. She doesn't even share her house with obnoxious roommates or pesky little brothers."

"What are you saying?"

"That she doesn't need to protect anything from anyone in here."

"But she's hiding something from us. I know it."

"Well, you should be looking at what's right in front of you. What's on her coffee tables? What's on her bookshelves? Duh— what are the pictures she's got hanging on her walls?"

"Didn't you notice? She doesn't have any."

"I dispute that notion," Jade says in an official voice. "It's amazing what you'll see when you stop to notice it."

Marina's not listening. "The attic. Let's go find the attic."

"You go find the attic. I'm going to stay down here. Can't make a quick getaway from an attic."

I'm gripping the arms of my theater seat, leaning forward. Dylan is at the wheel of Sara's Porsche Panamera, which she bought one-year used to replace the dismantled Boxter. They're driving back from the vineyard, and if I were still able to get out and about I would seriously consider standing in the middle of the road again and sending my son spinning. But I'm not, and besides, the Panamera is fully enclosed.

"Why would you buy the sedan when you could have got the convertible?" Dylan asks Sara.

"I had a convertible. Thought it was time for something more practical. More seats. Besides, you wouldn't be able to drive the convertible. Your hair would blind you."

"It must have been pricey. Custom paint, fully loaded."

"The previous owner paid for all that. The previous owner and my insurance company."

"Still. It's a nice ride for someone who sells candy."

"It is a nice ride," Sara agrees. "You like the way it handles?"

"I feel strangely at risk of getting road rash on my butt cheeks, but yeah. Other than that it's perfect."

They talk so easily that I feel a surge of jealousy. Did Dylan and I ever talk about cars, even in this limited way? Why not? What stood between us? And why does Sara's presence with my son, which is exactly what I want, prick me with regret instead of relief?

"You'll tell me if you need me to take over for you," Sara says.

"Sure."

Like he'll tell you he doesn't have his driver's license, I say under my breath. *Why didn't you make him show it to you, Sara? Good grief, even if he had it—that's a sixteen-year-old boy and a seventy-thousand-dollar car. Rule number one of parenting teenagers, Sara: assume nothing.*

"Maybe I could drive it back up to get Denica next week," he says, taking a curve a little too wide.

"Let's see if you can get us home today first."

He re-centers the Porsche in the lane, lowers the speed to a few miles above the limit, then returns to his not-so-subtle inquiries about Sara's financial status.

"Business must be good."

"It is. Very good."

"There weren't many people at your shop when I was there."

"You were there before we opened." Her smile teases just a little. "But summer is a chocolatier's slow season."

"How does that work?" he asks. "I mean, I'm asking as a businessman, right? I'll never be a lawyer or a doctor or anything like that, so how can a lowly game programmer like me make millions? What's your secret?"

Sara fidgets with the hem of her blouse. "Sell a great product."

"Easy as that?"

"Easy is the *last* thing it is."

"You don't have to sell your soul to the devil or anything like that?"

This time Sara is slower to answer. She puts her sunglasses on top of her head and turns to my son.

"Are you asking if I can help you and your sister, like I promised?"

He takes his eyes off the road to look at her. She points at the windshield meaningfully. He straightens up.

"I want to know if I can trust you. Because . . . you know."

She nods. "Ian says I should make sure I'm telling you the truth."

"Is that because you haven't been?"

"The truth is, business has been very good. I sell a great product. I've had some lucky breaks. And candy makers don't make as much money as I have."

"So I was right about that."

"A lot of my income comes from smart investments. Old money. Family money, you know?"

"Sort of."

"In other words, I started off ahead, see? I had capital to get the business off on the right foot, and I've worked hard to keep it there."

"You want to invest in another business?" Dylan asks hopefully.

Sara chuckles at that. "Are you good at it?"

"The best."

"Then I might."

"What'll it take?"

"Oh, wow. Uh, time, information, trust. But I'll support you. That's why I'm here."

"Okay," he says. "Trust, huh?"

"That's right."

"You should probably know that I don't have a driver's license."

———

At the end of the upstairs hall, a door that looks as if it should lead to a linen closet actually leads to a steep, narrow staircase into the attic. Marina has left the door open, and Jade finds it easily.

"I told you, right in plain sight," Jade calls out. She climbs the steps holding a stack of slim hardback volumes. "You found anything yet?"

"Maybe," Marina says. She's sitting on a window seat under a sloping roof when Jade enters the room. On her lap sits a stationery box, a white box printed with yellow birds. Little canaries fly around the sides and over the top in artistically appealing chaos. They fly through my stomach as well, put to nervous flight by the sight of the box's contents. Marina's fingers have left tracks through the thin layer of dust on the lid. I avert my eyes.

Similar lightweight dirt coats everything in the attic, but it's surprisingly clutter-free and spacious, with windows at both ends of the low roof. The walls and sloping ceiling have all been painted a powder-blue color at odds with the earthy tones of the rest of the house. An antique china cabinet with chipped white paint takes up most of one wall. Its shelves are loaded with old tools: muffin cups, dipping forks, spatulas, candy molds, ladles, a thermometer, wire cooling racks, and a dented copper pot. One of the six drawers in the bottom of the cabinet is fully open and tilts toward the floor. This is where Marina found the box now on her lap.

Next to the window seat, a cheap bookcase with peeling veneer sags under the weight of large cookbooks. Besides these items, there are file boxes containing old tax records—the more recent ones are held by Sara's accountant—Christmas decorations, a plastic bin full of stained table linens, and a closet full of designer clothes no longer in style.

"Give me a vacuum and I could turn this place into a nice apartment," Jade says, scanning the room. "Think she'd have me?"

"After chopping her car, no."

Marina is reading a handwritten note by the afternoon light coming in through the window.

The writing is my own, and I feel considerable embarrassment that my daughter is reading these letters. Definitely not the woman they were for. I assumed Sara had destroyed them.

Jade looks around and opens a few of the drawers under the cabinet. "She could open a Williams-Sonoma up here."

Marina is engrossed in the letters. Disgusted? Maybe. Hard to tell.

"What have you found?"

"Letters."

"I can see that. What kind of letters?"

"Love letters."

"Mmm. Anything worth sharing?" Jade leans over Marina's shoulder.

Quickly, Marina folds what she is reading and puts it back inside the box, then shuts the lid.

"Why can't I read 'em?" Jade wants to know.

"Because they're my dad's," Marina says. She puts the box on the seat and reaches for the volumes Jade has brought.

"So why does Sara have them?"

"They're from my dad, to Sara."

"Ah. The plot thickens."

"I don't get it. My dad loved my mom. His whole life. There was never anyone else."

"Maybe these were from before they met."

"All these are from the fall of '97. Right before Mom died."

Jade slowly seats herself next to Marina on the seat. "That would explain why he doesn't like to talk about what happened."

Marina doesn't want to talk about it either. She's already thumbing through the slender books of glossy black-and-white photos. There aren't very many students at the school, so it doesn't take her long to look up Rochester and find Sara and Misty smiling out at her from their postage-stamp windows, looking more like twins than Marina is prepared for. Aside from the differences in their clothes, there are only two things to distinguish the girls. Sara's hair is straight while Misty's has a wave, and only Misty's smile reaches all the way to her eyes. Sara's smile has something like sadness behind it, even at her young age.

"Check out that perm!" Jade points to a blonde with especially big hair. "Is she wearing *spandex*?"

"They must have been sisters," Marina says, picking up another volume. Some of the page edges are stuck together as if no one has ever looked through the book one page at a time.

Jade takes the book Marina already looked through. She's still ogling the trends of her parents' generation. "Mullets are definitely in the top ten worst hairstyles of all time."

Marina finds similar pictures of Misty and Sara in each year, differentiated mostly by Misty's easy self-confidence and Sara's increasingly bold fashion statements. Her freshman year: oversize hoop earrings that hit her shoulders. Sophomore: a zebra-print jacket. Junior: a sideways bob, short over her right ear and long under her left, replaced the long, straight hair.

"Where's their senior book?" Marina asks.

"These were the only ones. Did Sara have no friends?"

"Why do you say that?"

"Not a single signature in any of these books."

She's right. The pages are crisp, clean, with a hint of yellow age cast over the surface.

"Where did you find these?"

"Downstairs. There's a bookshelf in the living room—big picture books mostly, atlases, lots about South America."

Marina closes the yearbook and looks at the front cover. The size and shape look familiar. She leaves the book with Jade and puts the box of letters back in the china cabinet's drawer, then returns to Sara's bedroom. There, peeking out from beneath the bedsheets, is the corner of the book Sara must have been reading recently, the same size and thickness as the yearbooks. This one has a black cover with gold letters and tumbling pink geometric triangles. *On the Edge*, it says. The year is printed inside: 1989.

The missing senior yearbook doesn't have the fresh-off-the-press look of the others. This one has been vandalized by a Sharpie pen, its broad black tip slashing across the fields of most of the pages. The name *Sara Rochester* on the inside front cover has been struck and rewritten in large, childish letters, with an expletive for the middle name.

There are no signatures in this book either, but the pages have been softened by frequent turning and thumbing.

In their senior yearbook, Misty and Sara each have a page featuring several photos and a written summary of their high school achievements and highlights. Misty's is the only unmarked sheet in the two-hundred-page book. Marina feels she is looking at herself in these images. She feels at the same time that the woman looking back at her, two years younger than Marina is now, has nothing in common with her own life. She was an artist, the bio says. A dancer with bottomless energy. A smart student who wanted to open a dance studio in Los Angeles. A popular, life-of-the-party, well-balanced person whom everyone loved.

Sara's senior page is on the back side of Misty's. Her photos have been X'd out by that permanent marker. Someone has turned the bio paragraph into a solid black box, then used a bottle of lumpy White Out to paint a picture over the top. The effect looks strangely artistic, abstract and eye-popping like one of those optical illusions in which you can't tell whether you're looking at an old woman or a young woman. Only this line of white looks like a person looking back over his shoulder. His eyes and mouth are frowning.

Marina stares at it for a long time, then holds it farther away from her face. She tilts it slightly to the left, and the face becomes a handwritten word. *Liar*, it says, the two loops of the *L* forming the eyes and the tail of the small *R* shaping the cold shoulder. Chunks of dried White Out stick to the opposite page.

As she holds the book out, a blue envelope falls from the back cover and flutters to the floor. Marina retrieves it. Long ago it was crudely torn open at the top, but years of being sandwiched in the book have flattened and smoothed the jagged edge. It's addressed to Sara Rochester in Santa Barbara, California. No return address. The postmark on it is still legible. Marina del Rey, December 15, 1997.

The day before Misty's death.

I'm as surprised by this note as my daughter seems to be. Misty never showed it to me.

Marina withdraws the paper inside and unfolds it against the marred yearbook cover. Sara's name is at the top in handwriting that would be considered beautiful if not for the wobbling strokes that seem to suggest the letter was written with a trembling hand. Her eyes drop all the way to the bottom first, looking for the sender. It's signed *MRS. Misty Becker.* The title is in all capital letters and underlined three times.

She starts over at the beginning.

Sara, I know what you are. Stop pretending.

Downstairs, the door between the kitchen and the mudroom slams.

Marina startles. She shoves the yearbook back between the sheets and crumples the letter into the back pocket of her jeans.

Twenty-Three

"Misty wrote a letter to Sara?" I demand of the man in the theater.

"As you can see."

Again I twist in my seat. It's becoming increasingly difficult. My back is stiff. My head hurts. I can't quite bring him into focus.

"Did they fight?"

He isn't going to answer.

"Why can't I read the letter? What happened?"

The man lifts his hand toward the screen. *You'll see.*

"Was it Sara? Did she . . . ? Please, just tell me. I don't want to watch. That would kill me all over again."

"You can't just pick and choose what you want to know, Garrett. And remember—you're not dead yet."

———

One Sunday afternoon in early October Misty threw a party. Most of the guests were parents of Misty's dance students, and the gathering was a strange family-friendly event for both children and adults—a harvest festival complete with bobbing for apples, an open bar, and a hay ride through the neighborhood in the back of someone's pickup. Misty cast it as a pre-maternity-leave farewell, though Dylan's due date was nearly two months off and nothing would keep her away from that dance studio. She'd already decided to put him right on the bottle so she could get back to her meds as soon as possible. I suspect the emotional roller coaster was more trying on her than it was on me, because this time little Marina was in the picture. "She deserves better than this," Misty would say in the valley days.

The shindig was a huge success. I watched from the sidelines, sitting on a great pumpkin with an Indian Wells beer, happy to see my wife so . . . happy.

The next day I was late getting home from work and unintentionally ruined a surprise candlelight dinner. Misty kicked me out of the house.

I made the ninety-minute drive up to the Rincon, which had made progress since the September purchase. The living room suite was still on back order, but the bedrooms were furnished and the window coverings had finally been installed. But a delay in the building permit for our new porch threatened to postpone the project until spring, and a retaining wall that collapsed two weeks after closing sucked at our budget and set us back further than I had hoped it would.

Still, it was our getaway home, and so I got away. I arrived after dark, restless and angry. The city planning meeting that had delayed me that evening wasn't my fault. The LA traffic wasn't my fault. Misty's mean moodiness was not my fault. And yet everything in that beach house accused me of failure, mostly the intolerable silence that not even the surf could mask. If I was the right kind of man, the permit would have gone through on time, the wall wouldn't have fallen down, the living room would have a sofa and chairs, and Misty's happiness would last for more than twenty-four hours at a time. This weekend house—this was the thing that was supposed to prove what I could offer her. It was the thing to finally make her happy.

How far short it fell.

The ocean breeze was stiff and foretold a storm. It was too dark for a walk, too cold to sit outside. I called Sara, because I knew she would tell me what I wanted to hear. She would probably say it without me having to fish, because her heart was perceptive and generous.

I said, "I'm in town. Can I buy you dinner?"

She didn't answer right away. I imagined her looking at the clock. After nine thirty. She said, "Jason?"

I was an idiot. "No, Garrett."

"Garrett? What are you doing—"

"I need to get out of this house."

She couldn't have understood what I meant, but she laughed and said she did, then, "It's too late for eating. Come here and I'll fix you something warm to drink. If you're starving I have . . . stale pretzels."

On the way, I stopped in Carpinteria at a twenty-four-hour hole-in-the-wall for a spicy *pollo asado* burrito and my mood immediately improved, even though the rain started falling before I finished it off.

At the time, "here" was a studio apartment attached to Allegro, the State Street confectionery in Santa Barbara where Sara had done her apprenticeship and then become a full-time manager. In the parking lot at the rear I climbed a staircase with an unstable wrought-iron rail to the second floor and knocked on the green door as instructed. Sara confirmed me through the peephole before clicking through the locks and opening the door with a wide smile.

She was a chaos of flannel pajama bottoms, a T-shirt, and hair transformed by a recent shower into thick, limp strings. Her apartment was a disaster of genius proportions: furniture draped with cast-off clothing and baseboards littered with cast-off shoes. But she'd made an effort to clean up. I assumed that the mountain of clothing on the unmade daybed had just recently been relocated from the room's only comfortable chair.

"Sit, sit," she said, pointing to the threadbare recliner as I shrugged out of my wet parka. She shook it out in the bathroom shower stall and then hung it on the clothes hook, over a robe.

"No problem is so big that hot chocolate can't fix it," she announced, gliding into the kitchen, which I could see in its entirety from where I sat.

Her tiny kitchen table bore a dangerous tower of cookbooks and thick file folders with *Sara's Sins* written in her hasty handwriting across the front, her emerging business plans. Dirty dishes filled the sink, but a copper pot on the miniature gas range simmered with the scents of good memories.

Seconds later a steaming mug warmed my hands. Sara's crazy notion of hot chocolate was bittersweet and topped with black pepper–crusted marshmallows that crunched even as they melted. It was the best thing I'd ever poured over my tongue. "This drink might introduce entirely new problems of its own," I said, "like a rush on peppercorns. What's the other flavor in it?"

"An almond syrup."

"Mmm. Better than therapy."

I sat and sipped and we listened to the rain, and she didn't ask why I was there or what I needed. She probably guessed. She took a seat on the daybed, sat right on top of the clothes.

The muscles in my back and neck finally relaxed into the seat. "You serve this at the store?"

"I will when I open Sara's Sins."

"How's that coming?"

"Big setbacks." She shook her head and with her fingers lifted a sopping marshmallow to her mouth.

"What happened?"

"Wrecking ball took down the shop I was looking at." She didn't seem too broken up over this. In fact, she looked up at me through the steam of her cocoa and grinned as if it were all a stupid joke.

"What?"

"The owner neglected to tell his tenants the building had been condemned. Took off with their rent money first of October, and then the demolition crews showed up."

"The tenants were still there? People were hurt?"

"Not physically. But they had to clear out, and the building went down yesterday."

"Unbelievable. Tell me he didn't have any of your money."

"A ten-thousand-dollar check."

"Ouch."

"It was a deposit to be applied to the lease."

"What are you going to do?"

"Nothing."

I waited for her to explain.

"In more bad news, a San Francisco investor backpedaled on his promise last week, so my bank account is ten thousand dollars smaller than I had hoped it would be right now."

"You mean you're twenty thousand dollars in the hole?"

"Not at all." She sipped. "Timing is everything. It's the criminal landlord who's going to find himself holding a bad check. As for me, well, I pretty much break even in this tangle."

It took me a minute to sort out what she said, and by then she was laughing. "Wouldn't it be wonderful if he came after me for it?" she asked. "I have this fantasy of turning him in."

"Maybe there'll be a reward in it for you."

This tickled her own funny bone so hard that she had to hold her mug out over the carpet or risk slopping hot chocolate all over herself. I laughed because she was laughing. She clutched her stomach and tilted her head back, eyes closed, giggling, not at all behaving like a girl whose dreams might come to an end before she has a fair chance to prove herself.

The perfection of this moment gut-punched me. It did then and does again now, as I watch from a very distant place in time. That right there was all I ever wanted with Misty, to sit smack in the middle of life's difficulties and laugh at them. I wanted nothing more than to be hemmed in by dirty laundry and the chaos of dreams and the close walls of our human limitations with someone who could help me see the humor in it.

Sara never looked more like Misty than she did then, though the women under the skin were completely different.

"A reward!" Tears leaked from the corners of her squinty eyes. "Can you imagine what my parents would say if that's how I get my startup capital?" This scenario made Sara hoot again. "Daughter of upstanding citizens gets her lucky break by giving a criminal a rubber check."

She was laughing too hard then, just far enough over the top so that I could see the real pain trying to punch up through the crust around her heart. The bit about the money was genuinely funny. The truth about her parents' disapproval of her dreams was a drill in her heart that wouldn't stop spinning.

I put my own cocoa on the lamp table between the daybed and the recliner. I leaned forward and reached for her cup too. She was going to burn herself. Already there was a spot of brown on the leg of her pajamas. She was holding the cup instead of the handle. My hand closed around hers and I grinned at her.

"I want to be there when you tell them."

Sometimes when watching a movie, I'll shout at the lead character as if he can hear me: *Don't go into that house alone, you idiot! The killer's hiding in the closet! Don't steal that money! You'll lose your soul!*

Don't kiss that woman. It'll kill your wife.

I know he can't hear me. I don't try to stop him because it's already happened, and I don't want to relive it. This time, I look away.

———

In her own home, Sara enters from the garage. She passes the laundry basket that I once fell into—or thought I fell into—then comes into the kitchen with her purse. She drops it on one of the counterside chairs, then heads across the house to kick off her shoes and change upstairs. She gets as far as the living room. Marina and Jade are sitting side by side on her sofa reading magazines, exactly as they'd been positioned the day Sara saw them driving away from her vandalized car. The scene instantly reconstructs itself in her mind, knocking her speechless.

This works to Marina's advantage. She's still angry about Dylan's trip to the vineyard, so she jumps into the confrontation first by laying out her expectations. She wants to be told about plans to take Dylan away from the house. Sara knows nothing about sneaky teenage boys, Marina accuses, and even less about sneaky teenage boys with anxiety disorders.

I hate seeing my daughter in this mood. But I don't know what to think of Sara right now.

Sara half listens. She knows Dylan is fine. Great, even. She's trying to think of what to do about the girls' involvement in the destruction of her Porsche.

Nothing, for now.

Pandora is in Jade's lap, purring.

Sara apologizes for the miscommunication, though that's not how Marina has characterized Dylan's disappearance for the day. She promises to keep Marina in the loop. As she lowers herself into a chair opposite the two friends, Marina and Jade rise like a seesaw. Pandora mews and leaps away.

"I can tell you how Dylan and I spent the day." Sara is so earnest.

"Maybe later."

"Okay."

Marina puts a hand on Jade's arm to direct her toward the door.

"Wait," Sara says. Then she rushes to her purse, withdraws her checkbook, and hesitates. What on earth does it take to run a family these days? It must have some similarities to running a business. She writes a check and carries it to Marina, holding it out face-first, nervous about her own ignorance. The girls turn, Marina already gripping that tall, vertical door pull. When she sees the five-digit check—made out to her—her rebel act sputters and stalls. She stares at it. Her hand comes off the door handle but she won't reach for the money.

It would solve so many problems.

It would complicate everything Marina is learning about this would-be mother of hers.

Sara worries about Marina's hesitation. "Let me know if that's not enough for a month or so. Mortgage, utilities, credit card bill. Food."

Marina stares at the slip of paper, so tempted. Jade snatches it out of the air at the same moment Sara lets go.

"Don't be stupid," Jade hisses to my daughter.

The girls and the check are gone in seconds. It's much more efficient than chopping a car.

Sara watches them leave, feeling less satisfied with her generosity than she had hoped. She returns to the living room, trying to remember what she meant to do before she discovered the girls.

A bookcase from her downstairs office peeks at her through the open door. On the bottom shelf, Sara can see the thin spines of her old high school yearbooks. They've been pushed all the way to the back of the shelf, and their misalignment with the other books catches her eye. She must have jostled them when she pulled out her senior book the night before. The one Misty marked up. If Marina and Friend are going to be popping in unannounced, Sara thinks, it's probably unwise to keep these books out in the open. How long will it be before Marina sees through Sara's paper-thin story? She just hopes for enough time to make amends. That's the most she can wish for.

Sara carries the three volumes up to her room, where she fishes out the fourth yearbook from her ocean of sheets, then proceeds to the attic. She finds a space for them next to some tilting cookbooks. She almost doesn't stop to look at my letters, but the china cabinet is right there, and she wonders if there might be something in my own hand that she can show to my children. Proof of our partnership, maybe.

She opens the drawer, finds the yellow-and-white box. Inside, the bundle is tied up in a piece of gold elastic from one of her old chocolate boxes. She carries it to the window seat where the light is fading and loses herself for an hour, reading words I should never have written to anyone but Misty.

———————

This is how we all die: the first wheel of our lives slips off the pavement on the day we learn how to lie to ourselves. The second wheel goes when we discover that lying gives us something we need, even if only for a little while. And then we are destabilized. From there we fall and fall, like my truck headed for the belly of the earth.

Now I see it clearly.

The first lie I told myself was that Sara and I needed each other's laughter to survive. Laughing with another human being is always good, never harmful. Laughing heals.

Misty figured it out on a Saturday afternoon in November, after more than a month of secret meetings with Sara and shortly before Dylan's due date. She called my cell phone, excited. She was having contractions, but she didn't want to take Marina with her to the hospital, and the family scheduled to take Marina when the baby was born was out of town. She needed me to come home. I should have been thirty minutes away at my Los Angeles office, trying to tame a project that was over budget and behind schedule, when really I was an hour and a half up the coast in Sara's tiny apartment, waiting for her to get off work.

"Can you take Marina to your friend's house?" I asked, snatching my keys and running out Sara's door.

"Which friend? Can't you just come get us?"

"The one from the party. The one with the little girl Marina's age."

"Anna?"

I had no idea what the woman's name was. Maybe Anna was the daughter. "Yeah, her."

"Just come home. I can wait. Traffic won't be so bad right now."

I hurried down the wobbly iron steps outside of Sara's place, behind the shop, ransacking my mind for an excuse. "Look, Misty, I'm up at the Rincon house. I'm working on something—it was supposed to be a secret."

"I thought everything was done that could be done for now. When we were up last weekend—"

"There was just one more thing. I wanted it for you and the baby, so it had to wait until I knew you wouldn't be up again. I'm on my way right now, but it'll take longer than a half hour."

Misty was silent. I had no idea what kind of a surprise I'd need to come up with to cover this fib. I slammed the door of my truck and turned the ignition over with as much clatter as possible so she could hear, to prove myself a truth teller.

"Take Marina to Anna's and go to the ER. I'll drive straight there."

Her silence was the kind that sits on the edge of a knife. It might fall either way, into manic fury or pleasant surprise. The blade might slice it in half: angry tears and laughing accusations.

"I'm on the freeway right now. Are you okay?"

"Sure," she said, so quietly I could barely hear her.

"When was your last contraction?"

"A few minutes ago." All the excitement was gone, replaced by something new that I couldn't name.

"Maybe you shouldn't drive. I'm going to get off the phone and call an ambulance for you. Then I'll call back until—"

"I got it, Garrett. It's okay." Already I knew that it wasn't okay.

"No, wait. Is Marina there? Turn on the speaker phone and we'll—"

"See you when you get here."

"Fast as I can," I said, but she was already gone.

My hands on the steering wheel felt cold and unsteady. I wondered if Misty suspected anything before now, which lie had a hole in it large enough for her to see through. I doubted it. Her mood had been too bright. She might have noticed last weekend, when we rescheduled our missed dinner with Sara, but there was nothing to notice. Sara and I avoided eye contact, hardly spoke to each other, didn't even touch. Misty was at the center of my attention. Marina was at the center of Sara's.

Everything could be explained. Everything that *looked* like an affair could be explained as something else. My relationship with Sara was still young enough to be cast in a completely innocent light. All I had to do was end it and stay close to home.

I didn't want to, but I would. For Marina, for Misty, and for Dylan. Sara would understand. She would understand my rejection of her the way she understood her family's. I hated myself then. I never stopped hating myself after that. Even then my life was in a tumbling truck plummeting into a pit.

I rolled down the windows and turned up the radio. I spent the rest of the trip trying to think of some surprise to install at the beach house. Something that Misty didn't already have. Something that would thrill her. My mind was blank.

I didn't call Sara to explain. I didn't call Sara for another month.

Twenty-Four

The surfboard is flat on the beach, fins buried in the sand. Denica is on the board, belly-down, chin lifted, palms planted right by her armpits. Her long arms and legs look longer in the suit she's wearing, and Dylan is glad for a legitimate excuse to study her perfection as closely as he is.

"Keep your legs and ankles together," Dylan says again. "Then when you feel the wave begin to push, you pop up quick as you can. Bring your feet forward. Don't let your body go back over your legs, bring your legs forward under your body. Put your left foot under where your shoulders are right now, right foot where your hips are. Ready?"

"This feels silly on solid ground."

"You'll be glad you practiced here first. One, two, three."

The girl's arms are stronger than they look. She pushes up quickly, but her feet don't get as far forward as they should. They're too close together and too far to the back of the board.

"Wiiiiiipe ooouuut," Dylan croons.

Denica jumps off the fiberglass. "Show me again," she orders. Her fair nose is already pink.

Dylan takes her spot on the board, flat on his stomach. "Feet together. Body centered on the board. Chin up, paddle, paddle."

His fingertips brush sand. "You get lucky, you're in the right place at the right time, you have the right of way, and the wave gives you a shove. Hands here"—they press down alongside his ribs—"toes curled against the board, and *pop*." In one smooth motion his body springs. His feet land where his body used to be and he's up, arms floating. "Back foot ninety degrees, front foot forty-five, chest up, hips turned."

Denica doesn't wait for him to get off. She goes down on the packed sand and tries again. The grains shift under the weight of her palms, but this time she pushes harder and pops quicker.

"That's it. Do it again."

She gets back on the board. "This thing is huge. Shouldn't I start with something smaller?"

"The bigger the board, the easier it is to catch the wave. Don't grab the rails. Keep your hands flat. Right."

"Those waves out there don't seem too hard to catch." They're not even waist high, spilling over the top rather than plunging. She pops up again, more gracefully this time.

"Those'll be tough enough for your first time," Dylan tells her.

"Are they even waves, technically?" A handful of hopeful surfers have traveled for a few yards here and there across the white water.

"The best kind to learn in."

"Would Gabe call them waves? Because that's why I'm really here, see, because he said I couldn't do it."

Dylan laughs. "If you can stand up on the board in the water, you can surf."

Denica practices the pop-up until Dylan finally says, "That one was perfect."

"About time. My arms are mush. I won't have anything left."

"Sure you will. Wanna give it a try?"

In spite of her complaint she keeps practicing, and keeps nailing it. Dylan waits for her. There's nothing more to be said about her form, except that he doesn't mind watching her concentrate so hard on something he loves. He pretends indifference by looking out over the water whenever she stands.

"The truth is," she says, arms stiff as airplane wings, "I'm basically afraid of the water."

"Obviously," he teases. She socks him in the arm. "But I wouldn't have thought you're afraid of anything."

"Yes. Of poisonous spiders, of being wrong, and of planes crashing into the ocean."

She drops back down onto her stomach and scoops sand, then lets it fall between her fingers. Dylan listens to the spilling wave water, the kind of noise most people find comforting enough to lull them to sleep.

He says, "There's a lot to be afraid of in the water, especially if you've crashed into it thousands of miles from shore."

"Sharks," she says.

"Undertow."

"Jellyfish."

"All kinds of living things that you can't see."

"Drowning." She shudders.

He holds that one in his mind for a second, then continues, "Rip currents."

"Perfect storms."

"Shore breaks."

"Deadly nets of seaweed."

"Tsunamis."

Denica drops her forehead to the board. "You're not helping."

"I'm not the best person for this topic."

"The ocean?"

"Being afraid."

Denica rolls off the board onto her back, crossing her arm over her eyes to shield it from the sun. Dylan thinks she's not truly scared. She's trying to make him feel better. It's annoying. And nice.

"You don't have to worry about poisonous spiders out there," he offers. The corner of her mouth twitches. "And there's dolphins."

She sits up and faces him. "How can you be nervous picking grapes in a vineyard but not riding waves in the ocean? It's not logical. Didn't you spend your whole life thinking that your mother drowned in those waves?"

He did, which was part of the effect that he couldn't explain. "Apparently that's not what happened."

"Still." Denica wriggles her toes down into the damp sand. "People die out there all the time."

"My dad used to say that fear is just an idea about something that could happen but probably won't, and even if it did, the happening won't be as bad as the fearing."

"Do you buy that?"

"Sometimes."

"Is that what gets you out on the water?"

"No."

"Then what?"

"You wouldn't understand," he says. Then he mimics, "It's not logical."

"Try me."

He almost doesn't. He's enjoying her company and isn't ready to scare her off. On the other hand, if it's going to happen it might as well be sooner than later. A sweat breaks out on his palms. "I can be in a room full of people and be totally alone. Like they could squash me and wouldn't even notice."

She's nodding. He'd expected a blank stare.

"But out there, floating in the lineup and waiting for the next set—there don't even have to be any other surfers—it's like I'm not alone at all."

Still nodding. "You're right. That doesn't make any sense," she says. "But I think I get it."

He stoops down and picks up the board's leash lying in the sand like a string of seaweed. He kneels to lash the Velcro strap around her ankle, not too tight or too loose, alert to any clue that she wants to do it herself: a flinch, a yank, a protest. She is still, but when he runs his thumbs over the closure, he feels a low hum in her muscles, a shiver that isn't from a chill, a tremble as familiar to him as his own fear. He looks up the long line of her body. She's staring at the baby waves. Her hands are clenching and releasing.

He wants to say, "I won't leave you alone," but it's a cheesy promise that he might not be able to keep. It's easy to get separated, even in these shallows. So he stands, picks up the board, and tucks it under his arm. Now they're as connected as they can be. He waits for her to decide what she's going to do. He studies the water. It looks friendly. No rip currents today.

He waits some more.

Denica finally steps out with an accusing look over her shoulder. "Are we going or not?"

Sara stands out on the enclosed patio of the beach house and watches Dylan and Denica wading into the water. She did not let Dylan take the Porsche to fetch Denica. She chauffeured them both and then stuck around.

Behind her, Marina is reading a book with her feet up on the wraparound bench. Her bookmark is a folded sheet of lilac stationery, the letter stolen from Sara's yearbook. She slips it behind a page where Sara won't see it.

The charge in the air is hostile, so unlike the day Sara and I sat here drinking champagne.

"Dylan invited Ian and Gabe down for dinner," Sara says to Marina. "I thought I'd go pick up some takeout unless you'd rather do something else."

"Make yourself at home," she says without looking up from her book.

"I'm glad it goes both ways," Sara murmurs.

Denica is stomach-down on the board in the shallow waters, paddling, and Dylan is wading next to her, putting a little pressure on the back of the board to help keep the nose up.

"They're good for each other," Sara says to Marina.

Marina folds her book closed and scoots her chair back from the table. Sara turns around.

"No one's trying to cut in on you, Marina. Whatever kind of friends Denica and I can be to Dylan, we won't replace you. That would be impossible."

"I'm so relieved," she says. She gets up and reaches for her empty tea glass. She doesn't offer Sara anything to drink.

"I went to see your dad yesterday."

"I went to see him today," Marina says as if it's a competition.

"I asked them to give him a haircut. He was getting bushy."

"Now he looks butchered."

Marina pushes open the sliding glass door.

"Marina."

"What?"

"I'm so, so sorry for everything you've lost. Considering all the ways your dad and I messed up, you've turned out to be a truly amazing person."

"Dad wasn't the one who messed up, was he?" she says.

Sara's gaze slides back out to the ocean.

Marina lingers.

"Can I show you something?" Sara reaches for her purse. Inside is a small plastic photo book with a gold foil Christmas tree stamped on the cover. The photo sleeves are cracking a little, and the crimped plastic edges are brittle and yellow. She considered transferring the pictures to a new album before she shows it to Marina and Dylan, but she's not even sure where to buy these so-called brag books anymore. She hasn't seen one in years.

Marina is in a mood. "Is it a marriage certificate? A legal document showing your name change? Proof that you don't have any relatives named Misty Rochester?"

Sara stills at the sound of her cousin's name.

"You're angry at me for leaving. I understand. I deserve that."

"You deserve worse. You did more than just leave."

"I did," Sara said. "You've done my job your whole life, and you've done it well. To show up now must seem like an insult to you. I didn't mean it that way. I only want to help."

"I can't take help from someone I don't trust."

"Like I can trust the girl who stole my car and sold it for parts?"

The emotion in the air whooshes out like a bomb blast. Anger out. Guilt in. Wariness falling like ashes. I'm overcome by sadness.

Sara leaves the photos in the purse. Yes, it's the wrong time for that.

Marina is quiet, playing with the corner of her paperback. She pages to the folded letter and draws it up so that the edge protrudes from the top of the book. "I didn't have anything to do with that." She expects Sara to bite back. This letter is her own weapon. But Sara isn't looking at it.

Sara fingers the straps of her purse. "Okay." She seems disappointed in herself for saying anything about the car.

Marina flicks the edge of the lilac stationery. She's never met a person who accepts a deceitful answer as quickly as Sara seems to. Maybe because that's what Sara wants others to do for her. Marina's lips press tightly together. She turns her back on Sara and goes into the house.

Twenty-Five

Sara retrieves the promised take-out dinner but leaves before Marina serves it, reminding me of the first time we met. She departs apologetically as Ian and Gabe are arriving, Ian carrying a bottle of wine by the neck. The trio pass one another on the red porch. There's news of an emergency in her kitchens, she claims. One of the enrobing machines is broken and needs immediate attention to keep the week's production schedule on track. It's too late to get a technician out there before tomorrow. She knows a thing or two about the gadgets that coat her candies in uniform chocolate shells.

Even I can tell that Sara is far too preoccupied with the low stakes in this slowest month of a chocolatier's year.

She explains the meal that she's leaving behind, tells Ian that she hasn't ordered the wasabi plate before and isn't sure if it'll be too spicy for his palate. She's sorry if it is. She's saying too much.

Ian offers to help her fix the equipment. "I'm a fifth wheel here," he says, referring to being left with the kids.

"You'll be a fifth wheel there too," Sara says, though he's mechanically minded. Ian's fixed his share of crushers and pumps and presses.

Sara seems to be waiting for him to reply and when he doesn't, she blinks, like maybe he said something and she didn't hear it. Or she didn't even hear what she said herself.

Gabe sees the confusion on his dad's face and claps his hands together. "Hope it's an easy fix," he says, then goes into the house.

Sara leaves Ian on the porch and gets into her car.

———

Dylan and Denica dominate the dinner table conversation. She caught a wave today and can't quite find an equal thrill to compare it to. Her cheeks are sunburned. Her eyes are puffy from being on the water without sunglasses. They're eating Japanese fish tacos, a fusion spinoff of the Mexican tradition. These are stuffed with seared ahi instead of breaded halibut, and wasabi and ponzu sauces instead of mayonnaise and salsa. "What was it, Dylan, maybe up to here?" She levels her hand at the bottom of her rib cage.

Gabe laughs. "I've heard how you Californians measure the waves."

Denica smirks at her brother.

"It was maybe knee-high," Dylan says kindly. A skinny shred of cabbage sticks to his chin.

"Was not! I don't suppose anyone happened to get a shot of it?" Denica looks at Marina, who is making sure there is food in her mouth for the duration of this dinner with strangers. My daughter shakes her head.

"Exactly how does one measure a wave?" Ian asks Dylan.

"It's complicated. In Hawaii they call them very short—from the back of the wave, or about half the height of what you can actually surf."

"You must be part Hawaiian," Denica says.

"The rest of us usually call it from the trough to the peak, but even that's not consistent. Pros generally like to call them short."

"You mean they underestimate the actual size?" Ian asks. "Why?"

Gabe pounds his chest with a fist. "To intimidate the rest of us with their idea of a one-meter wave."

"Something like that."

"I don't like you underestimating my first ride," Denica announces.

"Knee-high is fair."

Ian says, "That can't be very helpful, not having a scientific way to measure them. How do you forecast? How do you call winners in the competitions?"

Dylan swallows a bite. "Bragging rights aren't very scientific. But there are people who try to be objective. Billabong has a system for their contests."

"I like objective," Ian says. "If I just guesstimated the sugar content of my grapes I'd be out of business."

"That's why you're not a surfer, Da." Gabe grins at him and Ian concedes.

"Da can't stand people who exaggerate," Denica tells Marina.

"Not true," Ian says. "I love you very much, sweetheart."

Gabe snorts.

Marina observes this exchange with ulterior motives. Ian might be an ally in her pursuit of truth. So when he asks about her work and her interests, she becomes suddenly conversational. For a short time they find common ground in overseas relief work—something Gabe has done and Marina hopes to do. Marina isn't interested in Gabe, though. She's polite but won't return his friendly banter. He doesn't seem discouraged. He pokes at her gently with words the way one fingers a sea anemone in the tide pools, just for the fun of watching the pretty thing close up.

When he loses interest in this, he challenges Dylan to a match in some Internet game. Denica claims to be uninterested but isn't about to hang around with her father and closed-up Marina. She follows the boys upstairs.

Ian gets up and starts clearing the table. Marina jumps up to help. They share the kitchen space easily, two people who've done this particular task on their own often enough not to have to say anything about it. Marina shows him which cupboard houses the trash can and where to find the dish soap. The rest is done in silence, an odd activity for a middle-aged man and a young woman who've only known each other for two hours. But neither one is self-conscious. Both are thinking about Sara. Each knows the other person is doing the same thing.

Marina hauls the empty take-out containers out to the side of the house, then returns and pulls out fresh towels to dry the plates he's just cleaned.

"I know Sara isn't our real mother," Marina says as she puts a plate back in the cupboard. Her eyes are on Ian, looking for a reaction.

He frowns at the soapsuds. "Is that why she left early?"

"You don't seem surprised."

Ian shrugs. He's not sure what Marina is aiming for.

"Why would she lie?" my daughter asks. "If she really wants to help like she says, she could just help."

"Would you let her?" Ian asks.

"Not sure. Does it matter? Why lie?"

Ian looks out the window that stands between the kitchen sink and the back patio. He thinks, then says, "Some things might be easier for her to do if she's your mother, married to your da."

Marina hasn't thought of this before. She holds a dry plate in front of her heart. "She's not his wife. I'll make her prove it. She won't be able to. She can't make any decisions about my dad."

"Decisions?" Ian asks.

"Life support, for example."

"Have the two of you talked about that?"

"No. In some ways it's worse that she hasn't brought it up. Secretive."

"Maybe it's just premature. But I was referring to things like taking financial responsibility of your father's affairs. Guardianship issues with Dylan. Maybe she just wants to be your mam."

"You think this is her version of a midlife crisis?"

"No." Ian turns off the hot water and unplugs the drain in the sink. "She cares about you."

"People who care don't lie. And they don't fake their own deaths, and they don't keep running away every time they're uncomfortable. And they don't pretend to be someone they're not."

Ian's sympathetic toward my daughter and defensive of his friend as well. "You can't run away from family, can you?"

"Sure you can."

"I meant blood is blood."

"I have another theory," Marina says. "Guilt."

Ian dries his hands. He's accused Sara of the same thing.

"If everyone believes she's our mother, no one would accuse her of killing our mother."

Now surprise registers in Ian's eyes. He holds on to the towel. "That's a grave accusation. Sara told me your mother took her own life."

"So she *has* admitted to you that she's a different person?"

Marina really wanted a different truth. Ian doesn't hear her question. He's remembering a completely different admission. *I killed their mother,* Sara once said—and he had thought, as did I, that she merely felt responsible for Misty's death.

Ian finally puts down the towel and rubs his eyes. "How did your mother die?"

"Suicide is the family story. But they never found her body. We don't have a grave, just a memorial in the front yard. So I wonder sometimes."

"How did you come to wonder if Sara played a part?"

"Here, look at this."

The letter that had fallen from the back of Sara's yearbook is in Marina's hands now, withdrawn from the back pocket of her shorts. She smoothes it open on the countertop for Ian to read.

December 15, 1997

Sara, I know what you are. Stop pretending. You've always wanted my life, everything from my successes to my wavy hair. It was cute in the beginning, when you'd ask to study with me so you could get grades like mine, or when you'd ask me to teach you how to apply makeup or flirt or dance like Jennifer Beal or Jennifer Grey. You worked so hard to be like me. But we were kids then.

Grow up, would you? I see through your sweet smiles and your dinner invitations and your pathetic baby gifts. I know what you're trying to do. Hands off my husband and stay away from my children. Get your own like the rest of us do—figure it out. The least you could do is learn how to cook. Chocolate will only get you so far.

I know how you think, and how dark you are inside. You won't be hearing from Garrett again, because he knows who the real wife is, the real mother. You're nothing but a pretender. Remember the time you took those plover chicks out of their nest in the sand? You said the mama abandoned them, but I saw you chase her off. I told you they'd die without their real mama, and I was right, wasn't I? You didn't have a clue what to do with those birds.

I know that you've thought of doing the same thing to my babies. I've seen the way you look at Marina. You want me to be scared, but it won't work. You can't chase me off now any more than you could when we were schoolgirls. You've got nothing. I'll protect my nest with whatever it takes. I'll defend my home to the death. I won't forget how you killed those baby birds.

Misty

"Who's this?" Ian asks, pointing to Misty's signature.

"Misty Rochester. My mother. The name on my birth certificate. I've seen pictures. She and Sara could pass for twins."

"Or maybe all the photos were of the same person."

Marina shakes her head. "Two people. They're related in one way or another. Sisters would be my guess. Hasn't she ever told you anything about her family?"

"A little."

Ian might say more if he were talking to a peer instead of to a woman his daughter's age.

Ian hands the letter back to Marina. "A little girl who accidentally kills a few chicks with her good intentions is a far cry from a murderous woman, don't you think?"

"Sara's told me so many lies that I can justify a few leaps to conclusion."

Ian shakes his head. "Now there's solid reasoning. Why are you telling me this?"

Upstairs, the guys give a unified shout-out over their game. Dylan laughs and says something that's unintelligible down in the kitchen.

"I want the truth. You seem like someone who cares about that."

"I thought that conversation was about waves and surfing."

"And the sugar in your grapes, and more."

Ian frowns.

"I want to find out who my grandparents are. I want to find out how Sara and Misty are related. I want to see the police reports about my mother's disappearance. And I want to know if Sara might have played any part in it."

"You should be able to do all that."

"I don't know how."

"Sara is my friend, Marina. I won't help you without talking with her first."

"So talk to her. I've got nothing to hide. Do you?"

Ian crosses his arms. He doesn't answer.

"She's the one who's hiding something, Ian. I don't know about you, but I want to know what kind of wave she is. No matter what surfers think is good for their egos, you should never underestimate a wave."

Twenty-Six

I never had to explain my relationship with Sara, because Misty never brought it up. We never spoke of that Saturday when she had false labor pains, when she found me in Santa Barbara after thinking I was in Los Angeles. She didn't speak of it, not even after I took her up to the beach house to see the new window I put in Dylan's room. I called in a favor and had a friend install the big bay with a toy box under the hinged seat. I opened a new credit card account to charge a telescope for our unborn son and then pointed it at the Channel Islands.

Misty accepted the "surprise" with the appropriate smiles, oohs, and aahs. But her total silence about the Braxton Hicks Saturday told me how much she understood.

For the next month I made sure Misty knew my every move. I invested in cell phones that further taxed our budget so she could text me as well as call. I checked in with her every hour. I found a way to make it to every one of her countdown appointments. I said I was sorry by being as devoted as I knew how to be. And still Misty's mood declined.

I counted the days until her due date, stocking the kitchen cabinets of both houses with baby formula and bottles. I called in a refill for her prescription and put it up on the center shelf of the medicine cabinet, right at eye-level, label out. She'd be able to start taking it the day she came home with Dylan if she wanted to. I changed my mind about the medicine cabinet and put the bottle in the bag she had packed for the hospital.

But when Dylan finally arrived with that mass of dark hair, one of the nurses laid him on his mother's chest and she pulled him in close. He latched on like this was as familiar as breathing.

"I thought we were going to put him on the bottle," I said.

"I changed my mind."

"Why?"

She smiled at me, one of the last uninhibited smiles I ever saw from her, and said, "Everything's okay."

The medicine bottle went back to our Marina del Rey home unopened and stayed in the cabinet that way for the rest of Misty's life.

On his third day home both Dylan and Misty fell asleep in the nursery during a feeding. I scooped him up, so careful not to wake either of them, and cradled my son in my left elbow. With my free hand I pulled an afghan up over Misty's shoulders, then I went to put Dylan in the crib. His lips were still smacking though there was no more food. As I leaned over, he startled in that way babies do, both hands shooting straight out as if I'd dropped him off a cliff. I laid him down, patted his tummy gently, and waited for his muscles to relax.

He looked just like his sister. They looked just like their gorgeous mom. They still do.

"What are you doing?" Misty was standing directly behind me, frowning. I was so wrapped up in my son's face that I hadn't noticed her get up.

"Hey," I whispered. "You two fell asleep and—"

My wife stepped in front of me and picked him up. I saw his body stiffen again. I'm sure I flinched too, then stared as she spun away and carried our son into our bedroom. She locked the door before I could follow.

That night I slept on a round ladybug rug on the floor of Marina's room. I could've slept on the couch, but then both Marina and I would have been alone, and sticking together seemed important to our family's survival somehow. I thought about calling Sara to tell her what was going on. The thought never turned into action.

In the weeks that followed, Misty's emotional state blackened. My begging her to notice was like putting a lit match to the fuel. She refused her pills. She refused to put Dylan on a bottle. She spoke to him quietly when they were together. Long-winded, conspiratorial whispers that fell silent whenever I walked into the room. Marina peppered her baby brother with wet kisses, and Misty would stroke our little girl's hair, smiling. Then she'd lift her eyes to me and that smile would fall.

At the time I didn't understand what had gripped my wife. Her OB quickly called it postpartum depression. Misty rejected the diagnosis. Even I thought the diagnosis didn't quite fit, but what does a guy know about such things? I filled her script and she refused to take those pills too.

Today parents and docs know more than we used to. In Misty's case, PPD wasn't a hefty enough diagnosis for a woman with her mental health history. Today the bleak void that swallowed my wife would probably be called postpartum psychosis, a rare disorder that even more rarely causes a mother to take the lives of her children. More typically an afflicted mother becomes her baby's fiercest protector and does battle with herself as both champion and enemy. And here's the cruel dagger of this particular psychosis: if a psychotic mother possesses enough self-awareness to think she might endanger her newborn, or fail him in any way, she won't think twice about taking her own life.

Had I known . . . but I didn't.

———————

December 14, 1997, was a Sunday. I remember this because I was watching the Raiders game with the volume turned almost all the way down, because both of our children fell asleep for their afternoon naps at the same time. Marina on the floor of her bedroom, fanny up and draped over a big stuffed bear, her face squashed into the ladybug rug. Dylan in the bassinet Misty put up in our room the day after she locked me out. Misty slept in the bed next to him. Out in the living room I cheered silently and only once forgot to object to officials' calls in the same way. At the half it looked like Oakland was going to trounce Seattle. It also looked like I was going to run out of jalapeño poppers, so right after the Raiders' third TD I ducked out to get another box from the freezer section of the nearest Vons. I was gone thirty, maybe forty minutes, which included a quick detour to the marina, where the damp ocean breeze did more for my puffy, new-dad eyes than a halftime show would.

When I returned, the front door of the house was open. Immediately I checked the bedrooms. Misty, gone. The sheets of our bed were rumpled and still warm, but Marina and Dylan slept alone in the empty house that had been left open to the world. I dropped my grocery bag on the chair that usually held Misty's purse, and my thoughts split apart like a broken rock. It took me a minute to formulate a plan. I couldn't leave the kids and I couldn't let Misty wander. Where had she gone? Why had she left the kids? Or had someone taken her? Was she in her right mind?

I woke Marina thinking she could help me. First mistake. My three-year-old cried and cried while I transferred Dylan to his infant carrier. He slept through his sister's wails and my fumbling efforts to get the stupid restraints buckled right. I carried him out to Misty's car and clicked the carrier into the base, then I went back for Marina, who had to be carried out in her socks. I didn't dare insist on shoes. When I tried to secure her in her seat, she fought me and cried some more. But I got her belted in without losing my cool.

I thought to get her something to put into her mouth. In the kitchen I filled a sippy cup with juice and grabbed a sleeve of graham crackers. Her screams filled the garage. She called for her mother through a wet throat. The jalapeño poppers stayed in their plastic bag in the bedroom, where they thawed into a soggy ruin long before I remembered them again.

Marina's face and hands were a snotty mess when I handed her the cup and the crackers. She hurled both to the floor as I climbed into the driver's seat and adjusted it to my long legs, thinking I should have left a note in case Misty got home first. No time. I pulled out of the driveway, closed the garage door, and bumped down into the street before I saw Misty. She was running toward us down the sidewalk in the yoga pants and socks she'd fallen asleep in. Her purse on its long strap slapped against her hip. I sighed heavily, so relieved. Marina's sobs had morphed into hiccups.

I pulled forward to close the gap between us and leaned across the passenger side to open the door for her while the car was still rolling. Misty plunged across a neighbor's grassy verge and jumped into the road right in front of the car. I hit the brakes. The sudden jolt silenced Marina. Misty came around to my door and yanked it open.

"Get out," she said. "Get out get out. Out of my car."

"Misty, what happened?"

She grabbed at my shirt though the seat belt still crossed my chest. "I know what you're doing. Get out. Leave my babies alone."

"You left them at the house! Where did you go?"

"Where are you going?" A nonsensical echo. "Where are you meeting her?"

"Who?"

"Sara. I'm not stupid. I hear you talking. I know that's where you went."

"No." I pried her hand off of my sleeve. "Misty, stop."

"Sneak! Look at you!" She started to cry. Marina picked it up again too. "You whisper but I hear it. I know what you say. You sneak out. You take my kids. You and Sara want my babies."

Marina and Dylan were *our* babies, and no one was going to take them. I scraped off her grip. "Get in the car," I said. Our house was only two lots away. "Get in or walk, I don't care." But I couldn't move the car without my door smacking her.

When I refused to leave the seat, she opened the back door and started unbuckling Marina, muttering. I caught only pieces. ". . . do to my baby girl? Shhh, shhh, Mommy's here . . . let the bad lady take you . . ." She lifted Marina out. The crackers tumbled to the asphalt in their brown wax wrapper. Marina clung like a sniffling monkey to her mother's neck.

Misty walked round to the other side of the car.

"Misty, what are you doing?"

"Shut up," she ordered. "They're mine. She can't have them."

She couldn't lift Dylan's carrier out of the base with only one hand, though she tried. Her yanking on the handle jostled him, and I finally got out of the car. "Hey, hey." I tried to be gentle. "Let's all get in the car. We'll go back to the house together."

Misty tugged until the carrier was listing in the belt strap. Dylan woke and joined his sister in crying.

"You're upsetting them." I leaned in between her and Dylan and put my hand over hers on the handle of his carrier.

Her strike surprised me. Though she held Marina, my wife drew her elbow back and caught me in the chin swift as a reflex. I took a bracing step back and raised my hand in front of my face.

"Don't touch my son," she hissed. She took a swipe at my arm, still connected to the carrier. Her hit was awkward and flimsy, more like a shove than a punch, and I had the better footing. With Marina still in the crook of her arm, she lost her balance and fell into the door.

I caught them both as Misty went down, one hand on her elbow, one on Marina's back. She sank more than fell, letting me and the door support her. Trembling, she folded into a cross-legged sit, asphalt pebbles sticking to the bottoms of her white socks. I knelt and held on to her. She crossed her free arm in front of her bowed head.

"Don't kill me. Please don't kill me."

"What? Misty, *no*. I love you. I would never. How can you think that?"

"You want me to die. You wish I were dead."

"I want you alive and well."

"You want *her*."

I was guilty of betraying her; I would have admitted to that straight up. But I'd stopped it. I'd proven my loyalty. Her melodrama pushed my patience to its end. She didn't have to go so far.

"Stop it," I said sternly. "I won't leave you. And no one is trying to take the kids away."

We sat in the street, Dylan keening and Marina snuffling, wiping her sloppy nose all over her mother's shirt. A light of clarity flickered somewhere deep in Misty's glassy gaze.

"You're a liar. I'm taking Marina and Dylan to my parents."

Twenty-Seven

In the kitchen of Sara's Sins she disassembles the enrobing machine as if for cleaning. It's a small machine that coats candies and other treats in an even layer of chocolate more efficiently than hand dipping. Her whole setup here in Montecito is a miniaturized version of her larger production headquarters on the north side of Santa Barbara. That's where they make the bulk orders and pack them for distribution. Here at her café storefront, Sara operates on a smaller scale for daily freshness and limited edition goodies. Even experimental taste tests.

The enrober's wheel has warped. It should be a smooth disk, solid. Imagine a water wheel without the buckets, the clean edge cutting into a river of tempered chocolate. The chocolate sticks to the disk, the disk carries it up to the scraper, the scraper directs it into a trough, the trough drops a perfect chocolate curtain over ganache and cookies and caramels. A warped wheel means the scraper skips. The flow of chocolate has swells in it. The curtain ripples. Not enough to stop production but enough to bother Sara's critical eye when she looks over the end result.

She's not sure how the damage happened. She asked around. Everyone shrugged, but Sara knows these things don't happen on their own.

The wheel is an easy enough part to replace, but it's all the way at the back of the machine. Everything must be removed to get to it. The process takes time.

That the machine needs fixing is not a lie. But the spare has been sitting in her office for three days.

She removes the trough. She detaches the scraper. She lifts away the front panel, unlinks the chain belts that turn the gears, carries off the stainless steel belts that move the confections. And as she peels back the layers of machinery, washes by hand all the chocolate-covered gadgets, moving closer to the heart of the problem, she imagines what it would be like to wash away all the deception, get cleaned up, and set the center wheel of her life spinning true one more time.

I watch her work. Even these simple labors are graceful moves. Words come to my mind unbidden: *It's not your fault*, I want to tell her. *It's not what you think.*

Now where did that thought come from?

———

I tried everything I could think of to keep Misty from running to Monterey. Sunday evening, after she had eaten and fallen into a quieter, more compliant mood, she allowed me to take her to the emergency room. I hoped that a doctor would see what I saw, but by then she'd transformed her outward distress into private plotting. We took the kids with us, and in the waiting room she entertained Marina with sewing cards, using shoelaces to attach tutus to a ballerina. In the evaluation bay she sanely answered all of the psychologist's questions, and she kept her knowing eyes on me. I was the villain to her heroine. She was going to outwit me. By the time she was finished, she made me out to be a well-meaning but overprotective, overreacting husband. Her lighthearted banter put my heart in a vise. She left with instructions to keep taking the medications she'd already been prescribed. She promised, then at home reneged.

She went to bed fully clothed. I didn't sleep, fearful that she'd bolt in the night. I called her parents after midnight, preempting the call I knew she'd make in the morning. Lena and Lionel Rochester cared deeply about their daughter and had spent years shielding Misty. They had set her behind a heavy curtain of specialists and euphemisms and positive thinking and built her up into a kind of feminine Wizard of Oz. I told them what I thought was going on, begged them to help me talk her back into taking the medications that would help us all. They promised phone calls in the morning and a visit later in the week. Lena said she'd heard about this amazing new infant formula that was supposed to be as good as breast milk. She promised to bring some.

What else could they do?

I worried about Monday. I was scheduled to go to the Rincon to supervise the concrete pour for the new porch. A bad time, but the people who issue permits don't care about things like newborns and holidays and winter. The subcontractors who schedule jobs don't either. I'd already torn up the grass and built the wood forms, framed the new, more spacious steps beneath the front door. Skimmed and tamped the dirt. Strung the lines that would guide the grade. It had been on the family calendar for two weeks.

Monday morning I called my buddy Sam Raglan, who had come to my rescue when I needed that bay window installed, and asked him to cover for me in case I couldn't get there in time. They were scheduled to be there at three.

Then I took the credit cards from Misty's wallet and closed our joint checking account, transferring the funds to one in my name only. I took the fuel pump fuse out of her car so it wouldn't start. Anything to keep her from bolting.

These are the behaviors of an abuser or a lover, depending on who's looking. I loved her madly, wanted to protect her as much as she wanted to protect our kids. There were those who said later I should have just let her go to Monterey. I couldn't. No child safety seat could have protected my children from a six-hour psychotic drive up the Pacific Coast Highway. Getting away from me wouldn't fix Misty's broken mind.

She called her parents as I'd predicted, but calmly. Afterward she told me that she changed her mind about going to see them because they were coming to us. She cleaned the house, scrubbing and dusting for their visit.

I invited Misty to come with me to the Rincon, bring the kids, get away. We could all put our handprints in the wet concrete. Her smile accused me of painting myself into this corner.

"Can't," she said. "Need to get ready for Mom and Dad."

"When are they coming?"

"Tomorrow."

The solution came to me spontaneously. I didn't even stop to evaluate it. "Let's do Christmas at the beach," I dared. "Have Mom and Dad go there instead of here, stay the whole week. We'll put up a tree, get the house its own decorations."

Misty was scrubbing the bathtub. I stood in the door. She pressed down on the drain. Scrubbed harder. "No." Her curly ponytail fell forward over one shoulder.

"It'll be fun for Marina. We'll drink hot chocolate on the new porch and—"

"No. No, no, no." She sprang up and pushed by me out into the hall, white cleanser sticking to the fingers of her blue gloves. "Sara's there," she said. She started to hyperventilate. "You keep her, I know it. In our home. Our home that's her home. It was never a surprise window. It was you. I see through you. She'll ruin everything."

I could hardly process what she was saying. I hadn't reached out to Sara since the day I stood her up at her apartment, and she hadn't made any attempt to contact me. She wasn't at the beach house. She didn't even have a key. I reached out for my wife. Misty ducked away.

After she was breathing normally again, Misty packed the kids into her car and said she was going to the store for Windex. I put myself in the passenger seat without an invitation. It was entirely possible she'd bypass the store and go straight to the freeway, and I wouldn't be left behind. She glared at me. I stayed.

When the car wouldn't start, I waited for another outburst, a raving about my secret plots. This time she'd be half right. But she said nothing. Misty climbed out and took her purse to my truck. She smiled the way she had in the emergency room, a self-congratulatory smile for staying a step ahead of me. For her good luck in stumbling upon a guarantee that I couldn't go anywhere in a broken-down car.

"I'll be back in ten minutes," she said as she pulled out.

I sat there in the half-empty garage for five minutes before finally believing I could do what I had to do.

———

Springs in the theater seat poke at me. It's impossible to get comfortable anymore.

"You haven't shown me anything I don't already know," I accuse Beret Man. But my stomach is in knots, fearing what's coming.

I feel weaker than I was. Not strong enough even to swivel my head in his direction. He leaves his seat. It snaps up without his weight to hold it down and rocks on its hinge. A few seconds later he comes to sit beside me, leaving a seat between us.

"Your wife didn't kill herself, Garrett."

"What?"

He folds his hands in his lap.

"But I remember . . ."

What is it I remember? What is it I thought I knew? I didn't watch her do it.

In this dim place with larger-than-life images flashing in front of my face, the memories in my head begin to blur. I close my eyes and try to bring them back into focus, but I fail.

The chain that connects Ian and Marina to the county sheriff's cold-case investigator is short. Mrs. Estella Dickens, a great supporter of Ian's winery who ate Sara's chocolate the night of that fund-raiser and who often puts up out-of-town family members at the McCleary B&B, has a nephew who is a detective with the Lompoc Police Department. The nephew has just helped close a cooperative case with the Santa Barbara County Sheriff's Office, and his contact there refers Ian to Deputy Sheila Wasson.

Deputy Wasson sits across from Ian and Marina now in a conference room. She's young and fit and unconcerned about her appearance. Short hair pulled back carelessly into a band—it can't rightly be called a ponytail. No makeup on her uneven complexion, nails short and cuticles torn, uniform slightly too big for her. She's reading the letter Marina found, the angry one Misty wrote to Sara that awful Monday when she came home with Windex to find me gone, run off with the kids in the car that wasn't broken down.

It's clear to me that she's here because she's kind, and not because she thinks Marina has compelling new evidence to reopen the case. Certainly not because she doesn't have other demands on her time.

The table is barely big enough for the three of them and the box containing everything officially known about Misty Rochester Becker's disappearance on December 16, 1997. The box is not very large. The files are not as thick as a daughter might hope for. The contents are fewer than Ian and Marina expected. But I remember. I was there when these were collected.

When she finishes reading the letter, Wasson consults a separate report.

"Your mother had a history of bipolar disorder," she says to Marina. Her voice is more feminine than her appearance suggests it will be. Softer, higher, gentler. "And she was being treated for postpartum depression after the birth of your"—she flips a page, scanning—"brother. This letter would confirm that she was dealing with a certain amount of paranoia on top of that."

"Can I read it?" Marina points to the report. Wasson slides it in front of her.

"Sara Rochester and Misty Becker were cousins." The deputy points to a paragraph that Marina reads. "Your father said they were estranged until he and your mom bought the house at the Rincon."

Marina looks up. "You knew about Sara?"

"The night your mother went missing he left you and your brother with Ms. Rochester so he could join the search."

Marina reads aloud, "'Husband took children to home of family member Sara Rochester, 1313 State Street, at approximately 2 a.m., then drove to Marina del Rey in search of missing wife.'"

"I'm not sure the note sheds any new light on the case," Wasson says.

"Was Sara investigated?"

"She was questioned. She hadn't seen your mother since early November. Her whereabouts the night in question were accounted for, and her story lined up with Mr. Becker's. I'm very sorry, but all the evidence does point to a suicide."

She reaches into the box and withdraws a brown folder, then from the folder withdraws a plastic bag marked and labeled with red tape. There's a photograph inside. Misty in a hospital bed, sitting up, smiling in spite of dark half-moons under her eyes. She's holding newborn Dylan, swaddled in a white blanket and capped with a blue knit beanie. Curly-headed Marina is on her mother's other side, leaning to drop a kiss on her brother's forehead. Only Misty looks at the camera.

Marina looks at the photograph for a long time. "We don't have any pictures of Mom and Dylan together."

In the blackness of my private theater, I begin to weep. It's my fault, the missing pictures. I told my kids they were lost in the move, after I sold the Marina del Rey house. The truth is they were lost long before that. I wasn't there when Misty pulled into the empty garage with the Windex and saw that her car and her children were gone. But I was there when police found the pile of ashes in the kitchen sink, the remnants of a furious burn that singed the hem of the café curtains hanging in the window. They were photographs, the detective told me then. Picture frames, film negatives, a photo album—our wedding album. Every last shred of visual proof that Misty had been a part of this family.

Except for this one picture, which Misty carried on the dashboard of her car, which I had repaired and driven away. When the kids and I arrived at the Rincon Monday afternoon, I took the photo into the house and put it on the kitchen counter. I wanted it to be the first thing Misty saw when she showed up. Because I knew she would show up. I knew she would follow her babies to the end of the world.

Deputy Wasson pinches the top of the evidence bag and turns it over to show Marina the back.

A note, scrawled with a ballpoint pen.

I'm so sorry.

A suicide note.

Marina sinks back into her chair. Ian watches her. He hasn't spoken a word since coming into the room.

"That's it?" my daughter asks. "Couldn't even be bothered to sign her name?"

"The only thing that makes this case stand out is that we never recovered her body." Wasson speaks as one holding a sleeping baby or an injured dog. The wrong tone will turn her words into knives. Instead, they're pillows. "You know the highway patrol found her car at Monastery Beach?"

Marina nods.

"She was from the area, Monterey. Her family said she knew the place. There are a lot of reasons why someone who goes into the water there in the middle of the night might never be seen again."

Ian reaches out to take the photograph from Marina. He props his jaw on his other hand, studies both sides. He taps his cheek with his finger.

"Was this all she left behind?" Ian asks.

Wasson looks into the box, then reaches in. Another evidence bag, larger than the one holding the photo. It's a long metal object with a forked end and a metal handle. A sea god—Neptune, Poseidon—or maybe a merman. He has a beard and a tail that looks like molded obsidian.

"A fondue fork?" Marina asks.

"There was blood on the tines."

"My mother's?"

"Yes. Just a small amount on the tips."

"I don't understand."

"Here's what we think happened: Your parents argued at their home in Marina del Rey. Your father took you kids to the Rincon, and your mother followed later"—Wasson lifts the letter Misty wrote to Sara—"perhaps after writing this. We have a mental health history. This note to Sara supports the family's claim that Mrs. Becker was battling some kind of psychosis at the time. Paranoia isn't unheard of in people who have a bipolar disorder. She followed you three to the Rincon. She and your father fought. She went after him with the fork, he wrestled it away, she was cut in the process. Based on the amount of blood we recovered it was a superficial cut. They calmed themselves, they went to bed, and in the night she left."

Marina looks deflated. She fingers the fork's handle under the plastic. "Sara has a set just like this one," she says.

Wasson notes that detail by tilting her head to one side and waiting for more. But Marina has nothing else.

"Did Mr. Becker say he and Sara were having an affair?" Ian asks. "Or did anyone else suggest it? Friends, neighbors?"

The deputy shakes her head but pulls the report back to her to confirm her own understanding. "No. This letter Marina brought today is the only hint of that. Which likely means it was a misperception on her part."

"Dad was completely loyal," Marina says. "Even afterward."

"Sara told me there *was* an affair between her and Garrett," Ian says.

Marina's attention snaps to him.

"When?" Wasson asks.

"Mm. Three, four weeks ago."

"I mean, when did the relationship occur?"

"I don't know exactly. A short time before Misty died. Disappeared."

"Sara told you this?" Marina wants to know.

"Aye."

"Can you clarify 'a short time'?" asks the deputy. "A year? A month?"

"I don't know the details. You'd have to ask her. But there's something else you ought to look into." Ian straightens in the chair. New lines have appeared around his eyes, aging him. Fatiguing him. He leans forward to push the bagged photograph back across the table toward Wasson. Note side up. "That's not the same writing as what's in the letter."

Wasson holds the two side by side. *I'm so sorry,* says one. *I see the way you look at Marina,* says the other. Even my untrained eye can see the difference in the capital *I*s, the tails of the lowercase *Y*s, the shape of the *O*s, the slant of everything.

"Does anyone know if Misty had a multiple-personality

disorder?" Ian asks. "I guess they call it something else now." He looks at Marina, who shakes her head.

"Not that we uncovered," the deputy says. She checks the post-mark on the note Marina provided. She looks at the police report. "Mr. Becker confirmed his wife's handwriting on the pictures. It was compared to"—she searches, then quotes—"'a handwritten recipe brought out of the kitchen.' So maybe your mother didn't write this letter. You said you found it in Ms. Rochester's house?"

Marina nods.

"Any thoughts on that?" The deputy looks at each of them in turn.

Ian sighs. "A handwritten recipe. I don't suppose it was signed."

Wasson purses her lips. She's tracking with this, I can see. "Maybe it's time to have another conversation with Ms. Rochester."

Twenty-Eight

A door whooshes shut and the screen I have been watching blinks out. Sudden darkness. A pregnant pause follows, the moment in the theater when everyone wonders if he should get up and go tell someone there's a technical problem. Or maybe someone else will do that. Or maybe the trouble will resolve on its own. Let's all take a little catnap.

My friend a couple of seats away from me is still, so I follow his example.

I hear a shuffle of feet in the aisle, a thigh bumping the arm of a chair in the darkness, steps leveling out as eyes adjust.

Someone takes the seat beside me.

"Enough of this," Sara says. "Seventeen years of pretending nothing ever happened."

Her accusations are always friendly.

"We never had the chance to talk about that night," she says. "I think it's time, don't you? You raised smart kids. Marina, that girl. She's just like you, pushing, asking questions. I thought they'd be so much easier to answer." A heavy sigh. "All of this was supposed to be so much easier. Just a chance to make some things right. You know?"

I do, I do.

Right now I want nothing more than to be ignorant of my true state, so that I can float around through this world bumping into things, passing through people, making tiny electric connections with them. I don't care if the encounters aren't real. I want to lay my hand in yours, Sara, and ask you to forgive me.

"That day we were supposed to meet at my apartment and you weren't there, and then . . . nothing. Silence. I figured you decided to tell Misty about us. Honestly, I hoped that's exactly what you'd done. It was right, Garrett. It was what your family needed. I know that what happened between us was mostly about the timing of sad circumstances. We were young, busy, lonely. Really—can you think of a more perfect storm? I want you to know that I was relieved you finally made the choice. I know you loved her. Only love could survive her particular roller coaster. And Misty, for all the pain she caused me, she deserved to be loved."

You deserved it too, Sara. Why has no one loved you that way? Or is it that you haven't let anyone?

"She sent me this letter. I don't know if you ever saw it. It wasn't . . . She wasn't herself, but I knew it was her. You understand, I know. But it was the worst I'd ever seen from her. It arrived the day she . . . the day she left us. I can't believe she left her babies. Dylan . . . oh, dear God, he was so little . . ." Her voice drifts off. "That's the part that still doesn't make sense to me."

She smells faintly of chocolate and mint. Her fingers touch mine.

"Your hands are cold."

It's true. I'm freezing. This theater could host the Ice Capades.

She sandwiches my palm in hers. Warmth radiates. I wish I could see her face, but my eyes never adjust to this darkness.

"So for six weeks, nothing—and then a knock on my door in

the middle of the night, you remember that studio over the shop? And you say, 'Sara, I need your help.' And you thrust this itty bitty baby into my hands. Dylan. Do you remember that? No explanation, just, 'Would you help me? It's Misty.' I think I said, 'Sure.' Something dumb like that. I would have done anything for you."

I don't remember exactly what she or I said. I do remember the fear. Dylan waking in the night, screaming, hungry. Feeding him the formula he didn't like from the bottle he wouldn't take, heart in my throat, scared. His mother had followed us to the beach house just as I'd expected. She'd come, we'd fought, and then she was gone again, and I couldn't decide what to do.

It's taxing to remember the details. I look to the theater screen for clues. It's still dead.

"I've never seen anyone look as scared as you did, Garrett. I've often wondered what that night must have been like for you." She gives my hand a gentle squeeze. "I wish you could tell me everything. I wish I could take that burden off your shoulders. Because I know—I see it in your children, in your home, in the wedding ring Dylan told me they cut off of your finger—I know you still carry it with you."

Do I? Yes. An invisible elephant squats on my chest. She speaks it into being, and for a moment whatever method I have used to distract myself from that particular pain fails. I can't get a breath. But this lasts only a short time. The air rushes in again and I can at least wheeze.

"You want to tell me about it?" The tease is back. "No. Well then. I see the duty falls to me. I came to tell you something, Garrett. But first I want to tell you some of what your kids and I did that night. Think of it as the kind of stuff teenagers wait twenty years to tell their parents about. You know what I mean?

I'm sure you wouldn't approve, but I'm hoping you'll be nice about it. Because I fell in love with your kids that night, Garrett. Your amazing son and daughter won me over, and I hope I can win them back."

———————

The film rolls again. The screen lights up. Sara's studio apartment, bright with lamp lights in the middle of the night. A string of white Christmas lights tacked into her one window, blinking behind the drawn curtain. Sara in the chair. Marina on the unmade daybed. Dylan sleeping in the carrier on the floor. The diaper bag that Misty kept packed in her car tossed by the door. When I fled the beach house, I didn't even know what was in it.

Sara's voice overlays the scene. "You couldn't have come at a worse time. You know that, don't you? The holidays, Allegro's busiest season. You came at two I think, two in the morning. I'd been at a Christmas party until midnight, and I was scheduled to be at work at three. Melting and tempering the chocolate, dicing the nuts and the dried fruits, mixing the ganache, packing boxes.

"Marina didn't go back to sleep after you left. She sat on my bed in these soft, footed jammies and she said, 'I wanted to give Daddy a kiss.'"

It's a silent film. Not even a piano playing in the background. Sara narrates the way my parents used to give slide shows. *Click, click.* Only we've advanced to the age of handheld video. Someone forgot to turn on the mic.

"I told her if she wanted to give the kiss to me I would save it for you when you got back. Is that the silliest thing you ever heard? It's something my dad used to say to me when I missed my mom. When I was little, before we . . . well. What do I know about kids, Garrett? I made it up as I went along. Marina believed it as readily as I did at her age. She kissed me on the cheek, right here."

Next to me, Sara must be pointing; on the screen I see it all. Marina, not shy even then, bounding off the bed and standing on her tiptoes to reach Sara's face. Sara's fingers, lingering there. Sara, rising and going to the kitchen, returning with a cookie that Marina eats in three bites.

Sara throws a hoodie over the sweatpants and tee she is already wearing. She digs through the diaper bag and finds a contraption meant for carrying an infant. Seventeen years late I realize I didn't leave a change of clothes for either of the children.

"I asked Marina, 'Do you know why your dad brought you here?' 'No,' she says. And I tell her, 'It's a Christmas secret. Can you keep a secret?' She says, 'What's a secret?'"

Sara laughs as she puzzles the straps and links the buckles. She squats in front of Marina and looks her in the eyes.

"I say, 'I'm Santa's helper. I make candy for Christmas. Would you like to help me make candy for Santa today?' Marina, her eyes got so big! 'Will I see Santa?' she asks me. 'No,' I say, 'he's busy at his toy shop today, but I will tell him you were one of his elves. He pays his elves in chocolate. Do you like that?'"

The scene unfolds before me. How can it be that I never thought of what Sara did with my children that night? Maybe because they came back to me safe and happy. And by then, their mother was dead.

What I see now is amazing and insane. Sara doesn't have a clue, and maybe that's what made it work. It takes her ten minutes and Marina's precocious help to get Dylan into that baby carrier on her chest. Misty and I always helped each other with that. She doesn't think to change his diaper first. All the jostling wakes him and I expect shrieking to ensue, but when he's finally snugged in, he lays his head on her heart and is asleep again in seconds.

He'll be hungry soon. The bottle he refused to take is still full in a side pocket of the diaper bag. He'll be angrier than anyone about his absent mother.

But for now, Sara is blissfully unaware of what's to come. She pats his back continuously. She goes to a drawer in her dresser and withdraws a little camera.

She snaps a picture of Marina sitting on her daybed. Sara says, "'Proof of employment,' I told her. But even I knew then that this was going to be the last time I'd see them. It was the way you said Misty's name. *It's Misty.* That was all you had to say, with those scared eyes, after all the weeks of silence. This was all I was ever going to get, even though I didn't know what that meant until later."

Sara leaves everything in the apartment. The diaper bag, the carrier, the car seats I have left outside her door on the balcony walk. She locks up, takes Marina's hand, and together the makeshift family of three walks down rickety iron steps in the dark to a slender alley between two buildings. A motion-sensing light illuminates the side door of Allegro's, and Sara pauses here, gets as far as slipping her key into the keyhole. But then she glances down at Marina and withdraws the key. They follow the breezeway to the end. It opens up on State Street. They turn past Allegro's front windows, dressed with snowy bunting and colored lights and wrapped presents. Mechanical dolls are dressed like carolers. Empty silver candy trays stand like Christmas trees waiting to be decorated. Marina stops to stare and Sara waits. Takes a picture. Doesn't tell her that she needs to hurry. Three people in pajamas on the busiest street in Santa Barbara at three in the morning. Not a police officer or a drunk in sight.

When Marina is ready, they enter through the front door and the lights go up like the curtain rising on a child's finest dream. Marina, still holding Sara's hand, starts jumping in place.

The shelves are made of glass that catch the sparkling lights. These are stacked with boxes wrapped in metallic silver paper and tied with red and green satin ribbons. Track lighting above, spotlights beneath. Everything glitters. Underneath the shelves, wire bins hold cellophane bags of foil-wrapped chocolate balls, marshmallow Santas and hollow chocolate elves, pralines, and colored jelly beans. At the back of the storefront, a domed glass case waits to be filled with the day's offerings, made by hand and sold by the pound. Another picture: Marina, eyes as round and bright as the glittering foil balls.

But Marina's attention is riveted to the center of the room. The masterpiece centerpiece. On a twelve-foot rectangular table, bronze-footed with a glass top, Santa's reindeer rise into the air, suspended by nylon lines that Marina can't see. The jolly man himself sits behind them in red velvet, tossing the reins, waiting for liftoff. The sleigh is a crystal bowl. Plastic, I'm sure, but magical from my daughter's point of view and filled to overflowing with red satin boxes trimmed in sequins.

Marina reaches up and takes one down. Boxes on top of it threaten to topple, but Sara is there for the save. She deftly rearranges the pile. All is stable again. Marina lifts the lid and Sara helps her lift out the present: a beautiful, handblown glass globe swirling with golden colors of sunset. She lets it hang from her fingertip by the matching ribbon. Marina touches it. Photo op. It turns and catches light from the overhead track, casting gold kisses on Dylan's face.

Marina's interest lasts for two seconds. She reaches into a red tin pail on a low shelf, plucks out a teddy bear finger puppet mounted on a straight candy cane. Sara's voice reaches me from a distance. "She says, 'Can I have it?'"

"You bet. Why would I say no?"

Marina holds it tight in her fist, tries to lick the candy while it's still in plastic.

"Here." Sara puts the glass Christmas ball back in the red satin box and carries it with her. She leads Marina behind the empty candy counter, behind the divider between the cashier and the kitchens. In the back on a counter is a bowl with broken peppermint pieces in it. Sara lifts the lid and gives a piece to Marina. A framework of wood cubbies, labeled with names and tasks, tops the counter. One of them says *S. Rochester*. Sara puts the satin box and the camera in it and turns to face her work. She dons plastic gloves. She gives Marina an apron way too large. She chops nuts with a knife that horrifies me. She pours cream and cocoa into a vat.

When Dylan begins to root for food, Sara sticks her finger in his mouth. Not what he's looking for. She pours an inch of whole cream into a measuring cup and dips her finger in it, offers him that. He tastes, throws his head back against the carrier's neck support, and begins to wail. Marina is worried. She goes to the dish of broken peppermints and digs one out for Dylan, a piece as big as his button nose.

"That's too hard for him, honey. He doesn't have his teeth yet, remember?"

Marina pops the candy into her own mouth. Sara picks up a plastic bottle. It looks like the kind you squeeze ketchup from in a diner, only this one is brown, used for decorating the tops of truffles and the bottoms of dessert plates. She squirts melted dark chocolate into the cream, stirs it with her finger. Gives Dylan a taste.

He settles down immediately. He can't get enough. For twenty minutes Sara lets him suck chocolate cream from her fingertip.

The red digital clock mounted over the cubbies says 4:55 when Sara's boss enters through the side door. "Mr. Sorvino," she tells me. "Like the actor."

Looks like the actor too.

Dylan has had his fill of chocolate milk at this point, but the effects of sugar and caffeine have yet to kick in. I see it taking shape behind his wide, alert eyes. Sara leans over the melter, which looks like a concrete mixer, stirring in chunks of chocolate. *Tempering seed*, she calls it.

Mr. Sorvino takes in the scene: Nuts on the floor. Marina, sporting a chocolate beard and sideburns. She kneels in front of a muffin tin, sorting tiny confetti candies by color. Purple in this cup, green here, red here, gold here. The white bottoms of her jammies are spotted with melted brown flakes that she has walked in. Dylan is starting to squirm.

The old man raises an eyebrow as he takes an apron off the hook by the door and lifts it over his neck. Sara drops another chunk of chocolate into the melter.

"Family emergency."

"You can't have an emergency here, Sara. City codes."

"No codes were violated in the making of this candy." Sara is smiling at him. "I called Erica. She's on her way. Here in ten. I'll take her shift this afternoon."

He shakes his head. All fatherly. Obviously Sara is an apprentice-turned-manager who can do no wrong. He looks around at what she's accomplished already, eyes come back to her.

"Please tell me that's cocoa butter smeared on the baby's clothes."

Sara looks at the stain seeping out high on Dylan's skinny thigh, where the leg hole of the carrier cuts into his cheek. She looks at Mr. Sorvino and stifles a laugh. She steps away from the melter.

"You've gotta take a picture of this."

———

On the screen, I watch Sara and the children return to her apartment before Erica arrives. In the theater, Sara talks over the sounds of plastic pages slapping against each other gently, like waves kissing the shoreline. "I wish you could see these snapshots, Garrett. They'd make you laugh."

The weight of her voice is far from laughter.

I watch as she changes the offensive diaper on the floor of her room. Everything in the wrong order. She should have gotten everything ready before she took the filthy one off. Trash bag, wipes, clean diaper. But she doesn't realize this until it's too late. Marina, crashing from the sugar and lack of sleep, slouches in the chair that I once sat in.

"Sometimes we can't figure out how to do something right until we do it wrong," she says. I don't think she's talking about the diaper.

"I couldn't go to Dylan and Marina and say I was an old family friend, could I? Dylan saw through that right away. 'How come we've never met you?' he asked me. And I couldn't walk in and say,

'Hey, kids—you don't remember me, but I was your dad's lover for a couple of months. Thought maybe I could help you out.'"

That unpleasant thought hangs in the air like a foul scent.

"Losing their mother was hard enough. And then you go and do *this*." As if the truck accident and the coma were hatched from my own evil plot. "How could I walk in and ruin your reputation? How could I say, 'Your dad loved your mom so much—but I seduced him, and it's my fault your mom died. I completely destroyed your family, but here I am. Can I make it up to you?'"

No, that wouldn't have ended well.

"I knew they never found Misty. So I thought . . . well, I guess I thought that maybe they would forgive their own mother more readily than they would forgive me."

Her words get jammed in my ears, and I can't hear what she says next. *I thought that maybe they would forgive their own mother more readily than they would forgive me.* Sara said this, but I hear it as my own thought, my own belief. And I don't know why.

"It didn't work, Garrett. I have to tell them who I am. They're going to figure it out if they haven't already. I have to tell them everything."

I know. It was what I wanted to do when it was too late to do it.

"I'm sorry," she says.

In this nostalgic movie, Dylan is naked except for the cock-eyed diaper. Sara bundles him in a blanket. Marina is asleep. Her pajamas are a mess. I've left the car seats at her front door. Sara goes down to her car. She puts the car seats in the back, latches them in less securely than the owner's manuals would advise. Then one at a time, she packs the sleeping kids in.

Where is she going?

To the beach house, of course. My kids need clothes. Oh no.

Sara went back to the beach house that night while I was gone. I forgot. How could I forget?

This fact causes a sweat to break out at my temples. My hands go cold.

Sara slams the car door and I flinch and once again, the theater plunges into blackness.

Twenty-Nine

Denica waits in Dylan's room, wandering through the wide world contained in this narrow space. Books, computers, access to outside. There's a notebook on the desk that stands out from the rest, a spiral bound with a blue-green striped cover, stuffed with scraps of paper and held together with a rubber band. Denica helps herself. She sinks onto the bed, starts to read the poetry Dylan has collected (the scraps) and written (the bound pages).

Dylan is in my room, pulling on a short-legged wetsuit so he and Denica can surf again. It's still warm enough for trunks, but the suit is like a second skin. Denica came dressed, drawstring shorts and a one-piece. Ian dropped her off and picked up Marina, even though everyone but Dylan can drive. Is licensed, I mean. It was more practical that way. Fatherly of Ian to do it. I appreciate it.

Denica pages carefully through the notebook, skimming, pausing here and there, stopping at one titled "Mother."

Now we abandoned boats tilt in crusty sand
Punished
Guilty of needing the sea

Dylan comes in a few minutes later, all zipped up. He sees the invasion.

"What the heck?" he says. He tears the book out of her hands. A few slips—ideas, couplets—fall to the floor.

"I didn't know you wrote poems," she says. Her eyes are wet, but he doesn't see. He's turned his back, closed the book, snapped the rubber band. He's looking for a place to put it, secret, but she's sitting right there.

"They're good," she says. "The one about your mom—"

"You shouldn't do that," he bites.

"I didn't think anyone else knew what it's like. Not even Gabe."

Dylan hears the snag in her voice. He turns around, notebook in hand, still angry. But a little less.

"He says I shouldn't be mad at her," Denica says. "It's not her fault she's gone."

Dylan has no idea what to say. Denica's mom didn't pretend to kill herself. Her dad isn't lying around in a coma.

"But it doesn't change anything. She's still gone whether I'm mad or not," Denica says.

She's wearing a perfume that he likes. Something like oranges. He wishes she wouldn't have done that. He wishes she wasn't older than he and didn't like surfing and didn't understand his poetry.

He wishes she might know what it was like to have a mother come back.

He goes downstairs to fetch the boards.

The heat of August keeps patrons away from Sara's Sins, that and the midweek slump. Already tourists are thinking of home, of school about to start. Vacation budgets are blown and the kids need school supplies, backpacks. A happy group of retired ladies comes through after lunch down the street. They pick up a few indulgences to go. Peppermint creams in milk chocolate for the grandkids. Chocolate peanuts for the book club. No caramels that will stick to dental work. No daring chili spices for delicate digestions.

After Sara serves them and the bell over the door chimes their good-byes, she ducks into the kitchen to retrieve the photo book from her purse, the one with the snapshots of her one night with my kids. Then she returns to the corner of the room, the cozy nook where she and Dylan had their first conversation. The space is the same but it seems colder today. Marina sits where her brother did, but forward on the edge of the voluminous sofa. Deputy Wasson sits back, sunken in, more at ease than anyone else. She's trying to make this friendly. Ian takes the matching overstuffed chair, both hands out on the arms like Lincoln in his memorial. He keeps pained eyes on Sara. Sara sits back down in a wooden chair borrowed from one of the tables. The hot seat.

"These are the pictures I mentioned." Sara hands the book to Marina.

Marina opens the book. She sees herself, her bedhead curls piled up on one side of her smiling preschool face.

She turns the pages slowly. Dylan in his carrier. Marina standing in front of the Allegro Christmas window.

"Marina, I'm sorry I lied to you."

My daughter lets her curtain of dark hair fall forward over her expression.

"I was trying to protect your dad. The affair was . . . accidental. I guess most of them are. I didn't want you to think he was at fault in what happened to your mom. He loved her so much."

Marina is deaf to Sara's apology.

"It's okay to blame me. I just want to help. You and Dylan are in a bad spot."

"Do you have any idea how Dylan is going to take this?" Marina asks. She turns to another picture.

Sara folds her hands as if to hold herself together. She looks at Ian, remembering his warning.

Deputy Wasson says, "So Mr. Becker dropped them off around two in the morning. Did he tell you when he'd be back, or where he was going?"

"He didn't say anything, just 'I need your help,' and something like 'It's Misty.' I didn't even know the two of them were in town. We hadn't talked since before Dylan was born."

"What time did Mr. Becker return to pick up the kids?" Wasson asks.

"It was the afternoon." She lifts her eyes to the ceiling, thinking. "Uh, around three. It should be in there." She points to the folder on the deputy's lap. "They asked me all these questions then."

"And Mr. Becker didn't say anything when he fetched the kids?"

"No."

"Why not?"

Sara licks her lips. "He was so distraught. He said he couldn't find her. And I felt—responsible. Like if we hadn't had the affair Misty would have been okay. I pieced it together afterward. The investigation, newspaper reports." Sara clears her throat. "My family had plenty to say."

"Let me give you a quick time line." Wasson opens the folder on her lap. "Monday, December 15. Mr. Becker takes the children to the beach house because he has a job scheduled there and is worried about his wife's mental state. At their home in Marina del Rey

Mrs. Becker burns the family photographs and sends you a hostile letter. Both actions support Mr. Becker's concerns. Then she follows her husband to the beach house. She arrives around 9:00 p.m. There is a confrontation of a physical nature"—her eyes dart up to Sara, but Sara is looking at her hands and doesn't react to this information—"but Mr. Becker calms his wife without intervention. They go to bed. At 1:00 a.m., December 16, Mr. Becker is awakened by his son's cries. He's trying to get his son onto formula so that Mrs. Becker can resume her medications, so he quickly takes the child outside for a bottle while Mrs. Becker sleeps. Afterward the baby won't settle, so he packs both children into the car for a ride until the baby falls asleep. When he returns to the house, Mrs. Becker is gone. Mr. Becker takes the children to you and then goes on a search for his wife."

Sara is nodding.

"When interviewed, he said he thought his wife might have gone to her parents' home in Monterey."

"They were a tight-knit family."

"But Mr. Becker drove to Marina del Rey."

"If Misty went to her parents' house, they'd take care of her," Sara suggested. "There wasn't any family in Marina del Rey. That's where her business was. Her dance studio."

Wasson nods. "He searched at the house, called her parents several times, called her friends, went to the studio. He was there until"—she consults the report—"10:30 a.m., after the studio opened. Then he drove back to the Rincon. Called us when he returned at noon and she was still missing."

I'm watching this café conversation with an odd discomfort in my belly. I wish I could see that trip, the drive to Marina del Rey, because I don't remember it. Why can't I remember it?

Shock is a rational thing with irrational effects.

Marina has paused in the photo book. She puts her finger under something in one picture and holds it up to Sara. "What's this?"

Sara leans in. It's the red satin box with a little bear and a peppermint cane sticking out one corner. A chocolate-faced Marina is holding it in her right hand. Her left hand is linked with Sara's. Both of them are grinning. Dylan is still strapped onto Sara, leaking a little around the leg.

"There was a Christmas ornament in the box, a glass globe, a really pretty handblown thing. We were selling them, you liked it . . ." Sara shrugs and looks away. She seems embarrassed.

Marina closes the book. She can't look at any more. "Has anyone ever told me the truth about anything?"

No one responds.

I'm sorry, my beautiful girl. I'm sorry I said that was from your mother. I wanted you to have something from her besides a legacy of pain. I thought for so long I could undo my sins.

The deputy says to Sara, "And you were at the chocolate shop the whole time, with the children?"

"No. We left there at four. Five? I don't remember exactly."

"And after you left the shop?"

"We went to the beach house. Garrett had forgotten to pack the kids a change of clothes."

"You had the gate code to get in?"

Sara's eyes dart to Marina. "Yes. I'd been there for dinner with the family a couple of times."

"When you were questioned you didn't mention visiting the house."

Sara blinks, shakes her head. She presses her lips into a thin line for a moment. Wasson waits with disciplined patience. "I don't know about that," she finally says. "I hardly remember the questions."

"So you went to the beach house, picked up some clothes, and then what?"

"We went back to my apartment."

"Is that all you did?"

"Yes."

"At the beach house."

"*Yes.*"

"You drove in, picked up some clothes, drove back out."

Sara reaches for the photos. She turns to a page near the back. It's a shot of the front of the beach house. To the right, the framed dirt that will become our new porch. To the left, the garage door is open and the naked bulb is bright. The landscaping lights are also turned on. The sun has yet to rise. My old pickup, parked inside. Sara's small Volkswagen bug, outside. Marina crouches in the open bay where Misty's sedan ought to have been. The red box sitting at her side, on the floor.

"You wanted to share your peppermint with an ant," Sara said to Marina. "It crawled onto your pajamas. All that chocolate. You screamed!" The picture is a bit grainy. "It was dark outside. Wrong speed film for that." She turns the page. Marina in mismatched sweater and leggings, socks but no shoes, in the backseat of the bug, holding a Happy Meal box with golden arch handles. "It's still dark. And I probably lost the receipt with the time on it when I threw away the wrappers. That's all I've got."

Wasson takes a photo of her own out of the folder and shows it to Sara. "Do you recognize this fork?"

"Yes. It's from a fondue set I gave Garrett and Misty as a house-warming gift."

"Was your affair with Mr. Becker going on when you gave the gift?"

"No."

"And it had ended before December 16?"

"Weeks before."

"Do you know what happened to the fondue set?"

Sara clears her throat and says, "I took it with me. I have it."

"You took it from the Becker home the morning of the 16th?"

"Yes."

"Why did you take it?"

"There was . . . I wanted to . . ." She takes a shuddering breath and looks at Marina. "The house was chaos. The fondue pot had fallen on the kitchen floor. The forks everywhere. A broken glass. And there was"—she swallowed a knot in her throat—"blood on the carpet. In the living room."

"Why did you take it?" Wasson repeats.

"I thought he might have hurt her," Sara whispers. "She could be crazy."

"Liar." Marina shoots off the sofa, stands, bends over Sara. "Quit lying to me!"

"I'm not lying, I'm telling you what it looked like. If your dad had . . . Oh, Marina! What would have happened to you and Dylan if you'd lost your dad too? If the police thought what I thought? They would have taken you, separated you! I cleaned up the blood. I picked up everything and put it in my car. That's all. I didn't count forks. I didn't know there was one missing."

"You *served* us from that pot!" Marina shrieks. "Dylan *ate* out of it!"

Ian sits forward and touches her wrist, grounding her.

"I thought if you still had the other fork, if you recognized it, maybe you would believe . . ." Sara is pale as cream.

"Did you write this note?" Deputy Wasson lays another photograph atop the one of the fork. The backside of the only picture of Misty, Marina, and Dylan together. *I'm so sorry*, it says.

Sara takes a sharp breath. "It was on the kitchen counter. I thought Garrett still had that. I left it for Garrett."

"What were you sorry for?"

"For not stopping the affair before it started. For ruining his family. I was so scared."

Marina has started to cry. "Did you kill my mom?"

"No!"

"Did you keep on with my dad after she was gone?"

"No!"

Deputy Wasson says, "Did you and Mr. Becker plot to kill his wife?"

"Absolutely *not*." Sara becomes the calm in the center of the storm. Has she expected this? Has she seen all the signs pointing to this moment? Because I haven't. This scenario, this line of questions—it's as unexpected as snow on the beach. Sara stands so she can look Marina in the eye.

"Your father came to the apartment to pick you up the next day. I asked him what happened. He said, 'She's gone.' I asked him again—what? How? 'They found her car at Monastery Beach.' And that was all. That was every word. I know what Monastery Beach is. He didn't have to explain. Misty and I grew up there."

The deputy also rises. "Ms. Rochester, you were never fingerprinted."

She shakes her head.

"I'd like you to come down to the office with me so we can get your fingerprints on file, compare them to what we found at the scene. And on the fork."

"I can tell you already my prints are probably on the fork, unless Misty ever used it, which she probably didn't. I used it, washed it, put it away."

"Maybe you could ride with me."

"Am I under arrest?"

"Your cooperation would be helpful."

"All I've wanted to do is help," Sara said.

In the close quarters of the café, the emotional charge turns the heavy scents of chocolate into a stench. This is why I couldn't ever eat it again. Not after that night.

Thirty

"She's not our mom," Dylan says, repeating Marina's announcement. They're standing in the upstairs hallway that cuts between their bedrooms. Night has fallen. The house is dark except for the light from Dylan's computers and Marina's desklamp, spilling out of the open doors.

"I think you knew," Marina says gently. "Didn't you? All the signs were there."

Dylan leans his back against the wall and crosses his ankles. He's flipping through Sara's strange little Christmas photo album, the one of their night together at the candy shop, the night of their mother's death. They're in the hall outside the bedrooms, and Dylan isn't really interested in the snapshots that are mainly of his sister.

"The first time I saw her she tried to tell me the truth," Dylan said. "I guess I wanted something else." At the back of the album Marina has inserted a paper photocopy of the picture in Wasson's evidence: newborn Dylan getting a kiss from his big sister, their mother looking at the camera, tired but outwardly happy. He stares at it a long time. Then he takes it out of the sleeve and hands the book back to Marina.

"They look like twins," he says. "'Cept for the hair."

"Cousins."

"It almost wouldn't have mattered, would it?"

"What do you mean?"

"That she wasn't exactly Mom. We could have pretended. She cared. She wanted to help. Isn't that what a mom does?"

"There's a chance she had something to do with Mom's death."

"I don't believe it."

"Why not?"

"She wouldn't have tried to help us."

"Guilt makes people do all kinds of strange things. She was here at the house the night Mom disappeared."

"So was Dad."

"Dylan, c'mon."

"So were you. So was I."

Marina turns toward her bedroom. "I'm going to bed now. You should too."

"I'll go when I want," he says. She doesn't miss the challenge in his voice. "You're not my mom either," he says. "I guess that makes you guilty of *something*."

He takes the photo into the room with him and slams the door.

———

The scene changes. My anxiety and fear are rising. I punch the seat in front of me and it bounces on springs. My fist feels nothing.

On the screen Sara is in a small room with a barred window and a table flanked by two chairs. A paper cup full of weak, oily coffee that probably tastes like wax scraped off of Dylan's surfboard. The steam makes a curlicue under Sara's drooping eyes. She looks older, more tired than she has before now.

It's late for a visitor, nothing outside the window but night, fallen.

Ian comes in and she stands, runs a hand through her short hair, which slopes where her hand has supported her sleepless head. He looks around.

"I hope you weren't expecting the Biltmore," she says lightly.

"I could teach them a thing or two about hospitality," Ian responds. "But they wouldn't let me bring you a toothbrush."

She indicates that he should take a seat. The chair's legs scrape the floor.

"They found my fingerprints on that fondue fork," Sara announces. "The one with Misty's blood on it."

"Can you explain it?"

"To their satisfaction? I doubt it. Like I said, Garrett and I used the set a couple of times. I could have been the last one to touch them."

"Have they charged you yet?"

"For killing my cousin with a fondue fork?" She bites her lip apologetically, then says, "No. The deputy said they can hold me for forty-eight hours before they have to charge me. I'd guess they're looking at everything all over again. Or running the new information by the DA. I don't know exactly how it works."

"I can recommend a good attorney."

"I might need one." She swirls the coffee in her cup. "Is that why you came by? To wish me luck?"

"No."

"Because I don't know what happened to Misty, but that probably doesn't matter. For all these years I've believed that her death was my fault. Everyone in my family said so—if I hadn't let myself fall into an affair with Garrett, Misty wouldn't have gone over the edge. Even Garrett believed that. He never contradicted them. They cut me out forever with a check. Can you believe that? 'Severance,' my father called it. Enough money that I shouldn't have to ask them for anything ever again."

"That's how you launched Sara's Sins."

"That's right. With my cousin's blood money. I told you it was a good name." She lifts a finger in the air and smiles sadly. "You know, they even asked me to change my last name from Rochester to something else, but I never got around to that."

"If they really believed you killed her, why didn't they have you prosecuted?"

"They didn't think I was guilty of murder, Ian. But even I agree that I destroyed a family. It was embarrassment they wanted to be spared. Scandal. A Rochester committed suicide—why? The public scrutiny would have been unbearable on top of their loss. In their eyes my affair with Garrett was practically incestuous. And I was a chambermaid to Misty's royalty. Imagine that story being told in their social circles. They cover up their reputation the way they covered up Misty's illness. And if it can't be covered up, they pay for it to go away." She looks up at him. "Why did you side with Marina?"

"There aren't any sides. She found Misty's letter to you. She asked me for help sorting it out. One thing led to another."

"That's how it happens, isn't it?" she says. "One thing leads to another. I loved Garrett as much as he loved Misty. Those kids. I still do. It was selfish love, I know that, so maybe it wasn't love at all."

Sara takes a deep breath.

"Why are you here, Ian? We're colleagues. There's no reason for you to keep coming around."

"Spoken like a woman who thinks all of us agree with her parents."

Ian leans onto his hip and takes his wallet out of his opposite pocket. He unfolds it to a photo in a plastic sleeve and hands it out to her. "My wife," he says. "Gemina."

Sara takes the wallet gently. Gemina is young and fair, with Denica's fine red locks, and freckled wings dotting her cheekbones. She wears a green scarf pulled up over her head and wrapped around her throat, like a Hollywood starlet from another generation.

"She's beautiful," Sara says.

"I killed her when I fell asleep at the wheel," Ian says.

"I'm truly sorry, Ian."

"I can't undo it."

"Of course you can't."

"So I don't keep trying."

Sara hands the photo back to him.

Ian's gaze lingers on Gemina's portrait. "You can't bring back Marina and Dylan's mother."

"But continuing to try seems like the right punishment. The very lightest sentence, in fact."

"Sisyphus, rolling his rock uphill."

"I guess."

"Sara, irreversible sins aren't unforgivable." Ian puts away his wallet, then leans forward, propping his elbows on the table. "I don't know what happened to your cousin, but I don't need to. It's enough that you believe you're to blame. But maybe you'll let me tell you something I learned after Gemina died."

He doesn't go on until she nods.

"I used to think that the only way out from under the weight of her death was to get pardon from everyone hurt by her dying. But a lot of those folks don't have the capacity for that. Not even after all these years. It's one of the reasons I left Ireland."

"But you just said that irreversible choices aren't unforgivable."

"Well, they are if you expect *people* to forgive you. Because you don't have any say in what they decide to do."

"So what did you mean? That you look to God for forgiveness?"

Ian stands up and puts his hands in his pockets, jingles some loose change. He turns sideways and looks up at the blank cinderblock wall. "Gemina and I used to argue about God a lot. She believed, I didn't. She used to say, 'God's perfect. It's our ideas of him that are wrecked.' I would say, 'Then he can't be perfect, because that idea would be wrecked too.'"

Sara smiles.

"And she would get right in my face"—Ian holds his hand right in front of his eyes—"and put her arms around my middle, and she'd say, 'Nothing's mightier than loving someone and expecting nothing in return. No fool human could have come up with an idea like that.'"

"Was she saying that you never loved her back?"

Ian laughs. "No. The first time she said it she was talking about our children. But she said it often of other people. In time I came to agree with her."

"So you believe God has forgiven you?"

"I believe God has given me a thousand chances to look at people and see what I might give them instead of what they might give me. They don't exist to forgive me. I exist to love them."

Sara swirls the coffee in her cup. "I don't know what I think of God."

"It wouldn't hurt to stay open."

"Maybe not."

"Do you still love Marina and Dylan?"

"Yes."

"Will you love them if they never forgive you?"

"How could I hold that against them?"

"Then whatever it is you think you did or should have done—keep loving them without expecting them to redeem you, Sara. God will find you there."

―――――

I've heard enough. This man is full of hot air. God never found me, after all.

"Shut it off," I demand, waving at the screen. But my protest is as weak as I have become.

"You expected your children to save you too," my companion says as if he can read my thoughts. "Only God can save."

"I don't want to see anymore."

"That's what you said when all this first happened. Now you don't get a say in what you have to face." He pulls the beret down over his eyes and tips his head back against the chair.

The film rolls on.

―――――

The dream again. The nightmare:

Young Marina, the open ocean, the tiny raft. A storm is kicking up and she's holding on, scared and tired of having been here so many times.

Already, a lashing on the raft snaps and cuts her across the cheek. It's giving way so soon. The wind is merely a howl. It hasn't even started screeching yet. She remembers that her float is made of her brother's bones and it's her job to hold them together in spite of the odds. But she can't. She's not big enough, old enough, strong enough. This is what she's guilty of, she thinks: of not being enough. Of never being enough for her brother or me to make up for her mother's absence. Tonight this makes her angry. Angry at her mother for leaving, at me for neither living nor dying, for abandoning her to my debts, my own inadequate efforts to create a mother for her out of material things.

I wish I had told you before now, Marina, how well you've done with what you were given—and with what I couldn't give. I am so proud of you.

Anger doesn't do any good in dreams. Or in comas. It doesn't hold a raft together. It will probably hasten her drowning.

Salt water washes over her face and she sputters. She lies on her belly, spread-eagled, her fingers cold and achy, and closes her eyes. I muster the end of my strength, rise from this red velvet seat, and walk to the screen. I raise my hands and try to touch her. The projector turns my hands into shadows and her back lies over my fingers. I know I can't protect her. I can't even really be with her.

The swells are engorged now. Whitecaps spill down watery hills in all directions, the avalanches of oceans. For just a little while longer, seconds at most, she can pretend she's in a rocking cradle. Then the lullaby will turn violent and she'll flip. If she's lucky she'll wake up before she breathes death in.

A light cuts across her face, like a door to a bright hall opening onto a midnight bedroom. The brightness stabs. Even though her eyes are closed, she squeezes them shut more tightly.

The light passes by again, sweeping over her squint, golden and warm. And again. She looks.

Tonight there is a dark shadow sitting on the water, long and lumpy. A jetty or an island, and at the end, a lighthouse. Never before has there been a lighthouse in her dream. Under the weight of nighttime it's impossible to see the building itself, only the yellow orb turning. The beam passes over Marina and then illuminates the deadly rocks at the base of the land mass, the sharp teeth of a slobbering giant. Child, teeth. Life, death. The storm is pushing my daughter toward the inevitable.

Then, a surprise. The earth rumbles. The revolving light rises into the sky like a moon on its arc, and at the peak it pauses, swinging through thick clouds. What appeared to be a lighthouse is now a lantern, a light in a box, dangling from a human hand by a wire handle. The long, lumpy jetty is now a long, slender arm lifting the light, seeking, searching, scanning the ocean. A rescue mission.

Marina watches it, rising to her elbows. The wake created by the shifting earth pushes her raft away from the rocks, stronger than the stormy swells.

That light—spinning, swinging, sweeping, stabbing—circles the world once before passing over her upturned face and catching her eyes. The gentle glint changes everything. The lantern jerks into reverse. The metal handle rattles. The arm descends until the golden light shines like a sun on my daughter's sopping, shivering body.

But it isn't a sun. Or a lighthouse or lantern or even a simple light bulb. It's a glass Christmas globe, dangling from a ribbon and lit from within. It sends out shoots of copper and silver and yellow warmth, held by slender and feminine fingers. Then another identical hand comes from the sky down into the water and scoops up the battered child and fragile raft before a wave dashes them both on the unforgiving rocks. Not a single bone is lost.

Marina sleeps until morning.

Dylan does not.

The night watch answers the intercom when Sara pushes the button.

"May I make a call?" Sara asks.

"It's four in the morning."

"I know."

"I'll bring a phone."

"I don't know the number." Sara wraps both hands around her cold coffee. "Would you look it up for me? A Monterey number."

Dylan rises when it's still dark, bothered by something in one of the photographs, but he can't remember what. Something that made him pause before moving on. Though he's forgotten what it was, the thing won't let him rest. He tosses and turns. He finally gives up.

He's not sure where Marina put the little photo book. He grabs a flashlight from the drawer in his nightstand and crosses the hall into her room, passing the beam of light over the pink-and-white perfection of her space. The very opposite of his: clean, controlled. The strangest room in the house. Calm in the storm. Christmas in summertime. A glint of gold foil catches the rays of the light.

The album sits on the desk, her cell phone on top of it, both squared with the edge. When he moves to pick it up, he's struck by that feeling in his chest that is so familiar "out there" but never here, within the secure walls of his home. He catches his breath. His heart races and then, suddenly, slows to a walk. A sweat breaks out on his forehead and then, as quickly as it came, returns to normal.

His sister is sleeping so hard that when his light crosses her face she doesn't even stir. Her breathing is as measured as artificial swells in a wave pool. Spread out on the bedspread next to her is a copy of the sheriff's report, which Wasson gave to Marina. She'd have had to put in a formal request for the report from the Monterey County sheriff, which would have more details about the discovery of Misty's car, and the interviews with her parents and extended family. Dylan takes these pages to read for himself.

Downstairs in the kitchen he pulls a Pepsi out of the fridge and pops the top. His hand is shaking even before he takes a sip of caffeine. So he drinks it standing in front of the window over the sink, staring out at the black ocean, holding on to the lip of the counter.

He doesn't have to see the water to know it's flat. It's a terrible morning for surfing. But it's a good morning for the gulls. They fly low, already looking for fish that only they can see.

Maybe she died out there after all.

Why not? The glassy surface hides so much from the human eye. Danger and depth and everything that Denica is afraid of. Maybe even poisonous spiders and dead mothers sucked into bottomless trenches. Because who really knows? Who can say they've seen it all?

Safe on the water, safe at home. Everything else is a potential threat. Why? In a blink Dylan understands that I was the ocean that covered our house in a flood of secrets, and now that I am receding, everything will be exposed.

We could have pretended, he said to his sister just the night before. Pretended that Sara was his mother, that there were no unanswered questions, that all was well in the world. We could keep pretending.

We tried that, I murmur. We did. That's exactly what I did. I pretended that I knew what was best, that I could raise my children without answering their most important questions, questions they didn't even know how to ask.

A new kind of fear presses in on my son. He's never been afraid of his own house before.

He drinks the soda slowly, waiting for it to give him boldness before he studies the photos he only glanced at last night. Something about the images is pricking at his lungs, threatening to pop them like balloons. He can't put his finger on the problem.

I can't either.

And then Denica's voice jabs over his right shoulder, demanding, *Are we going or not?* Dylan sits down at the counter and opens the book.

Thirty-One

"Aunt Lena?"

Sara's hands on the black veneer tabletop are clammy. When she sits back to put her hands in her lap, moist prints next to the phone base evaporate. My mother-in-law's voice comes over the speakers, thick with sleep.

"Who's this?"

"It's Sara." Then, though there are no other Saras in the world who would call her Aunt Lena, she adds, "Sara Rochester."

She sits in the uncomfortable metal folding chair with her leg crossed over her knee, trying to appear relaxed, maybe for her own benefit. But her suspended foot is wiggling like bait on a hook, anticipating shark teeth. Four and a half hours north in Monterey, Lena's deadly mouth might be open, but it's silent.

She finally musters, "What time is it?"

"Almost four thirty."

"What on earth?" She's more alert now, talking at full volume. I heard Lionel passed from a heart attack three, four years ago. It's easy to imagine her elbow propped on silk sheets in a wide bed, her hand reaching for the lamp on the bed stand.

"I don't know if you heard that Garrett Becker was in a car accident at the end of June."

"I'm the last person in the world to care about what happens to that man."

"Well, I'm not actually calling about him. It's about Marina and Dylan."

A pause. Does she have to remember the names of her own grandchildren?

I thought I'd put away my anger toward Misty's parents years ago. But there it is—not cast off on some faraway trash island in the Pacific, but tucked under a flap right in the center of my heart, rank and rotting.

Sara was with me the last time I spoke to Lena and her husband. It was in January after Misty disappeared, after the authorities had given up hope of finding Misty's body, after the memorial. Though Sara and I hadn't spoken to each other since that night, she agreed to help me take Marina and Dylan to her aunt and uncle's house for a visit. *They might cheer up Misty's folks.* I actually said that to her. Our drive to Monterey was silent and awkward.

At my in-laws' estate, a gray storm pounded the cliffs just beyond their living room window. Lena held Dylan, swaddled and sleeping, in her lap. Sara helped Marina stack chunky foam blocks in front of the fireplace. Her own parents, Barb and Stan, stood behind her aunt and uncle. *We had an affair,* I found myself saying to the four adults there. *Sara and me. It was short, it ended before Dylan was born. But that's why Misty . . .* I couldn't finish, and the silence in the room was like the silence on the other end of Sara's phone line right now.

Lena's voice over the speaker phone loses its edge but remains guarded. "I imagine they're nearly grown."

"They are," Sara says. "Twenty and sixteen. Almost seventeen. Marina's beautiful. She looks just like—"

"Why are you calling, Sara?"

Sara clears her throat. It sounds loud in the cold room. "They need family. They have no one."

"They have Garrett."

"He's in a coma. His prognosis isn't good."

"Garrett's family."

Sara is quiet. Lena knows I am an only child, that my parents died before Misty and I married.

"Then they have you." Now Lena's teeth show their jagged edge.

"I can't . . . I haven't earned their trust yet."

"Let them trust in your money, your success. That's what you're saying they need right now, isn't it? This is about money?"

"No. I can give them money. They need love. I mean, I love them too but—"

"Well, you're a fine one to pontificate about that."

Sara catches the tears that escape her eyes.

"They deserve a family. Grandparents. Dylan especially, he—"

"Garrett made his decisions."

Sara raises her voice. "They're Misty's *children*. Aunt Lena, please."

I didn't forewarn Sara that I planned to tell her family about the affair on that January day. I feared she wouldn't come, and I wanted someone to share the blame, someone besides the kids to buffer the wrath.

Sara's father was the first to react to the news. Stan yelled at Sara. *You what?* His thundering voice took Marina's attention off the foam blocks. I picked up my daughter, hoping she wouldn't cry. *You violated your cousin's marriage? You took advantage of her condition?* My defense of Sara was weak. *That's not what happened.*

But all Rochester eyes were on their own. Sara stood up and took what came. If she was surprised by my revelation, she was more accustomed to being the black sheep of the family. Her mother spoke next. *You've made a career of shaming us.*

You killed my only child, Lena moaned.

To me they said nothing. Sara stood there, not looking at me, and didn't defend herself. When the accusations finally stopped, she walked out of the house and kept on walking, the last time I saw her. She wrote a letter to me the next day. *I have to go . . .* I didn't respond. I never saw Misty's family again either. They shut me out.

"Garrett shut us out," Lena is saying to Sara. "He didn't want us in their lives. He wouldn't respond to our phone calls, he kept the kids locked behind that beach house gate, he returned the Christmas and birthday gifts we sent."

I did not! What kind of story is that? Why would I keep Marina and Dylan from their grandparents?

The man sitting next to me in the theater says, *This is the tale you told yourself.*

I glance at him. What's he babbling about?

Sara says, "Even if Garrett did that, is that how you want it to be forever?"

At the end of the phone line Lena falls quiet again.

"You can call them directly," Sara says. "I have phone numbers. I have the code to the gate. Garrett and I won't be there. Just you and your grandkids."

"Garrett made it clear—"

"It's their turn to decide. It isn't Garrett's choice anymore. But I think if he had a voice right now he'd tell you he changed his mind."

———————

The scene shifts before I know whether I've changed my mind or not.

It's morning. Marina comes downstairs and her brother is sitting at the kitchen counter. There are two empty Pepsi cans within reach. He's working on a third. The sliding door is open and salty air pushes into the house. Beside him, a broken orange peel sits on a napkin, and next to this, the black satin box that holds almost everything he knows about his mother. He's staring at a picture in the little plastic album.

"Did you take that out of my room?" she demands when she sees it.

"Did you want me to wake you up? You were snoring." The hint of a smile lifts the corner of his mouth.

"Was not." Translation: *It's fine you came in and got it.*

She shuffles through the kitchen toward the coffee carafe. Fills it with water and gets a pot going. Smoothes out her T-shirt over her drawstring shorts and glances over at Sara's book.

"Why didn't you let me go with you yesterday?" he asks. "To see Sara?"

"I thought you'd want to stay here with Denica." She sees the black box, runs her fingers over the lid.

"Next time ask me what I want."

She nods. "Where'd you get this?"

"It was Dad's," he says. My kids exchange a look: an assent to a truce. They can't shut each other out anymore. She is not the mother and he is not the child. They are siblings. Equals. Marina smiles. She seems relieved.

"Okay," Marina says.

He lets her look through the contents. She holds on to the picture of her and her mother. Dylan has put the other photograph—*Sara and I at the front door, holding champagne*—on the counter next to the little book. She picks that up next.

"You still think that's Sara?" she asks.

"Yeah. No wedding ring."

"Maybe Mom took the picture."

Dylan shrugs.

"This would have been right after they bought the place, do you think? The front porch wasn't in yet."

"Come here," Dylan says.

On this large screen in front of me, the camera angle shifts in a way that catches my attention. The broad angle of the kitchen, spanning from the fridge in the corner, across the sink and window, to the opposite counter where Dylan sits at a stool, narrows. The view jostles, like the camera's on someone's shoulder instead of on a stand. It rises, jiggles, shrinks, moves in for a close-up of whatever Dylan is looking at.

About ten, fifteen years ago film directors did a lot of experimenting with this kind of technique and I never liked it. It was supposed to make a viewer feel present in the action, as if their perspective wasn't staged. All it ever did for me was serve as a distraction, as it does now. Have these scenes from my life, the parts I lived and the parts I'm not shut out of, bumped around like this before? I don't think so, but it's impossible to say anything except that this is the first time I've noticed it.

For a second the only thing I can think is this: *Who's holding the camera?*

It focuses over Dylan's shoulder on the picture of Marina in the beach house garage, trying to share her peppermint with an ant.

"So let me see if I've got this right," Dylan says. He straightens up, puts his hands on the counter, and locks his elbows. "On Monday Mom and Dad fought, then Dad brought us here without her. She came up later that day—then what? More fighting?"

"Dad told the sheriff they got their argument straightened out, ate dinner, then went to bed. You got up in the night and wouldn't stop crying, so he took us both for a drive to get you to sleep without waking up Mom. When he got back Mom was gone."

"So after that he drives us to Sara's and then goes all the way down to Marina del Rey to look for her. But she'd gone the other direction, up north to Mortuary Beach."

"I think she was probably trying to get home, to her mom and dad."

"Why would she go there?"

Marina shakes her head. "Is it so hard to imagine? She wasn't that much older than I am now. I wish I could call Dad right now to help us sort out all our problems. Also, she was sick, and I guess they were really sympathetic about that."

"With the bipolar disorder?"

"That plus something postpartum. Depression to the nth degree. The sheriff says maybe a psychosis."

Dylan turns his attention back to the picture. "So we're with Sara, Dad's in Marina del Rey, and Mom's up north by Carmel. You and I need fresh clothes, Sara brings us back here. You feed the pests candy."

"That's what Sara and the report say."

Dylan lifts up the book. "Then what's wrong with this picture?"

I see it right away. And I can't interpret what it means. I can't make sense of the proof right in front of my face.

The camera lets the picture go and zooms in on Marina as

Dylan turns the album toward her. Close up. She looks, she thinks. The light goes on in her eyes. She lifts her eyes to Dylan.

"Dad's truck is in the garage," she says.

Right there next to my kneeling daughter, the old black GMC Sierra catches the glare of the light hanging from the middle of the ceiling. The front end of Sara's VW bug is visible behind the empty bay where Misty would have parked her car.

I'm trying to remember: How did I get to Marina del Rey?

"What does that mean?" Marina asks.

Dylan says, "That Dad never went to our other house?"

"You think he was here when Sara brought us?"

"It looks like he was here."

"But Sara wrote that note—'I'm so sorry.' The one everyone thought was Mom's suicide note. Sara says she wrote it because Dad wasn't here, as an apology to him. And us." She sighs. "But what's another lie from her, right?"

"She tried to tell us the truth. The first time I met her, after this"—he points at her black box—"she said, 'I'm not your mom.' Maybe we forced her into the lies. Maybe we wanted her to make things better even if it wasn't true."

I'm racking my brain. I can't come up with anything except the clear fact that I wasn't home when Sara came by. I wasn't home and I wasn't in my truck.

Why is the most significant night of my entire life a blank slate?

"If Dad was home, wouldn't she have left us with him after bringing us back? See, there are other pictures, after the house." Marina points. "But he's not with us. We're in different clothes. Here the sun is coming up. It doesn't make sense."

"It would make sense if Dad and Sara had a whole plan to do something to Mom."

"What do you mean, 'do something'?"

My son looks out at the ocean. He can't say it. Even now.

"You know that couldn't have happened," Marina says. "Dad *loved* Mom. The wedding ring, the loyalty. He and Sara were never together afterward—he was never with any other woman."

"That we know of."

"Why would they do something to Mom and then never speak to each other again?"

"We can't really know what they did or didn't do, don't you think?" Dylan leans across the counter and flips the pages back to the one of the garage. "Look at this again. What else do you see?"

Marina shakes her head. "It's dark. There's equipment by the garage. I don't know what that is—a generator?"

"I think it's called a plate compactor."

"What's a plate compactor?"

"It's for tamping the ground when you're getting ready to lay a foundation for something. Like a porch."

"So they were laying the porch. The sheriff's report said something about that."

"What else?"

"What else would it be used for?"

"No, what else do you see?"

"Just tell me—I don't know. A rake? A shovel? Something's leaning against the garage. These wood slats here look like a frame for the patio. Do you mean something else?"

Dylan slides off the stool and turns toward the dining room table. He steps out of the camera's frame. Marina watches him, sets the photos on the counter, then follows her brother. The camera stays fixed on the empty kitchen. Where did they go, and why can't I see?

I can hear, though. Papers rustling. A search for one in particular.

"Look here," Dylan says. "And here."

A long pause, and then Marina:

"Oh no."

Oh no *what*?

Why can't I see? I shout the question into the theater. Why now, after being allowed to see everything else, why won't the blasted camera turn six feet to the left?

"Where did you find this?" Marina asks.

"In Dad's office."

"There's got to be an explanation."

––––––––––

I'm at the mercy of this black box of a theater, this sunken chair I'm no longer strong enough to rise from, this blasted screen.

"It's like this," says the man farther down the row of plush seats. "You choose the boundaries of your life, the limits of the truth you're willing to tell."

I don't understand. Alternating scenes flicker in front of me: Sara, pacing in her cell. And that empty kitchen. Back and forth. Sara waiting for news, me waiting for the kids to return. What does either have to do with something I've chosen?

"I want to see what my kids are looking at. I want to see what Sara really did the night my wife died."

"This is the view you've chosen."

"No, it's not. Show me more."

"You don't really want to see. You said so yourself."

How can any man want the truth more badly than I do? I don't even want it for myself, but for Marina and Dylan. They need to know who they can trust when I'm gone, and until now I'd thought that person might be Sara.

"Garrett."

My name, spoken the way I say "Marina" or "Dylan" when I'm telling a buddy about her maturity or his brains. The name formed by paternal pride and a smile.

"What?" Now I'm the child. Petulant.

"Think: when you go to the movies, you agree to the deception."

"I don't like the word *deception*."

"Limits, then. You don't think too hard about what's outside the edges of the screen—all the equipment and techs and props and costumes. All the details that remind you the framed world isn't wholly honest might ruin your experience of the story. Because the Truth-with-a-capital-*T* is, you want a certain experience."

I fling my hand out over the empty seats. "This is my family, not some screenplay."

"It's the screenplay you wrote. You wanted your life to be a certain kind of experience, Garrett. You wanted your children to live a certain story. What you see is the bedtime story you told Marina and Dylan as they grew up. This is the tale that leaves stuff out."

"I'm an honest man."

"That's part of the truth you've tried to create."

"I'd know if I was a liar."

"From where I sit, most people don't have a clue about their true selves."

———

I'm back at the infernal kitchen, still empty. A room with no life in it.

"Would you stop it?" I shout. "Would you stop shutting me out?"

You stop it . . ., a voice echoes. Is it mine? *You stop shutting . . .*

"Tell me what's going on here!" I demand. "Show me what this is all about!"

I don't even know who I'm yelling at. The theater is my prison, and I don't want to be here anymore. I want to be with the people I love, starting with my kids. But even they are out of the frame of my life now.

"Get me *out* of here!"

The lights go out. The screen vanishes. I can't even see my own hands. The towering theater walls block light but allow sounds whispering on the other side to come through: the bumping of wind against the concrete, the sweeping of tree branches, and the rhythm of rain. I couldn't hear these things over what was playing on the screen. Now I know that I was protected, and I'm asking to be exposed.

Are you ready? The voice cuts through darkness.

A tremble vibrates my bones. I'm not sure.

"Yes," I whisper.

I can't hear you.

A light pops on, not a projector but a spotlight, not in my face but from behind, over the top of my head. Someone is standing in front of me in the next row of seats.

I can't hear you, the someone says. A woman with the voice of the man who has sat with me through this bizarre showing of my life. A woman with a terrible blunt wound right at her temple. Misty, smiling at me so kindly, so openly. My wife, taken from me by a powerful undertow and a terrible blow to the head by an underwater rock at Mortuary Beach.

Not exactly, she says.

I stand from my seat without any effort at all. I lift my hand to touch her beautiful face. The fresh wound hurts me as if it's my own pain, but it doesn't mar her loveliness at all. There is a trickle of blood on her cheek. I can feel the warmth of her skin before we even connect.

But we don't connect, not then. It's the hair that stops me, the silky sheen that catches the light, the curl right under her jaw. Her hair is as dry as the sun.

"What happened?" I ask. I am holding my breath. I realize she's holding her chin up at an odd angle. She has to look at me sidelong.

Are you ready?

"Yes." This time I am firm.

And then she's gone.

Thirty-Two

My wife is gone and I feel a pain in my heart as real as the day she died. It stabs through me like a skewer through fresh meat. I want to die.

"Don't go, don't go," I hear myself saying. "Don't leave me. I'm sorry."

It's a sorrowful echo from my past. *Don't go, don't go.*

The loss drives me down and I fall, nothing to catch me, nothing for me to catch. I go down the way my Suburban yielded to gravity. When my knees tap the ground, the darkness recedes. It runs away from me in all directions like I've knocked over a bucket of light. It spreads along the ground and then takes off. It soars upward and catches the sky. It closes over my head, catching me inside of its balloon.

Inside of my house. The home I've tried to make for my kids. Here I am for the first time since the morning I drove to work, then drove to the brink of death.

It's brighter than I remember it being. The sky outside is broader, the salt air sharper in my nose. The acrylic wall of the enclosed patio, which the years have turned cloudy with sand scratches, is as clear today as the day it was installed. Beyond it, I can see the curve of the earth, the Pacific drooping toward the horizon.

At my fingertips I can see the loops of the slate blue carpet, brushing against the whorl of my fingerprint. I can see that there are three strands in each loop.

The empty kitchen is ahead. Behind me, the door to the garage. To the far right, the living room, the front door, the stairs to the bedrooms. To the left, the dining room table, and Marina and Dylan are standing over an open file, thick with unique pieces of paper that won't stack neatly. Marina is holding one tissue-thin piece of pink, from a triplicate work order. I recognize it.

"There has to be an explanation for this," Marina says to her brother through tears.

"What if this *is* the explanation? The concrete for our new patio foundation was poured the day Mom disappeared."

Marina puts the sheet down and looks around. "There was something about it in the sheriff's report."

Dylan holds up the papers. "Dad told them it went down on the fifteenth. On Monday. But the signature at the bottom was for Tuesday. The sixteenth."

"So he forgot what day it was. I do it all the time, signing papers off by a day."

"Maybe that's what the sheriff thought. But what if the job was delayed? Look at the picture again. As of the wee hours of Tuesday, December 16—no concrete."

Marina is denying these facts with every muscle in her face. "This signature isn't even his. Who's Sam Raglan?"

My kids are far more upset about the minutiae than I would expect them to be.

When I arrived at the Rincon Monday afternoon, with Dylan and Marina in tow, Sam was already gone and the wood forms that should have held the concrete were empty. There was a voice mail on my cell phone. *Garrett, Sam here. Concrete crew got hung up at their last job, so we won't see them until tomorrow. But you're first on their schedule, coming at seven. Call me if you're around—if not I'll be back at six to see it through for ya. Later.*

I can't remember if I ever called Sam back.

Marina sinks into a dining room chair. "What are you thinking?" she asks her brother.

"You know what I'm thinking."

"I want to hear you say it."

"Why? So you can tell me it's impossible? That I'm being unfair to Dad?"

"He *loved* Mom."

"It's possible to love someone and kill them too."

"How can you believe that about Dad? It's crazy."

"You wanted to hear me say it."

"That doesn't make it true!" Marina shouts this.

And wanting something different can't make the truth untrue, I say. It pops out of my mouth like a thing that's been buried alive and has finally fought its way out.

Dylan clears the silence. "What we know for sure is that Dad was here when he said he wasn't."

"Dad's *car* was here."

"But if Mom was in her car driving up to . . ." Dylan drifts off, his mind chasing a distracting thought.

On the kitchen counter, Marina's cell phone starts to ring.

"What?" she asks.

He looks to Marina's phone. "You should answer that."

"What are you thinking? Mom's driving to Monterey. Dad's here. What?"

My son is staring at the water for answers. "I don't know."

Marina's tears have dried up, but the stress shows in the lines of her brow and the bags under her eyes, markers of a much older person. She pushes back the dining room chair and gets up to retrieve her phone.

Dylan says, "I'll see if I can figure out who Sam is."

Marina reads the caller ID. "831? Where's that?"

"Monterey," her brother says. "Weird timing, don't you think?"

"Hello?" Marina turns to look at Dylan. "Yes, this is Misty's daughter."

———

My memory begins to return.

I said I was ready. Am I? My house is gone and I'm racing up the Pacific Coast Highway in my wife's car. Dylan was the one who set me on this road. He was the first to imagine me in the driver's seat of Misty's sedan. The first to remind me that I can't wish the truth untrue. The children teach the adults to remember.

Clouds hide the moon and all the stars. I can't see anything beyond the headlights, but I know what's coming.

———

Lena Rochester wears large cocktail rings even in the daytime, silver and turquoise things that look overlarge on her aging stature. She has dressed for this occasion in an expensive duster jacket. It's storm gray, flecked with silver threads and all the blues of the ocean. Her knit pants move like water, and a mass of silver balls forms a heavy necklace at her slackening throat.

Before she approaches the front door of the beach house, she crosses the lawn and goes to stand in front of Misty's memorial stone. She bows her head and lets her hulking gunmetal-gray purse, trimmed with links of hammered silver, slide off her shoulder. She clutches it in front of her, exactly as she did the day we set the stone. I remember she didn't like the inscription. *In Memory of Misty / Wife, Mother, Friend.* I didn't mean anything by leaving off *Daughter*, there just wasn't enough room.

Marina notices from the living room window and takes the chance to prepare for the personality that looks so intimidating, that sounded so detached over the phone. How do you prepare to meet a grandmother who died before you were old enough to remember her? This was the story I told.

Lena bends down and touches the top of the stone with her accessorized fingers, then turns back to the house. As her pointy shoes click up the red tile porch, it's impossible not to see her in the role of real estate agent, which the Rochesters have performed for generations. But there is also a softness about her, something tender to balance the sharp business acumen, starting with her fading blue eyes and the snow-white hair that cups her cheeks like angel hands. All the dark Rochester looks came from her husband's side of the family.

I never noticed the softness before. I'm relieved to see it and wonder if it's new, or if I'm changed.

Marina opens the door before Lena has the chance to knock. My beautiful girl is nervous. She tucks her hair behind her ear and looks into the house as she pulls the door wider. "Come on in," she says.

But Lena is frozen on the porch. She raises her skin-loose hand to her lips and forgets her manners, staring and staring at Marina, and then finally breaking into a hearty laugh. She drops the big purse and flings her arms wide and finally mounts the steps to the house, then throws herself at Marina's neck. They're the same height. Lena grabs her shoulders and rocks her back and forth, then plants her bright-red lips in my daughter's thick hair.

"I see her in your eyes," she says. And her own sparkle wet.

Marina doesn't resist any of it. But in the grip of her grandmother's hug she does shoot a look of surprise at her brother. Dylan has just come out of the kitchen with an avocado and tomato sandwich in one hand and a table knife hilt-deep in mayonnaise in the other.

Lena pulls away. She turns to her grandson, smiling like the day he was born. "You must be Dylan."

She grabs hold of Marina's hand, tugging her across the living room so she can be close to them both. Lena's shaking her head. She glances briefly at the sticky knife, decides not to risk it smearing on her duster. But she reaches out and cups his bent elbow.

"I brought pictures of you as a baby," she says happily. "I would have recognized you on the street."

I believe she tells the truth. I imagine she's been checking out faces on the street for seventeen years, hoping.

Dylan is grinning. "Make you a sandwich?" he asks, showing her his.

"No, thank you. I'm too excited to eat a bite. But you must give me the number of your hairstylist," she says. "Your look is just spectacular."

———————

The locals call this place Mortuary Beach, and I am here to save my children.

I park Misty's car on the shoulder of Highway 1, under the low branches of an old, salt-whipped tree. The sun isn't shining even though it has recently risen. The winds are spitting sleet across the windshield, and clouds press down heavily. The beastly surf rattles its cage, daring me to come closer.

I take what's mine and leave what I want others to find. Her purse. Her wallet. Her medications. I close the door and leave the empty car unlocked. Why frustrate the search?

The old monastery sits just there on the other side of the highway. I stand on this skinny strip of asphalt, the only thing separating life from death. I could turn in either direction. Strange hope swells in me, but then settles back into the sea. Yesterday I might have looked for refuge in that place where they believe God welcomes sinners and liars. But not now.

Like the unwitting visitors who make the mistake of taking their eyes off the water, I put the monastery at my back and face my fate. I point my body home. I follow the ribbon road, jacket lapel turned up around my ears, shoulders hunched, thumb asking for a ride.

It's the only way to protect Marina and Dylan from a life without either of their parents.

Lena's hunger eventually returns as the afternoon turns to evening and the setting sun turns the living room pink. Gold light sprays the overflow of Lena's Mercedes Benz: scrapbooks and loose photo prints and memorabilia that Dylan and Marina helped her carry into the house. Misty's school pictures, dance recitals, family Christmases, our wedding. Dylan holds on to an image of him and his mother sitting in front of a paned window, looking at each other.

"You keep that," Lena insists. She turns to Marina, who's looking through our wedding album for the second time. "Next time I come I'll bring her dress. If we're lucky that style won't come back for years, but you should have it. We might be able to take off the sleeves and reinvent it, don't you think? Maybe slim down the skirt? There's enough fabric there to make dresses for all the bridesmaids! Your mother was such a beauty, no one was looking at the dress, thank the stars. Do you have a boyfriend, sweets?"

Dylan snorts. Marina blushes.

"Well, when all this dust settles you're going to have to get out more. That's all there is to it. Your father kept you cooped up with responsibilities that no young woman should have to . . ." She catches herself. Exhales an exasperated puff. "That was gauche. I'm sorry. I'm so very sorry that your father's in this state."

"I agree." Dylan looks at his sister. "You need to get out more."

"So do you," she shoots back.

"All in due time, right?" Lena says, looking at Dylan. "Your issues are hardly your fault. These things are inherited. We know that now. Your poor mother—we all could have done better by her if we'd known more even twenty years ago." Her silence lasts longer than any since she's set foot in the house. When she snaps out of it, she says, "Your dad did the best he could, I imagine."

"He looks so young." Marina shows Dylan our wedding portrait, which involves Misty laughing with her head thrown back and me watching her, bewitched. Our arms are linked together.

"Not much older than you are now," Lena says. "I didn't see

much of him after she died. Funny how we keep an image of a person in our head. That's the man I think of. But not so happy. Maybe we can pay him a visit before I have to leave."

Dylan heads upstairs, snapshot of his mother in hand, to retrieve a framed shot of us surfing together just last winter.

"You aren't driving back tonight, are you?" Marina asks.

"No, no, sweets. I'm not your age anymore. I'll get a hotel."

"You can stay here if you want." Marina says it like it doesn't matter, just in case Lena declines. "I can make up the master."

"Why, thank you. I might just take you up on that."

I love my daughter's smile. It's been hiding.

"Would you two like to go out for a bite to eat or should I order in?" Lena asks discretely while Dylan is out of earshot.

Marina almost answers reflexively, then she stops and thinks. "You'll have to ask him. He's been different, since Sara. I can't explain it."

Lena sinks back into the sofa cushions. "Ah, Sara. I can't tell you the number of times I've wondered if I misjudged her."

"What?" Marina looks up from the photos.

Dylan hits the landing at the base of the stairs with both feet and Lena startles. He leaped at least four steps. He hasn't done that since he was thirteen. She places her hand over her heart. "Oh! You keep that up and I'll be visiting your father by ambulance this evening!" Dylan hands over the framed print, enlarged to an eight by ten. Marina took the shot of her brother and me in our wetsuits standing on the stony shore right outside the house, arms thrown over each other's shoulders and boards flanking us like two more people.

"Oh my," she says. She might be talking about the wrinkles, deepened by my squinting into the sun, or the gray hairs marching backward on my head, or the drooping skin under my eyes. She taps the glass over my face with her finger. "Now, I might not have recognized *him* on the street. I could never understand why he cut us off. But this . . . if this is what his sorrow looked like, well . . . poor man." Her eyes snap to Marina, full of fresh concern. "I hope he was good to you kids. I hope he didn't—"

"Never." Marina holds her hand up to stop the thought. "He's a really good"—she chokes up—"a great dad."

"And that's a relief to this old heart." Lena shakes her head and draws her granddaughter into a sideways hug.

Dylan takes back the photo and sets it over the fireplace. "What did you say about Sara?"

"Oh, right. Now, she's the one who called me down—I told you that, didn't I?"

Marina closes the wedding album and wipes her eyes. "No. I thought she was at the sheriff's office."

"Where?"

"Ian said they could hold her for two days—"

"Hold her? Is she under *arrest*? For *what*?"

Marina looks to Dylan. She hardly knows where to begin, so he does it for her.

"They're looking into the possibility that Mom didn't kill herself."

"Didn't . . . oh my stars! Are you saying she's alive? Did someone find her? No, no. Listen to me, she would have called. You mean . . ." She closes her pale-blue eyes and takes a breath. "Did they finally find her after all this time? Can I finally bury my daughter?"

Dylan looks at his feet.

"No," Marina says quickly. "He only meant that there's some new evidence. They're checking it out."

"Evidence? Like what?"

"Like, um, it appears Sara and Dad had an affair."

"Why yes, we all knew about that."

"And Sara was here the night Mom went missing. She wrote Mom's suicide note. And her prints were on . . . something that had Mom's blood on it."

Lena is staring at Marina as if her words were foreign.

"Sara?" she finally croaks. "I never thought Misty actually killed herself because of Sara. She would have lived for you two, if not for the illness. It wasn't fair, what Barb and Stan did to her. We lost two daughters that way. Stan was the elder brother, you know, and Barb never resisted her husband. He still has so much power over her. But maybe . . ."

"Why did you wonder if you were wrong about Sara?" Marina asks.

"Well, I don't know now." Lena tries to remember. "I guess I always thought she was a victim of Misty's moods, but we were all so frightened for your mother then. She had such a promising future with her dancing, and then one day we realized she had problems far worse than a teenage phase. She and Sara were like sisters—so it was easy to blame Sara if Misty was upset about something. You know how girls can be, sweets. I guess it started there, and then got to the point where we all believed what we wanted to. It didn't help that Sara was of her own mind regarding her career." Lena wags her finger at Dylan. "I dare you to tell your great-uncle Stan that you plan a future in gaming, young man. He'll cut you off before he meets you. I never even thought we'd been unreasonable until after Sara was gone for good. I wanted her to come talk to me about Misty, see, so I wouldn't forget the stories." Lena composes herself. "But murder? Not even at the lowest point would I think Sara capable of that."

"Yeah, I don't buy it either," Dylan says.

"I saw you looking at Mom's memorial stone before you came in. Had you seen it before today?"

"Why sure, I was here when he put it in. The whole family was. Well, everyone but Sara. It was a moving service, really. Christmas Eve. It felt nothing like Christmas, though. Sunny and sad. You poor, poor babies. You were an angel, Marina. You"—Lena frowns affectionately at Dylan—"not so much. I think you knew. Yes, I think you knew."

"Sara wasn't there?" Marina presses.

"It would have been awkward, even before we knew about the affair. Her absence was expected. I can't blame her for staying away. Your father was still very insistent then that they'd find Misty's body, though I shudder to think what that would have been like. It was fitting for the ocean to have her. But he believed. That memorial stone has a compartment in the back for ashes—did you know that?"

They don't. By the time they were old enough to have understood, I didn't see the point of showing them. Dylan walks over to the window and has a look in the direction of the memorial.

"I really objected to that notion. Misty belongs to the sea. Keeping ashes in a garden rock—it's what people do with their pets! And this, my dears, this has become a rather gloomy conversation, don't you think? Let's eat. I'm finally starving. Dylan, do you like Vietnamese?"

I don't think Lena notices that his fingers are shaking, or that he closes them into fists and puts them in his pockets to hide them. But Marina sees.

"Can you bring something back?" he asks.

"Of course," Lena says, rising. "Marina, I just read this review of a little hole in the wall in Carpinteria, a five-star beef pho."

"That sounds good. What do you want?" Marina asks her brother.

"Answers," he says. "With a side of shrimp."

———————

I had five hours to reinvent my world before I had to face the questions. Five hours back from Monterey to Santa Barbara in the twenty-year-old Toyota Corona of a UCSB student with a final to take that afternoon. I don't know what he was doing in Carmel. He didn't care what I was doing hitching a ride there. I was so thankful for his silence that I didn't even mind George Strait and Shania Twain singing us down the road. They kept his mind off me. He got me all the way to Isla Vista for twenty bucks and a Jolt soda, and in exchange let me have several sheets of three-ring notebook paper from a binder crammed under the passenger seat.

At ten thirty in the morning I made a phone call to Misty's dance studio and asked the woman who answered if Misty had been there. I asked her to please call me if Misty showed up.

Other than that I spent the hours writing a love letter to my wife. In barely legible writing, jostled by nerves and an old highway, the fickle ballpoint pen coming and going. No doubt a love letter like that one has never been written in the history of men adoring women. A catharsis, an apology, a plea for her forgiveness.

When Dylan finds it in the back of the memorial stone while his grandmother and sister are out, I suspect he will call it a confession.

Thirty-Three

Monday, December 15, I expected Misty to follow me to the beach house, but she didn't come immediately, and this worried me. The sun set. I resisted picking up the phone. We were locked in a battle of wills, and this was a battle I needed to win, for the sake of the entire family.

Dylan slept as babies do after hours of wailing and resisting an undesirable nipple in spite of being hungry. He crashed hard. I hoped he'd stay that way for several hours, so Marina and I put him in the master bedroom, in a playpen where he wouldn't wake her. Marina was less easily coaxed to sleep: only five stories, two cookies, three sips of water, and fifteen minutes of holding my breath while her head grew heavy on my arm.

Downstairs I lit a fire in the front room's old wood-burning fireplace. Waited for Misty to arrive with police officers and a kidnapping charge.

He took off with my children!

As you can see, officers, they're safe in their own home. It's Misty's home too. It's a misunderstanding, see. She has a condition . . .

I called Misty's parents again and asked Lena and Lionel to stop here at the beach house rather than drive all the way to Marina del Rey Tuesday morning. I'd need their help talking Misty into taking care of herself. We would do a private, small-scale intervention. They quickly agreed.

The house was so silent.

In the family room I powered up the TV, surfed the channels, found *It's a Wonderful Life* in its closing scenes. Punched the Off button. Got up and wandered aimlessly.

In the kitchen I dumped out the formula that Dylan wouldn't take, made a fresh bottle, and set it in the fridge. I stopped and stared at the photograph of my wife and children. We needed to be taking more pictures.

I turned off the lights, all but the one at the top of the stairs, in case Marina woke and wandered. The outdoor floodlights at the front of the house brightened the living room. Through the wood blinds I could see the framed porch, ready for the concrete. Everything looks wrong when it's under construction. The threshold of the door, too high to step into. Wood forms where the new steps would be, staked to the ground. More dirt than grass, no Spanish tiles yet. Everything dirty. Sam had left our rented equipment at the end of the footprint in case anything needed doing before the concrete went down.

I returned to the garage and opened the double-wide door so Misty wouldn't try to traverse the mess in front when she arrived. She would be driving my truck. The garage door opener was tucked away in the console between the seats. She might not think to look there.

Nine o'clock came and went. An old chiming clock that had belonged to my mother ticked on the mantel, measuring my plans and finding them lacking. After all, I had done exactly what Misty feared I would do. My efforts to protect my family were probably about to backfire. I stared at that picture and hoped it wasn't true.

Tomorrow, I thought, *I'll take the kids to get a Christmas tree. We'll see if we can find Santa at the mall. Maybe I'll buy one of those newfangled digital cameras, if I don't choke on the price. I'll look into getting Misty the new Toyota Sienna that she wants, now that our family is growing. It's a good-quality van, and I can pick up some extra work to make the payments—*

The kitchen door to the garage slammed. Other than that Misty arrived without theatrics, alone, a small overnight bag on one shoulder and a large gym bag stuffed with clothes and toys for the kids dangling from her opposite hand. She had changed into one of her favorite outfits, a bright-pink sweater with matching rhinestone-studded shoes. I stood and faced her, the flickering fire at my back.

"They're sleeping," I said, pointing upstairs.

She went up without speaking to me.

I thought about tossing the fresh bottle of formula before she found it, decided not to.

Thought about going upstairs to be with her being with the kids. Worried about how she'd react. Didn't go.

Paced.

Sat down in the antique, leather rocking chair by the fireplace. It squeaked and creaked. I left it, fearing Misty's wrath.

Paced more. Sank into the new sofa that had finally been delivered after Thanksgiving.

Waited.

"Where is she?" The question jarred me awake. The fire was out and a chill came down through the flue. "I heard you talking to her. Where did she go?"

It was critical I wake quickly, but lifting the weight off my eyes took an effort.

"There's no one else here," I thought to say. "You and me, the kids. That's all." I blinked.

Misty was standing in the center of the room, her curls matted on one side of her head, eyes wide. She clutched Dylan to one shoulder. He belched. Misty eyed the phone on the end table. "She's here. I know her voice."

"It must have been a dream," I said.

This only made her angry. "What do you know about my dreams?"

She threw open the door to the garage.

"Sara!" she yelled. In her arms Dylan startled. He turned his head toward his mother's neck. She turned on the lights, padded out into the huge space and looked inside both cars, walked around them, looked under the bumpers. I jumped up to follow her, squinting.

"Misty." I tried to remember everything useful: Be calm, clear, nonjudgmental. Don't contradict her. I stepped into the garage with her. "We shouldn't leave Marina in the house alone. Come back inside."

At the mention of Marina's name my wife looked momentarily disoriented, like she'd been sleepwalking and was surprised to find herself in the garage. But once she set foot in the kitchen, she slipped back into her search for Sara, switching on lights as she went—kitchen, dining room, family room, then back. She checked the coat closet, then started opening kitchen cupboards.

"What's this?"

The fondue pot from Sara sat out on the counter, clean but not put away. It didn't have its own place yet; it never would. I left it out knowing that Misty would want to organize the kitchen herself, never imagining a scenario like this.

"It's a housewarming present. Remember?" She'd seen it before. I wasn't about to remind her who it was from.

She picked one of the forks out of the pot and gave the merman handle a closer look. It caught the recessed light over the cupboard and flashed near Dylan's perfect ear. "I've never used it."

"You haven't had the chance yet. Let's break it in tomorrow." I reached out, hoping she might give the fork to me. "After dinner we'll—"

"You've used it." She snatched it away. There's nothing particularly frightening about a fondue fork until it's cutting the air beside an infant's tiny head. "You and Sara."

Stay calm, clear, conciliatory.

"Yes. I told you she brought it the night we had dinner plans and you couldn't get here." True—but not the only time Sara and I had eaten from those forks.

"You and Sara," Misty repeated. "I've always been right about you. You can't say I thought that up."

"I've never said that."

Her arm swooped across the counter, catching the stainless steel pot and sending it onto the floor, taking a glass half full of water down with it. The cup shattered on the new hardwood and the remaining forks rolled. The power cord flopped out. Wide-eyed Dylan stared at his mother's jaw, his head bobbing.

"Misty, Dylan is scared."

"Of *you*." She pointed the fork my way.

"Please don't do that." I backed away. "Look at him."

She couldn't actually see his face, but she turned her head and her cheek brushed the downy top of his soft spot. She dropped her

voice to a murmur. "He's okay. Aren't you, baby boy? We're okay."
She bounced lightly on the balls of her feet and walked out of the
kitchen, past me, back out to the living room. I gave her space. I
still eyed that fork. She clutched it by the long stem.

"Can I hold him?" I asked her.

"No."

Back in the living room she placed Dylan on top of the large
cushioned ottoman that doubled as a coffee table for the sofa.
She leaned over him and waved the merman above his eyes. He
wiggled as his eyes followed the sparkling cut glass.

"Maybe we could get one of his rattles?" I suggested. I looked
for the kids' bag of clothes and toys. She'd taken it upstairs.

"Stop it!" She spun to me. "He's my son. I know best. I love
him. I'll protect him. While you . . . while you . . ." She rushed me
with her fists up and this time I caught her. I held firmly while she
pushed and pulled against my strength. The fork in her fist aimed
sideways.

I kept my voice low. I tried to catch her eyes but she wouldn't
look at me. "Misty, please listen. I love you. I love Dylan and
Marina. Sara was a mistake. I betrayed you and I'll be sorry about
it for the rest of my life. Please forgive me. Please believe me. I'll
make it up to you every day. I love you."

Her eyes were closed and her lips were moving and she was
shaking her head from side to side. But she stopped fighting my
hold. Still, I didn't let go.

"Misty, I love *you*. Only you."

"She's *here*. I can hear her whispering."

"Sara isn't here. She hasn't been here since before Dylan was
born. She'll never be here again." A warning went off in my mind.
Don't contradict.

She went still. "*Listen.*"

I came at the problem from a new angle. "Tell her to be quiet," I said.

Misty's eyes popped open. "She's upstairs with Marina." A gasp, a push. I held tight.

"Marina is sleeping. She's *safe.*"

"How could you leave her alone with Sara?"

On the drive back from Monastery Beach, I had plenty of time to think of all the mistakes I made in that five-minute span, but I was too far out of my depth. Psychosis was my uncharted territory. I shouldn't have put so much effort into reasoning with her. I shouldn't have tried to convince her of anything. Most of all, I shouldn't have restrained her. Dylan was safe, out of her arms and away from that fork. Maybe I should have let Misty keep searching for Sara. Maybe I should have gone out into the garage and picked an imaginary fight with Sara within Misty's earshot—kicked her out, insulted her, ordered her never to return.

"Sara. Is. Not. *Here!*" I yelled. And I shook her. I shook my wife, and everything she feared about me punched through her false reality like a tsunami through a plateglass window.

"He's trying to kill me," she shrieked.

"No, I'm not!"

My fingers had become sweaty slick on her skin. The fresh fear strengthened her, and when she tried to free herself from me by jabbing that fork into my hand, her wrist slipped right out of my grip. I saw the fork coming, I jerked away, and the two-pronged fork bit her own arm like a snake, striking deep. She yanked it out. Two skinny trails of blood raced down to the tip of her elbow.

She saw the blood and jumped away from me. "He's trying to kill me! He's going to kill me!"

She spun around, cornered in the living room. Standing by the sofa, I unintentionally blocked her way out—to the kitchen and garage, to the stairs, to the front door.

"I'm trying to protect you!" I shouted back.

"Sara!" she screamed.

Misty lunged at me, a fencer with a fork. I knocked her hand away and she lost her hold of it. It bounced off the fireplace screen and then hit the stones of the hearth.

"You hit me." She shrank like a child. Her hands were on the side of her head, shutting out the terrible noise that only she could hear. Red drops dripped from her wrist to the carpet.

I lifted both of my palms, face out.

"Stay away, stay away," she muttered. She bent at the waist and moaned, but her neck was craned upward. She looked at something beyond my shoulder, in the kitchen. "Get her away from me!"

My eyes darted to Dylan. He lay still on the ottoman, blinking.

"I won't let you do it," Misty said. "You can't have me."

"Please let me help," I said. I took a tentative step and her attention shifted to me. "I only want to help you." I reached out to her, but I was no longer her husband; I was only a threat.

She saw me coming. Her strong legs, conditioned by years of dancing, sprang out of their crouch. In two easy strides she reached the sofa. In one graceful leap she was over the back, completely clearing the tall sofa table behind it. Her body moved of its own accord, trusting itself for balance and safe landings. She flew. I don't think her eyes saw anything at all. She reached for the front door. Twisted the knob and drew it back, her legs still in motion.

"The steps!" I shouted. I lunged and knocked over the sofa table. Somehow I caught her. Every pore of my skin was brimming with liquid fear. The door yawned, her body tipped out over the empty wood forms, my fist seized a wad of pink sweater and yanked her away from the danger.

My moves were desperate, clumsy. We were both in motion and now off balance. She crashed into my chest. My chin knocked the back of her head. I threw my left arm around her shoulders.

Trying to contain the uncontainable is a violent endeavor.

Misty was facing away from me. She probably never saw the danger, blinded by her own terror. With her sweater in my right hand and my left arm hugging her collarbone, both of her hands were free. She stretched her long arms up over her head and went after my face with her fingernails. I tightened my hold on her shoulders. I squeezed. I let go of her sweater, then managed to keep her right hand out of my eyes. I twisted her arm behind her back and pinned it there. I ducked my head, buried my face between her shoulder blades, and held on, waiting for her fire to burn out.

It seemed like she fought me for hours. Her free elbow found my ribs. I swept her feet out from under her and she dropped to her knees. Without my arms to balance us we went sideways and fell into the toppled sofa table. We fell on her left hand, finally trapping it, her neck cradled in the nook of my steadying arm.

"Misty . . . honey . . . shh, shh, shh . . ."

She kicked at my shins. Her muscles strained against me. She is the reason Marina and Dylan are fighters.

"It's okay, it's okay. Everything's going to be okay."

In time her kicks became less intense. She gradually stopped struggling. But still she seemed coiled. I outlasted her, waiting until her breathing matched my own. I couldn't see Dylan, but his baby gurgles reached me from the other side of the sofa. The muscles in my arms and back ached.

The tension between her bony shoulders finally yielded. I

tested her by releasing the hand pinned between her spine and my ribs.

I took a deep breath. "That's it." Her fingers brushed the floor. She didn't straighten her arm. She didn't fill her own lungs with air. Her head in the crook of my elbow was heavy.

"Misty." I rolled her over. Blood was still oozing from the fanged puncture in her forearm. Her head was bleeding too. There was blood on the edge of the fallen table. Her eyes were closed.

"Oh no," I whispered. "Misty, Misty."

At her neck, under the surface of her skin, I could see the flaming red protest where my strong forearm had cut off her airway.

"No."

I had only meant to hold her back. I couldn't have choked her. I had saved her from a broken leg, a broken neck. But even as I looked at her throat, the pressure mark faded. She didn't start breathing again. She hadn't been breathing in time with me at all, I realized. She had stopped completely, and I had mistaken the rising and falling of my own chest for hers.

"Please don't go," I begged. "Please don't leave me. I need you. We need you."

I clutched her and wished she'd fight me. Resist, accuse. But she was more trusting of my touch than she'd ever been, completely surrendered. Her long hair grazed my arm. Her narrow shoulders folded toward each other when I squeezed. "Please, please. We'll leave California. I'll take you to New York." I crushed her to my chest. "They need good dance teachers there. They'll love you. I'll protect you. Oh, Misty, I'm so sorry."

On the other side of the sofa, Dylan started to wail.

Thirty-Four

While Marina and Lena order large Styrofoam bowls of pho thick with fish sauce and shrimp, Dylan sits in our front yard on the grass that has started to brown for lack of attention. He sits next to the memorial stone and the compartment he jimmied open with a flathead screwdriver. While I continue to weep, he unfolds my pages of notebook paper, rippled with moist air and starting to yellow at the edges, and he sits and reads. I wonder if he can hear my sorrow through the words.

When he's finished, he goes into the house and calls Denica. I can't read my son now. I don't know what his calm means. He tells Denica our story. Our true story.

"Now I know why it's always seemed like Mom was right here," he says.

"Everyone I know who's lost their mom feels the same way," Denica says. "The feeling doesn't go away, it just takes new shapes."

"She didn't abandon us—Dad did. I feel like everything I believed about my parents was wrong."

"Was it wrong, or was it just a limited view?"

He thinks about it. "Is there a difference?"

"You don't really think your dad abandoned you, do you?"

Dylan doesn't answer.

———————

The night Misty died, the neighboring rental property was empty. Still, I shut off the outdoor lights and worked by the moon. The crashing surf masked the scraping noise of my digging. I cleaned the wounds on her head and arm. The ground was wet and cold. I slipped her pretty shoes back onto her perfect feet. I wrapped her shoulders in one of Dylan's soft blankets. I kissed her wedding ring and promised to always wear my own. And I buried my wife in that shallow grave where we would never be apart, where no one would misunderstand our story. Because people who don't understand will judge.

This is the truth: we all tell the stories that we want to believe. We tell them for so long that we forget what we really know. Occasionally we convince others to believe them too.

In the end, Misty's psychotic delusions were more lucid than my sense of reality. She knew I would kill her. She knew I would turn to Sara.

I leaned the shovel against the house.

I tamped the ground.

I righted and cleaned the fallen table. I packed up our children in Misty's sedan and drove them to Sara's apartment, where I knew they would be loved while I was recreating their future. Because a father who then drives their mother's car to a place where he can invent her suicide is not truly loving them, though that's what he thinks he's doing.

Sam Raglan and the concrete company sealed the truth at sunrise while I was away, and when I returned, I had a new story to tell. An amalgam of truth and deception. And I told it over and over and over and over, turning it like a concrete mixer, until it became a blend that I could call 100 percent pure.

I told it to Misty's parents—*Please don't drive down today. She's run off. Wait and see if she comes to you. I'll look south.*

I told it to the sheriff—*We had a fight. She cut herself with that fork. She sped off without the kids. I took them to Sara's and then went looking for her. But she's unstable. She has this illness. I'm so worried. Look, she wrote a note on the back of this picture.*

I told it to Sara—*She found out about us. She couldn't cope. Her history with you was too long.*

I told it to my children—*Your mother loved you. If she'd been in her right mind she would have stayed. She never meant to hurt you.*

My will instructs my children to reduce me to ashes and cast me out to sea. It's a common request that shouldn't raise any eyebrows, coming from a man born and raised on sand. That's all I considered when I first put this wish in writing and handed it to my attorney, Jamie Blythe.

But now the truth is out: I don't want to hear the sounds of a shovel's blade cutting the earth even at my own funeral.

Deputy Wasson reads my pages too, and this is less shameful to me than when Dylan and Marina and Sara and Lena and even Ian and Denica eventually take their turns poring over my car-rattled writing. I expect the sheriff to judge. I don't hope she'll understand, or forgive. Her frowning scrutiny is only the beginning of what I deserve.

She releases Sara and orders a GPR survey of our porch.

Ground-penetrating radar is effective through tile and concrete. They find Misty in a matter of minutes. They free her a few days later with a violence that insults the care I gave in burying her. A jackhammer, a demolition saw, a breaking chisel. The bougainvillea trellis has to come down. Marina and her grandmother watch from the living room window in shock that might never wear off. Dylan stands on the lawn as close as the crews will allow, imagining me stooped where that crime scene investigator is bent over now. My son glares, arms crossed. Sara's hand on his shoulder. Shattered red tiles and hot-pink petals littering the grass at their feet.

In the theater built for me by powers I can't understand, I collapse in my seat. I curl my head down to rest between my knees and grab the back of my head with both hands.

"How could I forget? How dare I forget?"

"You didn't forget. You decided to believe something else."

Hide me. Take me. End this pain.

Thirty-Five

It's a Monday evening in late September, ten minutes before Sara's Sins will close. Denica is on the sofa under a photo of a sugar-dusted orchid, sipping a pumpkin mocha without the whipped cream. She's down from her father's winery, where harvest is in full swing and Ian will be preoccupied for at least another month. These days he sleeps early, rises early. Gabe has returned to the university. In the morning, she won't be immediately missed.

Sara has sent her employees home and offered to close tonight. One patron reads a book by the unlit fireplace. Two others talk in low voices over nearly empty mugs and a plate holding two forks and the crumbs of a chocolate torte.

"You promise me that this cocoa is sustainably farmed?" Denica asks as Sara clears crystal trays out of the display case and carries them back to the kitchen. "Because I looked at the packaging and it doesn't say anything about being fair-trade certified."

Sara returns from the kitchen and leans on the counter. "I promise. The cacao for my drink mixes comes from a little plantation in Ecuador. I visit once a year, usually in March. The farmer's name is Jorge Gomez, and he has a weakness for Bit-O-Honey candy. Latin America hasn't put slaves to work for more than two hundred years, and Señor Gomez is no exception. He has nine full-time employees."

"But why isn't he certified?"

"He can't afford the certification—and explaining why is practically a college-level course in economics. Look, it's good that awareness is being raised about slavery in chocolate production. Your passion is admirable. But while it's true that fair-trade chocolate isn't produced by slaves, it *isn't necessarily* true that non-certified chocolate *is* produced by slaves. Do you see how easy it is to be misled?"

"So how do people like me sort it out?"

"You keep telling people what you know . . . *and* what you don't know."

"That's hard if I don't know what I don't know," Denica huffs.

Sara laughs. "That's the problem we all face, isn't it? Especially when the world changes as quickly as it is. So you keep learning too."

The bell over the door chimes. Dylan and Marina come in, followed by their grandmother.

"We're closed for the night," Denica calls out.

"Family privilege," Dylan says. "We might have to boot you out." He quickly crosses the room and sits on the same sofa with her, but on the opposite end, a gap of awkwardness between them like their difference in age. Denica hands over her pumpkin mocha to share a sip with him.

Marina comes across the room more slowly, a slim book bag draped from one shoulder to the opposite hip. She's come from one of her extension courses. New term at the university.

Lena lingers in the doorway, closes her eyes, and takes a deep breath through her nose. "Oh my," she murmurs. The copper threads of her autumn blazer catch the café lights.

Sara comes out from behind the counter and gives Marina a hug.

"How are classes?" she asks.

"Dull. Hard to concentrate."

Dylan says, "You'd find it easier if you had one of these before class every day." He holds up Denica's mug.

"True. It might put me into a sugar coma," she says, and the mention of a coma silences everyone for a few seconds. But I find it makes me want to laugh.

Denica too. She tries to suppress it, but she can't, and everyone breaks smiles in her direction.

"What is that you're putting away?" Lena approaches the counter, eying the glass plates in Sara's hands.

"These are cherry and ancho chili clusters," Sara says. Her voice lacks confidence, as if Lena is the master artisan and Sara an impostor. The bells on the door jingle as the couple who ate the chocolate torte leave, and the man at the fireplace closes his book and lifts the last sip of his drink to his lips.

"In milk chocolate?" Lena asks Sara.

"Dark, actually. Uh, sixty-five percent."

Lena's eyes dart to the other tray.

"These are clove-caramel truffles," she says. She glances at Marina.

"I'll take five of each," Dylan says.

"He'll be diabetic by daybreak," Denica says to Marina.

"You'd think. But he's one of those guys."

"Disgusting," Denica says. But she looks at Dylan as if he's the very opposite and takes back her mug.

"Is it too late for me to buy a sampler?" Lena asks.

"Yes," Sara says, turning her back on Lena's disappointed expression. "But if you come back here I'll make a fresh one as a gift."

"Oh, you shouldn't."

"Isn't your birthday coming up?"

Lena slips behind the counter. "My stars. How on earth do you remember such things?"

Sara takes a gift box off a high shelf in the back room, then begins to fill it from the nearly empty glass trays. Sara doesn't tell Lena what each candy is. She works quickly, busying her hands and eyes.

Lena notices all of it. She goes to the display case and removes the last remaining glass tray, which bears a single chocolate-dipped marshmallow rolled in cracked peppercorns. I remember the hot chocolate Sara made for me. Lena pops it into her mouth and chews and *mmms* and sighs like a little girl.

When she is finished she says, "Until I lost Misty, I never understood what it meant to have your life's purpose taken away from you."

Sara concentrates on setting each piece of candy into its rippled gold foil cup.

"It would have been a great loss if you hadn't pursued your purpose, Sara. I'm very sorry I didn't understand that."

"It's okay," Sara says into the box.

"I think not. Your parents made up all kinds of reasons to be offended by you, and I just made their opinion my own. Now it's my turn to have a strong opinion about you, broaden their horizons a bit."

The box is full now, and Sara sets the snug lid in place. "Good luck with that."

"Oh, I don't need luck, my dear. Do you have an annual report?"

"A what?"

"An annual report—you know? A publication of your earnings for investors?"

"Yes, I know. I mean, I do, but why—"

"I'll give one of those to your father for Christmas. Show him how you've grown his money over the years, right? And I'll upstage your mother at her own party with a dessert tray full of these confections of yours. But I won't say where I got them from until they've gorged themselves. That ought to force them to change their story about you, don't you think?" She takes the box from Sara and giggles. "Happy birthday to me. I'm just tickled."

Lena leaves Sara in the kitchen and returns to the kids, who are chatting out in the café about school—Dylan in his senior year, working with a tutor provided by the school district, Marina at the extension, and Denica taking yet another year off before attending college somewhere, anywhere. She'll make up her mind when she's forced to. She kind of likes attending the college of life, she declares.

Sara hangs up her apron and puts away the remaining chocolates, most of them going into a box for Dylan and another box that Denica will take back to Ian. She washes her hands. She shuts off all the lights at the front of the café, leaving a gold dome over the sofa set and her family.

Her new family.

She carries the boxes of candy out and sets them on the table.

"I was thinking," she says. She stops and clears her throat. "Maybe Marina and Denica might want to go to Ecuador with me in the spring. College of life."

Denica leans forward. "Seriously?"

Marina is looking at her brother. "What about Dylan?"

Lena guffaws. "A few boxes of these ought to keep the two of us out of trouble for a few weeks. What do you say, Dylan?"

"I can handle the house by myself," Dylan says.

"'Course you can. The question is, can you handle a crazy old lady?" Lena asks. "I have a feeling your big sister hasn't taught you how to party, young man. And for heaven's sake, you'll be a legal adult a year from now. That's downright embarrassing."

This puts everyone but Sara into stitches. She hasn't had much practice with this sort of thing yet.

"I'll take you to Venezuela when you graduate," Sara says to Dylan.

"I'd rather go to Ireland."

There's Sara's grin. "That would work too."

"He's never even been out of the state," Marina says. "Out of the country—"

Denica says, "If I can surf, he can make it to Venezuela and back. Do those pop-up drills, Dylan. You know what I mean."

He looks to Lena. "Maybe I'll practice by making a few dry runs to your house between now and then."

"After you get your license," Marina says.

"Think I can borrow your car?" he asks Sara.

She shakes her head. "Not on your life."

"I'll buy you one of your own," his grandmother says. "What do you like?"

––––––––––

A crowd of busy seasonal workers fills the winery with energy. Denica is helping to toss plucked grape clusters into the crusher when Sara arrives. The younger woman waves a greeting, then points to the northwest, where her father is.

Sara parks in a place that seems out of the way and hikes a short distance to where the workers are concentrated. She quickly picks out Ian's red work shirt.

"I've come at a bad time," she says. He looks up, smiles at her approach. His hands and clothes are stained purple. He holds the curved picking knife that is a permanent part of his gear between August and October.

"No, no," he insists. "But if you were dressed for it I'd put you to work. Just keep up."

His employees are making noise, a kind of spontaneous singing and hollering that is spirit boosting. The grape leaves are rattling as the workers cut purple clusters off the vines and drop them into bins at their feet. They seem to have a rhythm to their work—grasp, cut, drop; grasp, cut, drop—and when the bins are full, they make a dash to the tractors. Many of the workers jog with the bins balanced on one shoulder, some even on their heads. They dump the bins and run back to the vines. The air is filled with the scents of musky sweat and earth and grape juice.

"Everyone seems in a rush," she says.

"Sort of. Have to get the grapes into the winery before they warm up. We work fast, in small batches."

"I just wanted to thank you," she says, bending to pick up a cluster that has missed the bin. His hands are buried in grape leaves. "For knowing what was needed."

He nods. "You're welcome."

"This giving without expecting a return—it's a little scary. I don't know how to be a mom."

He releases another cluster. "Sara, they're not asking you to be their mother. They're both adults." Grasp, cut, drop.

"Then what do they need?"

"Just you. They need you to be you. Don't pretend, don't put on a hat, don't try to be someone you're not."

"You're a good friend, Ian."

"Why yes, I am." He grins at her.

Grasp, cut, drop.

"You could do this in your sleep," she says.

"True." His bin is full. He bends at his knees and hefts the full load, carries it toward the tractor to dump it. "Though I can't run these to the tractor on my head anymore."

Sara walks with him.

"I've been kicking around the idea of starting a foundation to further research for people who have bipolar disorder."

"Something in your cousin's name."

"Yes. And maybe a partner organization, support groups for family members. Resources, meetings, that sort of thing."

"I like it."

Sara is fidgeting with the zipper pull on her vest. She clears her throat.

"Would you be my cofounder?"

"Aye."

"Just like that—*aye*?"

"The best word in the world."

"I can't imagine you'd have the time."

"For you, as much time as you need."

Her foot comes down on a stone and tips her sideways. Her shoulder bumps Ian's the way it did the first time I saw them together at the winery. "I'll need a lot of time. I don't know the first thing about running a foundation."

"We'll learn together."

"And I'll . . . well, I'll need someone to teach me how to not shut people out anymore."

Ian tosses his entire load into the tractor's half-ton container. "Aye," he says. "I'm good for that too."

"Then would you have dinner with me? When you're free? I mean when the harvest is over?"

He makes a comical show of rolling his eyes. "We've eaten dinner together." He heads back for the trellis sagging with heavy vines, the empty bin swinging in his hand.

She jogs to keep up with him now, light on her feet. "You don't do a very good impression of me."

"I thought you didn't date," he says.

"Aye." She winks at him. "But you can't *always* love someone and expect nothing in return, now can you?"

———

The nurse at the station has no idea that I can see her make the call to my daughter. The woman isn't even confident that I can hear what's spoken at my own bedside.

"He's taken a turn for the worse," she says. "I would suggest you come as soon as possible."

I watch them come. Marina and Sara in the shiny new car, breaking speed limits to the UCLA medical center where I've been for more than three months. Dylan's nowhere in sight. His absence makes it that much harder to lift my head. My limbs have already reached their deadweight.

They drive in silence. They reach Ventura before Marina says, "I really want to go to Ecuador with you."

"Then I hope you'll come."

"Is it bad for me to want to get away?"

"No."

"Then why do I feel so bad?" she asks.

Sara hesitates. "Getting away isn't the same as running away. Getting away will make you stronger, more caring when you go back. Running makes everything . . . harder."

Marina stares at her hands. "Sometimes I want to run."

"We all do. Some of us actually make a break for it."

Marina raises her eyebrows.

"Exactly," Sara says. "You're not running, Marina. You and Dylan are on the brink of new things. It's going to feel strange for a while."

Marina leans her head back against the headrest and reclines the seat. She closes her eyes. "You know what?"

"What?"

"I really like not driving."

Sara laughs. "Let's see how you like it in Ecuador."

———

The screen is darkening. The theater is stuffy and warm. The wait makes me sleepy. All I want to do is close my eyes. I finally give in.

Why won't Dylan come?

Forgive me, please forgive me.

The man in the beret is close at hand. He picks himself up and moves to the seat at my left hand.

I'm glad they know. Carrying the lie around has worn me out.

He puts his hand on my shoulder.

Will you make everything better for them now? I don't deserve a dying wish, but that's mine.

He gives my shoulder a squeeze so firm it pinches a nerve and a burst of pain shoots down my arm. I can't take that as a yes.

The scent of sweet peas fills the room. Someone is holding my hand. Soft, smooth, feminine. Short nails.

"Dad?" she says. "Dad, we're here. Sara and me."

And your brother?

My other hand is picked up and sandwiched between two cool, dry palms. "Hi, Garrett."

Marina touches the finger where my wedding band should be. Sara strokes my skeletal fingers.

"He's so skinny," my daughter chokes out.

Don't cry, Beautiful.

Her strong daddy was always this weak—someday she'll see that also, that I was as weak as she is strong.

Forgive me that too.

She composes herself.

"Dad, I want you to know that we're going to be all right, Dylan and me. Lena—Grandma—is helping us out. She's got the house, the bills. Dylan really likes her, you know. He's doing well. This girl Denica, a new friend, she'll be good for him. The panic's down. And Sara. Sara's helping too. I just don't want you to worry about us."

There's life insurance. I know you thought I forgot that, but there's a policy—ask Jamie.

"We're going to have a service for Mom this weekend. Up in Monterey. With her family."

Your family too now. Thank God, thank God. They found you. I had to hide you to hide myself, but they found you.

"Her ashes—we want to scatter those at home, right there on the water we look at every day. Would you be cool with that?"

So very, very cool. A tremble overtakes my muscles. Relief. Gratitude. Exhaustion, like the kind that comes at the gym on the last, heaviest set.

"I know you did it so you could be with us," Marina says. "I know you didn't want us to be alone, and you thought maybe Mom's family would take us away from you, or worse. I might have done the same thing. I just want you to know I understand, and I'm not mad about it."

She squeezes my hand again. "Dylan is still working through things. He'll come around. Don't worry about that. He's got a good team. There's this man Ian—you'd like him. He's pretty cool. I think Dylan will open up to Ian when it's the right time."

I don't want to leave that job to some other man. I want it for myself, but some opportunities are only available once in life, and when they're gone, they're gone forever.

The man in the beret stands in front of me now. I didn't notice when he moved. The theater has fallen away. Nothing exists but a darkness and a faint breeze and these two invisible, merciful women holding my hands. Beret leans forward and scoops me up by the armpits, irresistibly strong. He expends no effort at all to lift me up. My fight is weak. He's a Navy Seal and he's lifting me out of a roiling ocean of regret—Marina's perfect storm—me limp in his arms while he gives the helicopter the signal. Up, up, up.

Not now, not yet.

Sara says, "I love your children very much, Garrett."

"I love you, Daddy."

Then the rushing wind carries the rest of their words away.

Thirty-Six

My name is Garrett Becker, and I'm pretty sure that this time I'm dead. I've passed the point of no return, the moment when the heart stops beating and the lungs stop breathing and the brain stops messaging. The screen is black. The curtain has fallen.

But death isn't what I expected. Like a burst of lightning I'm back at the twisted fence in downtown Los Angeles, pouncing on it, gripping the strained wire links. Only now—the chains aren't there. My idea of them vanishes under my fingers, and my hands slap flat against a plywood barrier much taller than I am. They slide down the rough plane and my feet hit the ground. I crane my neck. The skyscraper is rising without me. In a few more months, granite cladding will stand where this plywood is. I step back out of habit and scan someone else's work in progress. Judge it. And find I don't really care.

Sun fills the space around me, warm. Later than the morning rush, but still morning. Not a drop of rain.

"Garrett."

I turn on the sidewalk. She's there in her crisp dark-blue jeans and a sweater the intense pink of bougainvillea petals, her mocha eyes bright. That black hair in its ponytail curls across one shoulder. She holds out her hand, and the first thing I fear is that I won't be able to touch her. I'll want to hold her, I'll try, and it will be like clutching air. My first pain in death. When I don't move, she leans forward and takes my hand for herself. She's soft, and warm, and alive.

"He said I could meet you here," Misty says, and she glances over her shoulder.

Across the street on the opposite corner is the man in the maroon beret, his turtleneck unfit for California summer. He's of a different era. He winks at me.

"A friend of yours?" But I already know the answer.

"A guide of sorts. More like a director. A spiritual director."

I tentatively encircle Misty, and she leans into me without fear. Her hair smells like Marina's sweet peas. I touch my lips to the strands. "Forgive me, please."

"It wasn't your fault."

"I betrayed you. That was my fault."

"A human mistake."

"I failed you."

"Then you have to say that I failed you too."

"No—"

"Garrett, I forgive you. What we did, we did for love. We loved our children imperfectly well." She laughs.

I want to cry. "I wanted to undo everything. I wanted you back."

"Here I am."

I pull away just enough to see her clear and smiling eyes. She's whole right now, healed of everything from the wound at her temple to the psychosis in her mind to the fear in her heart. Even that light scar on her left cheek has faded to nothing.

"You're not still angry about Sara? About all the lies I told the kids?"

"No."

"Don't you worry for them?"

"No."

"Why not?"

"Grace."

A strange word. An archaic word.

"I don't know what that is," I admit.

"Grace is what happens when we realize that God is more powerful than everything we ever got wrong. He is bigger than any lie we ever told, any delusion we ever believed. Our children are in good hands."

"God's hands."

"Everything that's happened has been a mercy—don't you see, Garrett? Sara's their family now. She's good family."

"She doesn't know a thing about mothering."

"She knows plenty about what our kids need."

"Chocolate, you mean?"

Misty laughs. "Loss. And hope."

She links her elbow in my arm and turns me around on the sidewalk. Her feet are shoeless. Her dark-blue socks match her jeans. In spite of the filthy street, they're as clean as if she just pulled them out of the dryer.

Though I can't see the ocean from here, I can smell it rolling in on the fall breeze that also keeps the smog away. We head toward the blue expanse. We cross the street. We approach the man in the beret.

"Where are we going?" I ask Misty.

"To meet the giver of grace."

"Is it a long walk?"

The guide clasps his hands behind his back and asks, "Are you in a rush?" I'm surprised by his voice out here. It's the distant but rich call of the ocean in a seashell.

"I guess not," I say.

"Good," he says. "Come see before we go."

———————

The water is slate blue trimmed in white foam. It wraps around the Rincon in slender layers like a dress flowing over a woman's curves. Well out beyond the lineup, our children sit astride their surfboards, torsos clad in black Neoprene, legs dangling in the water. When was the last time I saw Marina ride? It's been too long.

Thick plastic containers sit forward near the noses of the bobbing boards, and I know without being told that one contains Misty and one me. Their faces are wet. Dylan's by the sea, Marina's by her eyes. He's waiting for her to take the lead. She's frozen, staring at the temporary urn in front of her.

Dylan guides his board next to hers and lifts the box she can't bring herself to lift. He carefully breaks the seal and puts the cap down in front of him. The breeze reaches in and stirs the ashes as he hands it back to her. Dust floats on wind above their shoulders. Tiny flecks kiss their cheeks.

He uncaps his own container and puts that lid with the other, holds the box in both hands, and looks at his sister.

"This can't be them," she says.

"It isn't," her brother says. "You know it, right?"

She nods without speaking.

"And what we're doing is just . . . a symbol. Like a poem. Got it?"

"Some poems are hard for me to get."

"Right. Well. Don't try so hard. Just feel it."

A shiver runs through her shoulders. "Okay."

"I didn't mean literal—"

"Dylan. Are we gonna do this or not?"

"All right," he says. "Here we go. One . . . two . . . three."

Reading Group Guide

These questions contain plot spoilers!

1. Garrett believes he is dead. Sara believes she is responsible for Misty's death. Misty believes Sara bears ill will toward her and her children. Marina and Dylan believe their mother committed suicide. Each of these beliefs contains some truths tangled up with some falsehoods. What makes it so difficult to sort out truth from untruth in the things a person believes? Consider such factors as family history, age, personal experiences, time, inaccessible facts, wishful thinking, and so on.

2. At any time did you believe that the narrator was Misty? What did you feel when the true narrator was revealed? Describe a time when you discovered that something you believed to be true was proven false. What emotions did the discovery stir up in you? Relief? Confusion? Anger? Happiness? Betrayal? Disbelief? Was it difficult to let go of the old belief? Why?

3. "This is how we all die," Garrett says. "The first wheel of our lives slips off the pavement on the day we learn how to lie to ourselves. The second wheel goes when we discover that lying gives us something we need, even if only for a little while. And

then we are destabilized. From there we fall and fall." What do you think Garrett means?

4. When Dylan won't accept that Sara is not his mother, Sara decides that lying about it might be best for Dylan. What factors bring her to this conclusion? Is lying to someone ever more loving than telling the truth? How were Garrett's lies motivated by love?

5. "This is the truth," says Garrett. "We all tell the stories that we want to believe. We tell them for so long that we forget what we really know. Occasionally we convince others to believe them too." Do you agree or disagree? Explain.

6. Ian claims, "I believe that God has given me a thousand chances to look at people and see what I might give them instead of what they might give me. They don't exist to forgive me. I exist to love them." How does this belief distinguish him from Sara and Garrett, who are desperate for the forgiveness of their own sins?

7. Is ignorance bliss? Is knowledge freedom? How might the truth of their mother's fate forever change the lives of Marina and Dylan, for better or worse?

8. How do you define grace? How might Garrett, Sara, or Misty define it?

About the Author

PHOTO BY MICHAEL HEATH

Erin Healy is the bestselling coauthor of Burn and Kiss (with Ted Dekker) and an award-winning editor for numerous best-selling authors. She has received wide acclaim for her novels *Never Let You Go, The Baker's Wife, House of Mercy,* and *Afloat.* She and her family live in Colorado.

An Excerpt
from *Stranger Things*

The house appears to be a tragedy.

It's an abandoned structure that sits far off the road, a ruined place gutted by fire and battered by weather. Stone walls hold up a metal roof. Where the two meet, fat spiders lie in wait for their next meal. The trees that surround the place are indifferent, and someday the weeds will swallow it completely.

That's one way of seeing it.

Close your eyes. Spin around. Drink the air. Then look again:

The house appears to be a triumph.

It's a peaceful home nestled under sheltering trees, its stone walls a fortress against harsh weather and unwelcome visitors. The metal roof catches sunshine and sends water sliding into a rain barrel at the bottom of a gutter, where white birds have come to bathe. On the shady porch, strong with new boards and fresh paint, a graceful swing waits for its occupant to return. A glass topped off with lemonade and ice sweats on the rail.

Darkness sweeps in. A cloud passing over the sun brings the tragedy back to life. A chill creeps up the path leading from the grove. The glass of lemonade falls to the rocks and shatters.

Then wind shoves darkness out of the way. Sunshine raises

the triumphant house from the dead. Orange poppies spring out of the ground. A woman in an ocean-blue dress emerges from the house to pluck some for her table.

A black scorpion lies in wait among the flowers.

Here, light and darkness jostle for attention. Both visions are real, but which one is more true?

Listen: there are footsteps on the path. People are coming. People who will give an answer to this question. There will be an argument. Expect worse than a civil dispute.

But keep an eye on the woman picking poppies.

One

The closet where Becca was trapped held every nightmare she'd ever had, plus one that had never violated the borders of her imagination until now.

Outside of the closet, a gas lamp burned in an empty room. The lamp's unnatural white light and dizzying stink came into the tight space through a crack in the locked door. Sawdust from the unfinished floor stuck to Becca's sweaty palms and formed a gritty paste. Her breath was noisy and her heart was a frightened cat trying to claw its way out of her throat. If she wanted to avoid a split lip, she should follow orders: shut up, sit down, stay put.

Becca got to her feet and pressed her cheek against the wood, looking through the gap for her opportunity to disobey. To survive. Better to live with a split lip than die without one.

Outside the closet, only fresh floorboards made the burnt-out carcass of a room suitable for humans. It seemed there was no electricity here. There was definitely no heat. For the most part there was fear, and something else that Becca couldn't name: a sensation that the place was unstable, that the floor might open up and swallow her.

She wrapped herself up in her arms. If she could keep her head, she might be able to see her way out.

Jett, the boyfriend who turned out to be a liar, was gone now. He'd promised her a candlelight picnic and privacy, when what really awaited was a crumbling house and a man who looked her over as if she were something to eat.

That man, who had an unfortunate resemblance to her step-dad, had forced her into the closet. She raked at his grip with her free hand; she kicked at his knees, at his groin, and screamed. But he hefted her in as if she weighed no more than a pair of shoes and he was just tidying up the house. She beat on the door with her fists, and though it rattled, it held firm.

At first she had feared for Jett. Would the man kill him if he didn't get away? Her eye found the crack for the first time and she looked out—shouting, questioning, pleading—and saw something more terrifying than a murder. Cash exchanging hands. The man gave Jett a thick bundle of bills. Jett caressed those bills, kissed the stack, and left the house without her.

His betrayal silenced her. She pressed her hands to the door, which was now a shield separating her from worse horrors, and wondered if there was a handle she could grip from the inside. Something to prevent the man from opening it. No. The panel was smooth and flat.

But he seemed uninterested. He stood in the shadows of the opposite corner of the room, where the glare couldn't reach, and studied the illuminated panel of his phone. He tapped, he scrolled.

He said, "You're not as strong as you think. Accept that as quick as you can."

She wasn't sure he was talking to her. The crack in the door put him in a tight frame. He had Hollywood looks equally fit for an unwitting hero or suave bad boy.

He continued, "Things'll go better for you when you do."

Slowly she lowered herself to her knees and moved her finger-tips over the surface of the ground, searching for something besides sawdust and spiders, something useful for self-defense or escape. A nail, for example, that she might slip between the door and the wall to dislodge the latch.

"What's your name?"

She didn't answer. Dust clung to her hands.

"Jett said your name is Becca."

"Then you don't need me to tell you," she snapped. She remembered the fake ID—Jett's idea, so she could get into his favorite club. The card was still in her jeans pocket. She fished it out, thinking new thoughts about the things he had often talked her into doing there after just a couple of beers.

Today the manager had asked her if she wanted a job.

In the closet, Becca rose from the floor and leveled her eye with the crack.

The man's eyeball was there, staring into her black hole. She flinched and knocked her head against the underside of a stair. The ID card dropped from her fingers and lightly slapped the floor.

"You're right," he said. "I don't need you to tell me anything." His words were thick against the wood, for her ears only, though as far as she knew they were alone. "In fact, don't speak at all. Or I'll shut you up myself."

She believed he would.

"What are you doing here?" he demanded of someone else. An unexpected visitor? He moved and the crack filled with light.

"Hey, Uncle Phil." The voice was thin with undertones of whine, like Becca's little brother's. But a kid her age stepped into the skinny view, an athletic boy, all-American clean. She recognized him at once. Brock Anderson. They'd gone to high school together before she dropped out, but she knew him by reputation: star pupil, king of the wrestling mats, and when the adults weren't looking, the Tom Sawyer of troublemaking.

Uncle Phil? Brock would be no ally of hers. Would he?

Brock took in the run-down room. "When I told you about this place I didn't think you'd actually be interested. It's a dump."

"I'm waiting for someone, and you don't want to be here when he comes."

"Was that Jett I saw leaving?"

"As you should be."

"I need to talk to you," Brock said.

"We both have phones."

"I wanted to see you."

The pair stood on the other side of the gas lamp and faced off like bright halves of the moon. Behind them, the ceiling bent their dark shadows at an aggressive angle.

"You here to ask for money?"

Brock sniffed and looked embarrassed.

"Get out. And don't ever follow me again."

"Look, I'm freaking out. I lost my scholarship!"

"Not my fault," Phil said.

"It wasn't my fault either. And you know Mom can't pay for Cornell."

"No, after her latest incompetence she probably can't afford a Happy Meal."

"But you're rolling in cash. Mom says—"

"Do you think she can say anything that would matter to me?"

"Why do you think I'm the one talking?" Brock spread his hands wide. "Help me out here!"

Taking advantage of their argument, Becca lowered herself to her knees and patted the floor for the ID card. Now was the time to tinker with the latch if it could be done at all.

"I don't give handouts," Phil growled.

"Then make it a loan."

"I'm not a bank either."

"Then . . . then . . ." Shadows shifted across the crack in the closet door. Becca found the card, slipped it under the latch, looked out through the crack at the two men who faced off, one desperate, one indifferent. The plastic met resistance.

Brock was saying, "Let me work for you, just one year. Now through next summer. Give me something to do. Anything."

At this Phil's expression changed from irritated to amused. His eyes darted to Becca's closet. She snatched the card back to her racing heart.

"You think you can earn enough for Cornell that fast? Just what is it that you think I do?"

"Mom says something criminal." Brock's laugh was a snort. "Not that you care what Mom thinks."

"Anything successful must be criminal. It's how she excuses her résumé of failures."

"That's what I said."

"I doubt it."

Brock gestured to the ruins. "I think you flip houses. You've got enough of them."

Phil watched him, tapping his phone against his chin.

"I can work, Uncle Phil. I'm good with a hammer and paint-brush." Brock crossed his arms.

"Tell me how you lost your scholarship."

"Wasn't my fault."

"Do you have a story or not?"

Brock rolled his eyes. "Teacher gave me a D at the end of the term, a totally subjective grade. She was completely unfair."

"Old hag with an ax to grind? Teacher for fifty years, angry about today's slacker youths?"

"Not exactly. She's the one who brought us up here on a biology field trip that one time."

"So I have her to thank for the house."

"I guess. It's when I first saw it."

Phil looked at his watch. "Contest the grade."

"Tried. But Ms. Diaz is some kind of darling, won a bunch of teaching awards. Everyone's all gaga over her. Hot too. Probably sleeping with the principal."

"Oh, that type," Phil said.

Type. Becca knew Ms. Diaz, and it took no special brains to guess that Brock had finally met a teacher who wouldn't be charmed by his flashy intelligence into letting a few assignments slide.

"You mean *your* type," Brock challenged, and his uncle laughed agreeably.

"Unattainable," Phil said. "Until she learns she's not." He put away his phone, his thin tolerance of Brock replaced by some kind of fresh interest.

In her closet, Becca believed she had glimpsed her imminent future with Phil and felt sick. It would take more than silence to save her skin; she knew it the way she knew when her stepdad was about to throw a plate at her head. She worked the card back into the door, and it went in far enough to tap the latch before snagging in some unseen joint of the hardware and refusing to dislodge.

Brock was saying, "So, about a job?" when the gas lantern

popped and Becca jumped, bumping the door. The latch jangled and the card remained pinched. She held her breath. Brock's head turned toward the closet.

"What was that?"

"I think I could come up with something for you to do," Phil said as if he hadn't heard Brock's question. But he was moving toward Becca. She pressed herself against the back wall, then thought there might be a better way. She had just enough room in the short storage space to throw herself at the door if he opened it.

The story continues in *Stranger Things* by Erin Healy.